Culture Wise
JAPAN

The Essential Guide to Culture, Customs & Business Etiquette

Edited by David Leaper

Survival Books • London • England

First published 2009

All rights reserved. No part of this publication
may be reproduced, stored in a retrieval system or
recorded by any means, without prior written
permission from the publisher.

Copyright © Survival Books 2009
Cover photo © Jorgen (🖥 www.shutterstock.com)
Maps © Jim Watson

Survival Books Limited
26 York Street, London W1U 6PZ, United Kingdom
☎ +44 (0)20-7788 7644, 🗐 +44 (0)870-762 3212
✉ info@survivalbooks.net
🖥 www.survivalbooks.net

British Library Cataloguing in Publication Data.
A CIP record for this book is available
from the British Library.
ISBN: 978 -1-905303-40-3

Printed and bound in India by Ajanta Offset

ACKNOWLEDGEMENTS

The editor (who wrote chapters 2, 7, 9 and 10) would like to express his gratitude to the writers who helped bring this book to fruition: James Knudsen (chapter 3); Jason Schindler (chapter 4); Andy Hockersmith (chapter 5); Erin Irving (chapter 6); and Lauren Shannon (chapter 8). I would also like to thank Chiharu Kawai, Michael Hassett, Yoshie Okada, Dennis Schneider and Gerry Leaper for correcting grammatical, factual and other errors (any mistakes are entirely my own).

Mina Onuma deserves a special mention for ploughing through various chapters and enlisting her friends, Takehiro Nakamura, Hiroshi Takada and Takahiro Moji to help, as well as being on hand to answer queries in the final stages. Also, 'thanks' to Nitin Goel for his support, but most of all to my loving wife, Sohyun Joo, who (probably) unknowingly kept me going on this project. Andy Hockersmith would like to thank Misako Goto, Etsuko Ohta, and Charles Cabell. Lauren Shannon would like to thank David Leaper for the opportunity and his incredible patience.

Finally a huge thank you to Joe Laredo for his perspicacious editing and the publisher for tolerating the countless delays. Others who deserve a mention include Peter Read for his additional editing and proof-reading, Rachel Wright for final checks, Di Tolland for DTP and photo selection, and Jim Watson for the cover design and maps. Finally a special thank you to all the photographers (listed on page 230) – the unsung heroes – whose beautiful images add colour and bring Japan to life.

THE AUTHOR

David Leaper is a New Zealander who has been living abroad since 1995, when he went to Japan. He has lived in Japan on and off for a total of eight years, dividing his time between Mie-ken, Chiba and Tokyo. Although he left Japan in 2008, he remains an avid follower of sumo and drinker of nihonshu, when he can find it. Currently, he and his wife are living in Seoul, South Korea, where his work in teacher education leaves him busier than he wishes to be. *Culture Wise Japan* is his first book.

What readers & reviewers have said about Survival Books:

'If you need to find out how France works then this book is indispensable. Native French people probably have a less thorough understanding of how their country functions.'

Living France

'It's everything you always wanted to ask but didn't for fear of the contemptuous put down. The best English-language guide. Its pages are stuffed with practical information on everyday subjects and are designed to compliment the traditional guidebook.'

Swiss News

'Rarely has a 'survival guide' contained such useful advice – This book dispels doubts for first-time travellers, yet is also useful for seasoned globetrotters – In a word, if you're planning to move to the US or go there for a long-term stay, then buy this book both for general reading and as a ready-reference.'

American Citizens Abroad

'Let's say it at once. David Hampshire's Living and Working in France is the best handbook ever produced for visitors and foreign residents in this country; indeed, my discussion with locals showed that it has much to teach even those born and bred in l'Hexagone – It is Hampshire's meticulous detail which lifts his work way beyond the range of other books with similar titles. Often you think of a supplementary question and search for the answer in vain. With Hampshire this is rarely the case. – He writes with great clarity (and gives French equivalents of all key terms), a touch of humour and a ready eye for the odd (and often illuminating) fact. – This book is absolutely indispensable.'

The Riviera Reporter

'A must for all future expats. I invested in several books but this is the only one you need. Every issue and concern is covered, every daft question you have but are frightened to ask is answered honestly without pulling any punches. Highly recommended.'

Reader

'In answer to the desert island question about the one how-to book on France, this book would be it.'

The Recorder

'The ultimate reference book. Every subject imaginable is exhaustively explained in simple terms. An excellent introduction to fully enjoy all that this fine country has to offer and save time and money in the process.'

American Club of Zurich

'The amount of information covered is not short of incredible. I thought I knew enough about my birth country. This book has proved me wrong. Don't go to France without it. Big mistake if you do. Absolutely priceless!'

Reader

'When you buy a model plane for your child, a video recorder, or some new computer gizmo, you get with it a leaflet or booklet pleading 'Read Me First', or bearing large friendly letters or bold type saying 'IMPORTANT - follow the instructions carefully'. This book should be similarly supplied to all those entering France with anything more durable than a 5-day return ticket. – It is worth reading even if you are just visiting briefly, or if you have lived here for years and feel totally knowledgeable and secure. But if you need to find out how France works then it is indispensable. Native French people probably have a less thorough understanding of how their country functions. – Where it is most essential, the book is most up to the minute.

Living France

A comprehensive guide to all things French, written in a highly readable and amusing style, for anyone planning to live, work or retire in France.

The Times

Covers every conceivable question that might be asked concerning everyday life – I know of no other book that could take the place of this one.

France in Print

A concise, thorough account of the Do's and DONT's for a foreigner in Switzerland – Crammed with useful information and lightened with humorous quips which make the facts more readable.

American Citizens Abroad

'I found this a wonderful book crammed with facts and figures, with a straightforward approach to the problems and pitfalls you are likely to encounter. The whole laced with humour and a thorough understanding of what's involved. Gets my vote!'

Reader

'A vital tool in the war against real estate sharks; don't even think of buying without reading this book first!'

Everything Spain

'We would like to congratulate you on this work: it is really super! We hand it out to our expatriates and they read it with great interest and pleasure.'

ICI (Switzerland) AG

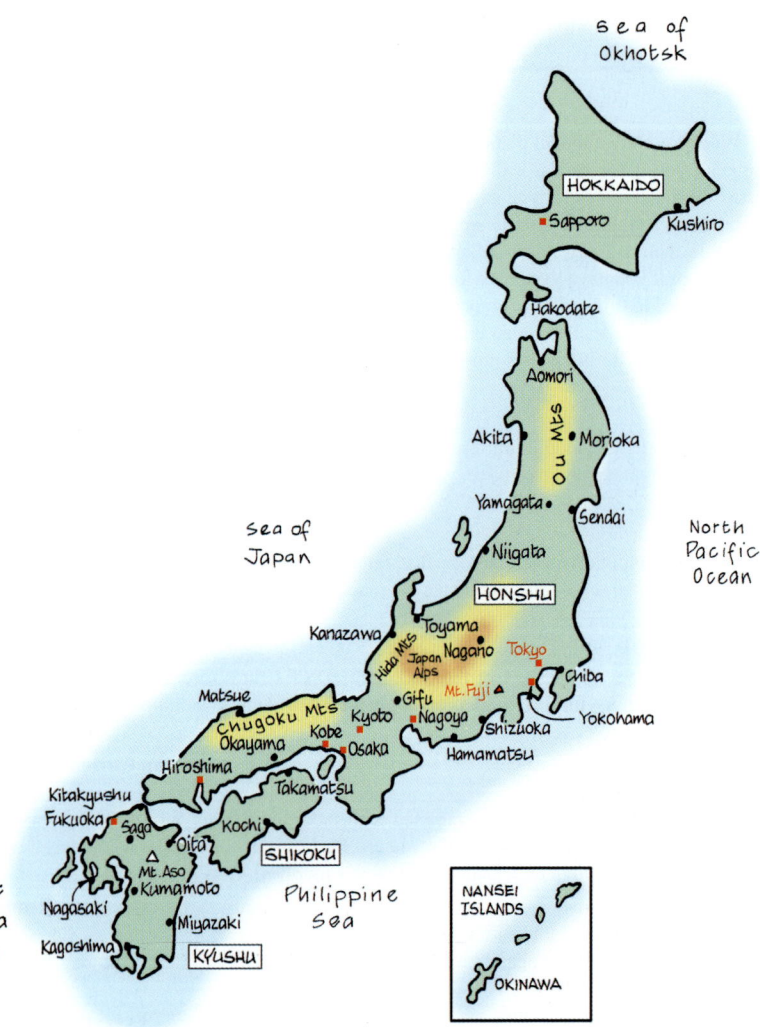

CONTENTS

1. A CHANGE OF CULTURE — 13

Japan is different — 13
Culture shock — 14
Families in Japan — 20
A new life — 21

2. WHO ARE THE JAPANESE? — 23

Timeline — 23
The people — 28
Humour — 35
The class system — 36
Children — 36
Attitudes to foreigners — 37
National icons — 39

3. GETTING STARTED — 51

Immigration — 51
Bureaucracy — 52
Accommodation — 53
Buying or hiring a car — 57
Emergency services — 58
Health service — 59
Insurance — 62
Education — 63
Council services — 66
Utilities — 67
Staying informed — 69
Banking — 70
Taxes — 72

4. BREAKING THE ICE — 75

Community life — 75
Sexual attitudes — 77
Meeting people — 79
Invitations — 81
Respecting privacy — 83
Taboos — 84

Expatriate community	86
Confrontation	87
Dealing with officials	88

5. THE LANGUAGE BARRIER — 91

Learning Japanese	91
Other languages	96
Slang & swearing	97
Body & sign language	98
Forms of address	99
Greetings	101
Telephone, email & letters	102

6. THE JAPANESE AT WORK — 105

Work ethic	105
Holidays & leave	106
Finding a job	108
Employment agencies	112
Salary	113
Contracts	113
Starting or buying a business	114
Business etiquette	116
Employing people	119
Trade unions	120

7. ON THE MOVE — 123

Driving	123
Public transport	129
On foot	133

8. THE JAPANESE AT PLAY — 137

Dress code	137
Eating	138
Drinking	142
Cafes, bars & restaurants	143
Nightlife	147
Family celebrations	148
Funerals	152
Clubs	153
Popular culture	153
The arts	160

9. RETAIL THERAPY — 167

Customer service	167
Opening hours	168
Queuing	168
Sales & discounts	168
Types of shop	169
Vending machines	171
Markets	171
Department stores	172
Supermarkets	173
Food	174
Alcohol	177
Clothes	177
Books, newspapers & magazines	180
Collectables	181
Mail-order shopping	181
Returning goods	182

10. ODDS & ENDS — 185

Climate	185
Crime	187
Flag & anthem	187
Geography	188
Government	191
International relations	192
Pets	194
Religion	194
Time difference	197
Tipping	197
Toilets	197

APPENDICES — 201

Appendix A: Embassies	201
Appendix B: Further reading	203
Appendix C: Useful websites	207
Appendix D: Provinces & regions	212
Appendix E: Useful words & phrases	214

INDEX — 219

Mt Fuji

INTRODUCTION

If you're planning a trip to Japan or just want to learn more about the country, you'll find the information contained in *Culture Wise Japan* invaluable. Whether you're travelling on business or pleasure, visiting for a few days or planning to stay for a lifetime, Culture Wise guides enable you to quickly find your feet by removing the anxiety factor when dealing with a foreign culture.

Adjusting to a different environment and culture in any foreign country can be a traumatic and stressful experience, and Japan is no exception. You need to adapt to new customs and traditions, and discover the Japanese way of doing things; whether it's a drinking and *karaoke* session with your colleagues after a hard day at the office, playing *pachinko* or *Pokémon* with your kids, or a celebration dinner of Kobi beef or Fugi with your neighbours.

Japan is a land where almost everything is done differently: where toilets give you a wash and blow dry and may even talk to you; where people live in tiny six-*tatami* rooms with miniature furniture and sit on the floor; where food consists of raw fish and even stranger concoctions, washed down with *sake* or *shochu*; where everything comes in small sizes, from tiny (*kei*) cars to micro homes, *netsuke* to miniature trees (*bonsai*), *sushi* to gardens; and where people bow all the time, talk in riddles and you never know what they are <u>really</u> thinking.

Culture Wise Japan is essential reading for anyone planning to visit Japan, including tourists (particularly travellers planning to stay a number of weeks or months), business people, migrants, retirees, holiday homeowners and transferees. It's designed to help newcomers avoid cultural and social gaffes; make friends and influence people; improve communications (both verbal and non-verbal); and enhance your understanding of Japan and the Japanese people. It explains what to expect, how to behave in most situations, and how to get along with the locals and feel at home – rather than feeling like a *koi* out of water. It isn't, however, simply a monologue of dry facts and figures, but a practical and entertaining look at life in Japan.

A period spent in Japan is a wonderful way to enrich your life, broaden your horizons, and hopefully expand your circle of friends. We trust this book will help you avoid the pitfalls of visiting or living in Japan and smooth your way to a happy and rewarding stay.

Gokouun o inorimasu! (good luck!)

David Leaper

February 2009

detail from 19C woodblock print

1.
A CHANGE OF CULTURE

With almost daily advances in technology, ever-cheaper flights and knowledge about almost anywhere in the world at our fingertips, travelling, living, working and retiring abroad has never been more accessible, and current migration patterns suggest that it has never been more popular. However, although globalisation means the world has in effect 'shrunk', every country is still a 'world' of its own with a unique culture – and Japan is certainly no exception.

> 'There are no foreign lands. It is the traveller only who is foreign.'
> Robert Louis Stevenson (Scottish writer)

Some people find it impossible to adapt to a new life in a different culture – for reasons which are many and varied. According to statistics, partner dissatisfaction is the most common cause, as non-working spouses frequently find themselves without a role in the new country and sometimes with little to do – other than think about what they would be doing if they were at home. Family concerns, which may include the children's education and worries about loved ones at home, can also deeply affect those living abroad.

Many factors contribute to how well you adapt to a new culture – for example, your personality, education, foreign language skills, mental health, maturity, socio-economic conditions, travel experience, and family and social support systems. How you handle the stress of change and bring balance and meaning to your life is the principal indicator of how well you'll adjust to a different country, culture and business environment.

JAPAN IS DIFFERENT

Many people underestimate the cultural isolation that can be experienced in a foreign country, particularly one with a different language. While most foreigners have no problem accepting that Japan will be different from their own countries, they may be surprised at just how different it is. Even if you've studied Japanese extensively before arriving, you'll find that you still have plenty to learn about the nuances and shared understandings that are so important in Japan.

When you move to Japan, you'll be faced with a host of challenges – possibly including a new job, a new home and a new physical environment

– which can be overwhelming; and all this before you even encounter the local culture. You may have left a job in your home country where you were in senior position, extremely competent and knew everyone. In Japan, you may be virtually a trainee and not know any of your colleagues or the Japanese way of doing things. The sensation that you're starting from scratch can be demoralising.

Japan has many extremes of climate and weather, and you mustn't underestimate the effects that this can have on you. The heat and humidity of summer can lead to a lack of energy, poor sleep and dehydration. In winter, the thermometer may tell you that it isn't that cold, but you'll certainly feel cold. Housing isn't well insulated and typically without central heating. Even if you move to a major city, many things that you're used to and take for granted in your home country may not be available in Japan, e.g. certain kinds of food, opportunities to enjoy your favourite hobby or sport, books and television programmes in your language. This lack of 'home comforts' can wear you down. You'll also need to contend with the lack of a local support network. At home you had a circle of friends, acquaintances, colleagues and possibly relatives you could rely on for help and support. In Japan there's no such network, which can leave you feeling lost.

The degree of isolation you feel usually depends on how long you plan to spend in Japan and what you'll be doing there. If you're simply going on a short holiday you may not even be aware of many of the cultural differences, although if you are, it will enhance your enjoyment and may save you from a few embarrassing or confusing moments. However, if you're planning a business trip or intend to spend an extended period in Japan – perhaps working, studying or even living there permanently – **it's essential to understand the culture, customs and etiquette at the earliest opportunity.**

> 'If you reject the food, ignore the customs, fear the religion and avoid the people, you might better stay at home.'
>
> James A. Michener (American writer)

Although Japan does have minorities, it's one of the most monocultural countries in the world. There's a prevailing opinion amongst Japanese that foreigners cannot understand 'Japaneseness' simply because they aren't Japanese, that foreigners, by their nature, are different and will act in strange and unpredictable ways. Even in the main cities, where foreigners are common enough, the locals may cling to negative stereotypes and be unaccustomed to (and intolerant of) non-Japanese ways of thinking.

This prevailing mind-set won't make it easier for you to adapt to life in Japan, but by being open-minded and maintaining a positive and generous attitude, you'll help break down stereotypes and play your part in opening up Japan to the outside world.

CULTURE SHOCK

Culture shock is the term used to describe the psychological and physical state felt by people when arriving in a foreign country or even moving to a

A Change of Culture

new environment in their home country (where the culture, and in some cases language, may vary considerably by region and social class). Culture shock is a common experience among those who travel, live, work or study abroad, when in addition to adapting to new social rules and values, you may need to adjust to a different climate, food and dress. It manifests itself in a lack of direction and the feeling of not knowing what to do or how to do things, not knowing what's appropriate or inappropriate. You literally feel like a 'fish out of water'.

> 'When you travel, remember that a foreign country is not designed to make you comfortable. It is designed to make its own people comfortable.'
>
> Clifton Fadiman, (American writer)

Culture shock is precipitated by the anxiety that results from losing all familiar rules of behaviour and cues to social intercourse: when to shake hands and what to say when you meet people; how to buy goods and services; when and how much to tip; how to use an ATM or the telephone; when to accept and refuse invitations; and when to take statements seriously and when not to. These cues, which may be words, gestures or facial expressions, are acquired in the course of a lifetime and are as much a part of our culture and customs as the language we speak and our beliefs. Our peace of mind and social efficiency depend on these cues, most of which are unconsciously learned and recognised.

The symptoms of culture shock are essentially psychological. However, there are also physical symptoms including an increased incidence of minor illnesses (e.g. colds and headaches) and more serious psychosomatic illnesses brought on by depression. Culture shock can even cause physical pain. You shouldn't underestimate the consequences of culture shock, although the effects can be lessened if you accept the condition rather than deny it.

Stages of Culture Shock

Severe culture shock – often experienced when moving to a country with a different language – usually follows a number of stages. The names of these may vary, as may the symptoms and effects, but a typical progression is as follows:

1. **Honeymoon stage** – The first stage, commonly known as the 'honeymoon' stage, usually lasts until a few days or weeks after

A Change of Culture

arrival (although it can last longer, particularly if you're insulated from the usual pressures of life). This stage is essentially a positive (even euphoric) one, when you find everything is an exciting and interesting novelty. The feeling is similar to being on holiday or a short trip abroad, when you generally experience only the positive effects of a change of culture (although this depends very much on where you're from and the country you're visiting – see box).

> Every year, a dozen or so Japanese tourists need to be repatriated from the French capital after falling prey to what has become known as 'Paris Syndrome'. This is what some polite Japanese tourists suffer when they discover that Parisians can be rude, or that the city doesn't meet their expectations. The experience can be so stressful that they suffer a nervous breakdown and need to be hospitalised or repatriated under medical supervision.

2. **Rejection or distress stage** – The second stage is usually completely opposite to the first and is essentially negative and a period of crisis, as the initial excitement and 'holiday' feeling wears off and you start to cope with the real conditions of daily life – except of course that life is nothing like anything you've previously experienced. This can happen after only a few weeks and is characterised by a general feeling of disorientation, confusion and loneliness. Physical exhaustion, brought on by a change of time zone, extremes of hot or cold, and the strain of having hundreds of settling-in tasks to accomplish, is a symptom of this stage.

You may experience regression, where you spend much of your time speaking your own language, watching television and reading newspapers from your home country, eating food from home and socialising with expatriates who speak your language. You could also spend a lot of time complaining about the host country and its culture. Your home environment suddenly assumes a tremendous importance and is irrationally glorified. All difficulties and problems are forgotten and only

the good things back home are remembered.

3. **Flight stage** – The third stage is often known as the 'flight' stage (because of the overwhelming desire to escape) and is usually the one that lasts the longest and is the most difficult to cope with. During this period you may feel depressed and angry, as well as resentful towards the new country and its people. You may experience impatience and frustration at not being understood and discontentment, sadness and incompetence.

These feelings are inevitable when you're trying to adapt to a new culture that's very different from that of your home country, and they're exacerbated by the fact that you can see nothing positive or good about the new country, but focus exclusively on the negative aspects. You may become hostile and develop an aggressive attitude towards the country. Other people will sense this and in many cases either respond in a confrontational manner or try to avoid you. You may have difficulties with the language, your house, job or children's school, transportation – even simple tasks like shopping may be fraught with difficulties – and the fact that the local people are largely indifferent to these problems only makes matters worse. Even if they try to help, they may be unable to understand your concerns, and you conclude that they must be insensitive and unsympathetic to you and your problems.

> Transition between your old culture and customs and those of your new country is a difficult process and takes time, during which there can be strong feelings of dissatisfaction. The period of adjustment can last as long as six months, although there are expatriates who adjust earlier and (although rare) those who never get over the 'flight' stage and are forced to return home.

4. **Recovery or autonomy stage** – The fourth stage is where you begin to integrate and adjust to the new culture, and accept the customs of the host country as simply another way of living. The environment doesn't change – what changes is your attitude towards it. You become more competent with the language, and you also feel more comfortable with local customs and can move around without anxiety. However, you still have problems with some of the social cues and you won't understand everything people say (particularly colloquialisms and idioms). Nevertheless, you've largely adjusted to the new culture and start to feel more at home and familiar with the country and your place in it, realising that it has its good as well as bad points.

5. **Reverse culture shock stage** – The fifth stage occurs when you return to your home country. You may find that many things have changed (you'll also have

changed) and that you feel like a foreigner in your own country. If you've been away for a long time and have become comfortable with the habits and customs of a new lifestyle, you may find that you no longer feel at ease in your homeland. Reverse culture shock can be difficult to deal with and some people find it impossible to re-adapt to their home country after living abroad for a number of years.

The above stages occur at different times depending on the individual and his circumstances, and everyone has his own way of reacting to them, with the result that some stages last longer and are more difficult to cope with than others, while others are shorter and easier to overcome.

Reducing the Effects

Experts agree that almost everyone suffers from culture shock and there's no escaping the phenomenon; however, its negative effects can be reduced considerably and there are a number of things you can do before leaving home and immediately on arrival:

- **Positive attitude:** The key to reducing the negative effects of culture shock is to have a positive attitude towards Japan (whether you're visiting or planning to live there). If you don't look forward to a trip or relocation, you should question why you're going. There's no greater guarantee of unhappiness in a foreign environment than taking your prejudices with you.

  It's important when trying to adapt to a new culture to be sensitive to the locals' feelings, and try to put yourself in their shoes wherever possible, which will help you understand why they react as they do. Bear in mind that they have a strong, in-bred cultural code, just as you do, and react in certain ways because they're culturally 'trained' to do so. If you find yourself frustrated by an aspect of the local culture or behaviour, the chances are that your attitudes or behaviour will be equally puzzling to the natives.

- **Research:** Discover as much as possible about Japan before you go, so that your arrival and settling-in period doesn't spring as many

surprises as it might otherwise. Reading up on Japan and its culture before you leave home will help you familiarise yourself with the local customs and make the country and its people seem less strange on arrival. Being aware of many of the differences will make you better prepared to deal with them. You're less likely to be upset by real or imaginary cultural slights, or to offend the locals by making cultural gaffes. Being prepared for a certain amount of disorientation and confusion (or worse) makes it easier to cope with it.

There are literally hundreds of publications about Japan as well as dozens of websites for expatriates (see **Appendices B** and **C**). Many sites provide access to expatriates already living in Japan who can answer questions and provide invaluable advice. There are also 'notice boards' on many websites where you can post messages or questions. Try to find people in your area who have visited Japan and talk to them about it. Some companies organise briefings for families who are about to relocate abroad.

- **Visit Japan first:** If you're planning to live or work in Japan for a number of years, it's important to visit the country before making the leap to see whether you think you would enjoy living there and will be able to cope with the culture.
- **Learn Japanese:** As well as adopting a positive attitude, overcoming the language barrier will be your greatest weapon in combating culture shock and making your time in Japan enjoyable. The ability to speak Japanese and understand the local vernacular (see Chapter 5) isn't just a useful tool that will allow you to buy what you need, find your way around, etc., but the key to understanding Japan and its culture. If you can speak Japanese, even at a basic level, your scope for making friends is immediately widened. You may not be a natural linguist, and learning Japanese can take time and requires motivation. However, with sufficient perseverance virtually anyone can learn enough to participate in the local culture.

> 'Americans who travel abroad for the first time are often shocked to discover that, despite all the progress that has been made in the last 30 years, many foreign people still speak in foreign languages.'
>
> Dave Barry (American writer & humorist)

- **Be proactive:** Join in the activities of the local people, which could be a carnival, a religious festival or some sporting activity. There are often local clubs where you can play sport or keep fit, be artistic, learn to cook local dishes, etc. Not only will this fill some of your spare time, giving you less time to miss home, but you'll also meet new people and make friends. If you feel you cannot join a local club – perhaps because your Japanese isn't good enough – you can always participate in activities for expatriates, of which there are many in the major cities. Look upon a period spent in Japan as an opportunity to acquire new skills, attitudes and perspectives. A change of culture can help you develop a better understanding of yourself and stimulate your creativity.

- **Talk to other expatriates:** Although they may deny it, many expatriates have been through exactly what you're experiencing, and faced the same feelings of disorientation. Even if they cannot provide you with advice, it helps to know that you aren't alone and that it gets better over time. However, don't make the mistake of mixing only with expatriates, as this will alienate you from the local culture and make it much harder to integrate.

- **Keep in touch with home:** Keeping in touch with your family and friends at home and around the world by telephone, email and letters will help reduce and overcome the effects of culture shock.

- **Be happy:** Don't rely on others to make you happy, or you won't find true and lasting happiness. There are things in life which only you can change. Every day we're affected negatively by things over which we have little or no control, but to moan about them only makes us unhappier. So, be your own best friend and nurture your own capacity for happiness.

Culture shock is an unavoidable part of travelling, living and working abroad, but if you're aware of it and take steps to lessen its effects before you go and while you're abroad, the period of adjustment will be shortened and its negative and depressing consequences reduced.

FAMILIES IN JAPAN

Family life may be completely different in Japan and relationships can become strained under the stress of adapting to culture shock. Your family may find itself in a completely new and possibly alien environment, your new home may scarcely resemble your previous one (it may be significantly smaller or larger and have completely amenities) and the climate may differ dramatically from that of your home country. If possible, you should prepare your family for as many aspects of the new situation as you can, and explain to your children the differences they're likely to encounter, while at the same time dispelling their fears.

> 'And that's the wonderful thing about family travel: it provides you with experiences that will remain locked forever in the scar tissue of your mind.'
>
> Dave Barry (American writer & humorist)

Culture shock can affect non-working spouses and children more than working spouses. The husband (the breadwinner is usually the husband) has his work to occupy him, and his activities may not differ much from what he had been accustomed to at home. On the other hand, the wife has to operate in an environment that differs considerably from what she's used to. She will find herself alone more often – a solitude intensified by the fact that there are no relatives or friends on hand. However, if you're aware that this may arise beforehand, you can act on it and reduce its effects. Working spouses should pay special attention to the needs and feelings of their non-working partners and children, as the success of a family relocation depends largely on the ability of the wife and children to adapt to the new culture.

Good communication between family members is vital and you should make time to discuss your experiences and feelings, both as a couple and as a family. Questions should always be invited and, if possible, answered, particularly when asked by children. However difficult the situation may appear at the beginning, it helps to bear in mind that it's by no means unique, and that most expatriate families experience exactly the same problems, and manage to triumph over them and thoroughly enjoy their stay abroad

A NEW LIFE

Although you may find some of the information in this chapter a bit daunting, don't be discouraged by the foregoing catalogue of depression and despair; the negative aspects of travelling and living abroad only have been highlighted in order to help you prepare for and adjust to a new life. The vast majority of people who travel and live abroad naturally experience occasional feelings of discomfort and disorientation, **but most never suffer the most debilitating effects of culture shock.**

As with settling in and making friends anywhere, even in your home country, the most important thing is to be considerate, kind, open, humble and genuine – qualities that are valued the world over. Selfishness, brashness and arrogance will get you nowhere in Japan – or any other country. Treat Japan and its people with respect and they will do likewise.

A period spent in Japan is a wonderful way to enrich your life, broaden your horizons, make new friends and maybe even please your bank manager. We trust that this book will help you avoid the pitfalls of life in Japan and smooth your way to a happy and rewarding future in your new home.

> 'Twenty years from now you'll be more disappointed by the things you didn't do than by the ones you did do. So throw off the bowlines. Sail away from the safe harbour. Catch the trade winds in your sails. Explore. Dream. Discover.'
>
> Mark Twain (American writer)

2.
WHO ARE THE JAPANESE?

From a militaristic past that includes some of the darkest moments in world history to a present that espouses pacifism and economic development, Japan has undergone perhaps the greatest transformation of any country in the world and remains a land of contrasts and seeming contradictions – especially to Westerners.

> 'Before seeing the flower is the best moment'
> Japanese Proverb

While the bursting of the economic bubble in the '90s has taken some of the glitter off its success story, Japan remains among the world leaders in many industrial and technological fields, such as shipping, cars, home computers, technology and leisure equipment.

But what lies behind this inscrutable economic monolith? For most Westerners, Japan is a distant, indistinct country that comes to mind only when they're using its efficient products or seeing a clip from a sadistic Japanese television show; their only exposure to its people is when encountering busloads of camera-clicking tourists. Yet those willing to look beyond such restricting adjectives as 'small', 'polite' and 'expensive' will find a Japan markedly different from their expectations. They will find a sophisticated and varied culture, a country with a diverse climate and natural abundance, inhabited by a quietly proud and hospitable people.

To help you become more familiar with Japan and the Japanese, this chapter contains information about its history, the Japanese character and the country's cultural icons.

Demographics

Population: 127.5mn (2008)

Population density: 343 inhabitants per km² (879 per mi²). Tokyo has a density of 13,416 inhabitants per km² (34,400/mi²)

Largest cities: Tokyo 8.2m; Yokohama 3.2m; Osaka 2.6m; Nagoya 2.1m; Sapporo 1.7m; Kobe 1.5m; Kyoto 1.5m

Ethnic minorities: Ryukyuan (900,000), Ainu (24,000)

Expatriate groups: Korean (693,100); Brazilian (250,000); Chinese (171,100); Indian (150,000); American (64,000); British (23,000)

State religion: Japan is a secular country – in 1945 state support of Shinto was abandoned

Most followed religions: Shinto and Buddhism, followed distantly by Christianity

TIMELINE

While it doesn't have the eons of documented history of some of its neighbours, Japan's recent past is rich with internal strife and external aggression. The main events are listed below:

The Prehistoric Period

35,000 years ago – First signs of human habitation. Stone tools and dwellings show that these first inhabitants had a hunter-gatherer lifestyle.

13,000-300BC – The Jōmon period, named after the Jōmon people, hunter-gatherers who migrated from northeast Asia.

300BC-300AD – The Yayoi period brings a swift transition to a rice-cultivating civilisation, as migration from the Korean peninsula pushes the Jōmon further and further north on Honshu, Japan's largest island. Parts of the country begin to unite under powerful landowners, and social classes evolve.

The first written reference to Japan (then known as Wa) appears in the *Book of Han* (Chronicles of Chinese History) and tells how, in 57AD, a Japanese messenger brought a tribute to the Chinese emperor Guanwu, who conferred his seal upon him. Remarkably, the seal was found by a farmer in 1784 and is now a national treasure on display in the Fukuoka City Museum.

300-538 – The Kofun or Yamato period develops in the province of Yamato, which is present-day Nara. The area controlled by the province stretches from the island of Kyushu to what is now known as the Kansai region. Ideas from Korea and China, in particular Confucianism and Taoism, spread and become established.

The Classical Period

538-710 – The Asuka period also has its power base in Nara, regarded as the first capital of Japan, characterised by Buddhism introduced from the Paekche Kingdom in Korea.

710-794 – In the Nara period, the capital is rebuilt based on Chang-an (Xian), the capital of the Tang dynasty in China. In this period, Chinese characters are first used to record Japanese creation myths in the *Kojiki* (Record of Ancient Matters) and the *Nihon Shoki* (Chronicle of Japan).

794-1185 – The Heian period begins with the transfer of the capital to Kyoto. This period is looked upon as a 'golden' era of peace and cultural development. At the same time, the increasing incompetence of the nobility deepens the poverty among the lower classes, and a new 'warrior class', the *samurai*, forms. The later decades are marked by war as different clans fight for supremacy.

The Medieval Period

1185-1333 – The Kamakura period is heralded by the victory of the Minamoto clan at the battle of Dannoura. After seizing control, they shift their seat of power to Kamakura (in Kanto), where Yoritomo Minamoto becomes the first *Shōgun* (military dictator), leaving the emperor as a figurehead in Kyoto. The Minamoto extend their administration to rule over the entire island of Honshu, unifying Japan for the first time, while surviving Jōmon people are forced northwards to Hokkaido, where today they are known as the Ainu.

Who are the Japanese?

Giant Buddha, Kamakura

1274 & 1281 – Mongolians make two attempts to invade but are defeated by a combination of stout defence and typhoons, which the fortunate Japanese dub 'divine winds' or *kamikaze*.

> "The King of the island has a very large palace all covered with fine gold as our churches are covered with lead ... there is a great abundance of pearls, round and large, and of wonderful reddish colour and more valuable than white. There are also many precious stones. For this reason the island, Cyampagu [Japan], is very rich and marvellous."
>
> Marco Polo (Portuguese explorer). This description in *The Travels of Marco Polo*, written in 1299, was enough to inspire Columbus to set sail on his infamous 1492 voyage to look for a shortcut to the Orient. Instead he stumbled upon the Americas.

1333-1573 – The Muromachi period comes about after a victory by the emperor's army restores the capital to the Muromachi district of Kyoto. However, two branches of the emperor's family continue to fight over the succession until 1392, when the southern dynasty surrenders.

1467-77 – The Onin wars, fought between regional warlords and the *Shōgun*, weaken the central government. The period that follows, until 1603, is often called the *Sengoku Jidai* (the era of the country at war), during which various factions battle for control.

1543 – The Portuguese land in Kyushu and begin regular trading. They introduce firearms, which are quickly adapted and improved by the Japanese, and are first used in a major battle in 1548.

1568 – Warlord Oda Nobunaga's army enters Kyoto and in a series of battles defeats rivals to the military dictatorship (*Shōgunate*).

1573-1603 – The Azuchi-Momoyama period sees Nobunaga's establishment of rule in his castle at Azuchi, Kyoto. After his assassination in 1582, Hideyoshi takes control from his castle in Momoyama and completes the military unification of Japan.

1592 & 1597 – Unsuccessful invasions of Korea.

1600 – Victory at the Battle of Sekigahara allows the victorious warlord, Ieyasu Tokugawa, to take the *Shōgunate*.

The Early Modern Period

1603-1867 – The Edo period commences with the *Shōgun*'s relocation of the capital to Edo, a small fishing village with a natural harbour (renamed Tokyo in 1868). This period is one of repression and isolation as the

Tokugawas forbid almost all contact with other countries on pain of death. It's also a mostly peaceful period in which a new class of wealthy merchants emerges.

1853-54 – Commodore Perry of the US Navy arrives in Japan demanding the establishment of trade relations with the United States. In 1854, the Treaty of Kanagawa is signed, the first of a series of unequal trade agreements between Japan and other major European powers.

The Modern Period

1868-69 – Civil war (known as the Boshin War) ends in victory for the forces of the emperor, who defeat the *Shōgun*'s army and abolish the *Shōgunate*, restoring the emperor as head of government. This is known as the Meiji Restoration.

1869-1912 – The Meiji period ensues as Japan strains to adapt to a new era.

1890 – An Imperial edict sanctions a national assembly and leads to the promulgation of the Constitution of the Empire of Japan in 1898.

1894 – War with China over Korea breaks out. To the surprise of Western observers the Japanese are victorious. In international negotiations following their victory, the Japanese are made to renounce some of their claims to mainland China but are given Formosa (Taiwan) in compensation.

1904-05 – The Russo-Japanese War occurs after tensions arise over Korea. It starts with a Japanese surprise attack on Russia's warships in Port Arthur and decisive Japanese naval victories, again to the surprise of Western nations. This is the first victory for an Asian country over a European country in the modern era.

1910 – Japan annexes Korea.

1912-26 – The Taisho period is one of democracy as the poor health of the emperor allows the *Diet* (parliament) more control.

1914 – The outbreak of the First World War sees Japan join the Allies. They use this opportunity to seize German possessions in China and the Pacific.

1921 – Prime Minister Hara is assassinated by a right-wing extremist.

1926-89 – The Showa period.

1931 – The Mukden Incident: the Japanese army blows up a section of railway in South Manchuria and blames it on Chinese rebels as an excuse to invade Manchuria. The Japanese call their new state *Manchukuo*.

1937 – The Marco Polo Bridge Incident: a skirmish between Chinese and Japanese soldiers results in Japan launching an invasion of China. Japanese forces attack Nanking, killing as many as 200,000 people. Many historians consider this to be the start of the Pacific War.

1938 – Japanese and Soviet armies fight over the border between Manchuria and Outer Mongolia. The Japanese suffer a heavy defeat at the Battle of Nomonhan.

1940 – Japan moves troops into Northern French Indo-China (Vietnam) and declares a 'Greater East Asia Co-Prosperity Sphere' in which Japan is the dominant power. This expansionism results in an oil embargo by the US and Britain. A US memorandum demanding

Who are the Japanese?

Japan's withdrawal is regarded as an ultimatum, and the decision to attack US and European territories in Asia is made.

> **1941-45** – After the surprise attack on Pearl Harbour, the Japanese enjoy a period of superiority before Allied forces gain command of the sea and air, and throw the Japanese back in a series of increasingly bloody and desperate battles.

1945 – The Pacific War ends after the nuclear bombs dropped on Hiroshima and Nagasaki persuade the Japanese to surrender. An occupation government under General MacArthur introduces a constitution that retains the emperor as a figurehead.

1950-52 – The Korean War gives Japan's economy a boost as Japan acts as a supply base for United Nations armed forces.

1952 – The US occupation of Japan ends.

Modern Japan

1964 – The Olympic Games are held in Tokyo.

1972 – The Winter Olympics are held in Sapporo.

1976 – The Lockheed scandal causes several high-ranking politicians to resign, including Prime Minister Tanaka, who is arrested for accepting US$18mn in bribes.

1988 – A 3 per cent consumption tax is introduced.

1989-present – The Heisei period begins as Akihito ascends to the throne upon Emperor Hirohito's death.

1989 – A bribery scandal forces Prime Minister Takeshita to resign, and the ruling Liberal Democratic Party loses its majority for the first time.

1990 – The Tokyo stock market crash begins a long period of economic depression.

1993 – Opposition parties take control of parliament and choose the prime minister for the first time since 1955, before carrying out reforms of the electoral system.

1995 – Kobe is hit by an earthquake in which 5,100 die. Aum Shinrikyo, a religious cult headed by Shoko Asahara, releases sarin gas in the Tokyo subway, killing 12 and injuring thousands. Prime Minister Murayama makes the first official apology to other Asian countries for Japanese war crimes in the Second World War.

1997 – Despite a public outcry, the government raises the consumption tax to 5 per cent, plunging a fragile economy back into recession.

1998 – The Winter Olympics are held in Nagano.

1999 – A nuclear accident at a processing plant kills four and exposes a further 70 to radiation.

2001 – Koizumi becomes prime minister. The stock market sinks to a 17-year low. In response to the '9/11' terrorist attacks, Japan sends naval units to support the US, the first time Japan has posted military vessels on active duty outside its territorial waters since the end of the Pacific War.

2002 – Kim Jong Il admits that North Korea had kidnapped Japanese citizens in the '70s and '80s and forced them to become language teachers. Five of the victims are allowed to visit Japan. The Football (soccer) World Cup is staged jointly by Japan and South Korea.

2004 – Japanese armed forces are sent to Iraq, the first overseas posting since the end of the Pacific War.

2006 – Koizumi steps down and is replaced by Shinzo Abe.

2007 – Abe's Liberal Democratic Party loses some 20mn pension records and the public express their disapproval by voting against it in the upper house elections, causing the party to lose its majority.

2008 – Japan is hard hit by the world recession and is again haunted by the spectre of deflation caused by crashing commodity prices and a surging yen.

THE PEOPLE

The traditional values of the Japanese have been shaped by their country's geography, their reliance on rice cultivation and its long history of importing ideas from abroad. In the past, Japan's rugged geography and local rivalries often made travelling difficult, making the Japanese naturally suspicious of outsiders, while the intensive cultivation of rice necessitated close cooperation to achieve high yields. In addition, the influence of

Confucian ideals and the spread of Buddhism served to emphasise the need for order in society and the belief that everyone has a role to play and should be content with it for their entire lives. The period of stability between 1603 and 1867 cemented these roles to a ritualistic extent, and they're still much in evidence today.

Recent decades have muddied the traditional picture of Japan's ritualised, highly ordered society. After 1945 there was increased movement from the country to the cities, and a corresponding decrease in the proportion of Japanese growing up in extended families. Then the 'lost years' of economic stagnation brought a loss of confidence in institutionalised organisations, which were blamed for getting Japan into difficulty, and the Japanese began to question the very foundations of their society and sought change.

This section explains the traditional characteristics of the Japanese and how they've adapted to more recent influences and trends.

The Importance of Spring

In few other countries does spring have such an impact on the national psyche as in Japan. 1st April, not 1st January, is the beginning of the year for most things Japanese. It's the date on which schools, the financial year, new employees, government statistics and contracts typically commence. Beyond this, spring is the appearance of Japan's national symbol – the cherry blossom. The blossoming is tracked daily in the national media from its first appearance, usually in Okinawa in February, until mid-May, when the last trees bloom in Hokkaido. When the first blossoms appear, the Japanese hold picnics and festivities under the cherry trees – these are simultaneously a celebration of the new and a recognition of the ephemeral, the blossom itself a symbol of the joys of youth and of the transience of human existence.

> In March 2007, a public apology was issued by the Meteorological Agency for a computer glitch that caused it to predict the beginning of the cherry blossoming three days earlier than it should have. Because so many events are planned around the appearance of the cherry blossom, the cost of this blunder was estimated to run into millions of yen.

Worship of the New

From regarding cherry blossom as the metaphor for the human condition it's a short step to the idolisation of youth that is a defining characteristic of the Japanese. Children and young people are adored, especially young sports stars, who can find themselves the centre of national attention at the first sign of precocious talent. Perhaps the clearest example of this is the high school baseball tournament that takes place at Koshien Stadium every summer. The entire 11 days of the tournament are covered live on national television, and Japan grinds to a halt to watch the final. Players who shine in this tournament are lauded by the media and snapped up by professional baseball teams.

This fascination with youth reaches into all areas. When it comes to pop music, a large slice of the charts is dominated by junior and senior high school girl bands singing in their school uniforms about the tragedies and joys of love. Part of the enduring fascination of the *kamikaze* pilots of the Pacific War was their youth, and in the world of commerce, Japanese businesses draw their new recruits almost exclusively from college graduates in preference to older applicants, who often find it difficult to find jobs.

With the downturn of the economy in the early '90s, many young Japanese found themselves in part-time jobs, and discovered that while living at home they now had the time and money to travel independently and enjoy their spare time. However, the subsequent upturn in the economy saw companies preferring to hire graduates, while many *freeta* found themselves stuck at home.

The importance of the new extends to produce. The Japanese will pay over the odds for seasonal fruit and vegetables when they first become available, and buying the new season's rice is the natural thing for Japanese households to do, even though they pay a premium. Buying habits that emphasise the new are also seen with imported goods, Japan being the number one overseas market for *Beaujolais nouveau*, France's most popular young red wine.

> In May 2007, at the first wholesale auction of the season in Sapporo, a new record for a pair of melons was reached when Marui Imai Inc., a department store, paid ¥2mn (US$20,000), more than doubling the previous high of ¥800,000 (US$8,000).

The same applies to architecture. Old buildings aren't valued, but preferably knocked down to make way for skyscrapers. (One of the many apparent contradictions of the national character is that every year millions of Japanese travel to Europe to look at old buildings.) One only needs to visit Kyoto to see evidence of this: despite its being the only large city to be spared bombing in the Pacific War, except for its gardens and temples it now looks much the same as any other Japanese city.

The Cult of Cuteness

Arising out of Japan's adoration for youth and the new is the popularity of all things 'cute' (*kawaii*). It's difficult to go anywhere in Japan without being assailed by objects claiming to be the ultimate in 'cute'. Of course, almost anything compact can be thought of as cute, and there are an awful lot of small things in Japan, but 'cuteness' for the Japanese goes far beyond considerations of size. It's a difficult concept to pin down, but it relates to the humanising of functional objects. This tendency can be seen everywhere in Japan – from the plastic characters that hang off mobile phones to the latest household robots and animation. The Japanese even go so far as designing a 'Roadworks' sign showing a pile of dirt with smiling eyes on it!

Cuteness is a particularly desirable quality in females – and here it has more to do with 'babyfication'. Women's fashions in Japan aren't so much smart, pretty or beautiful, as cute. Images of Japanese and Western icons such as Hello Kitty (see **Icons – Symbols** below) and Mickey Mouse are found on clothing not out of a sense of irony or cynicism, as might be the reason they're sported by teenagers and students in the West, but because they're considered to be cute. (The young Japanese girls who wear T-shirts and accessories emblazoned with the Playboy 'bunny' would be shocked if they found out its true significance.)

Cuteness also manifests itself in the mannerisms of Japanese women, who often act younger or seem less mature than their counterparts in the West, attributes that are apparently attractive to Japanese men. Indeed, cuteness has become so popular that it has splintered into different 'cults', such as 'erotic-cute' and 'gothic-cute'.

Who are the Japanese?

Groupthink

In countries with a rice-growing tradition, there's a need for people to work together to get the most from the harvest. In Japan, this emphasis on the group rather than on the individual has infiltrated every aspect of society. Quite simply, if you aren't a member of a group, you're nothing. The induction into group culture starts early, when children learn that they're part of a family unit that eats and sleeps together, and is later emphasised by punishments that might include being put outside (as opposed to the Western punishment of being banished to your room).

The education system places a strong emphasis on group behaviour, which has been blamed for the high incidence of bullying and suicide among high school students. The importance of group identity continues into adulthood. If you ask Japanese workers what they do for a living, they will usually give you the name of their company rather than their occupation, as the company is the group they belong to.

Seniority Rules

One of the ways that Japanese organise their world is by a hierarchy of age. If you're the same age as somebody else, you automatically become part of the same peer group, or *doukei*. Anyone older than you should be treated with respect by deferring to them and using respectful forms of address. Similarly, you expect younger people to treat you with respect and you can use plain language with them. For this reason, your age is important information, and usually one of the first things a Japanese person will ask you.

Shyness

Strong group identity leads to another characteristic that Japanese often ascribe to themselves: shyness. But when they describe themselves as being 'shy', the Japanese really mean that they prefer not to act individually. The prefer to consult others belonging to their group to find out what action is agreeable to them in order not to inconvenience anyone.

Reinforcing this tendency are the crowded conditions of Japan's cities, where privacy is at a premium. Windows in Japanese apartments are often small or frosted so that residents cannot see into their neighbours' living rooms, and packed commuter trains force people to withdraw into the only 'space' available to them – their own minds. It's no wonder that the personal stereo was invented in Japan, that games consoles are so popular and that mobile-phones-cum-mini-entertainment-stations have become ubiquitous.

Hikikomori is the Japanese term for 'hidden away' or 'confined', and it refers to those who withdraw from society. Typically, they're young males who have suffered bullying and who isolate themselves in their parents' home. According to the Ministry of Health and Welfare, a person who has remained 'confined' for six months is officially classified as a *hikikomori*.

Modesty

The Japanese are very difficult to compliment. They will emphatically reject any kind of praise and are unlikely to boast of proficiency in any endeavour. If a Japanese person admits to playing a sport, it usually means that he has practised intensely for long hours, spent a lot of money on coaching and dedicated himself to improving his skill in it; even so, he's highly unlikely to admit to being good at it. Being recognised as outstandingly good at something would disrupt group harmony.

> *Otaku* **is the Japanese word for the geeky kind of person who becomes obsessed with a specific subject at the expense of developing social skills. They tend to congregate in the Akihabara electronics-shopping district of Tokyo, where** *otaku***-targeted businesses have developed, including specialist video stores and 'cosplay' (costume play) cafés, where** *otaku* **are served by girls dressed, for example, as French maids.**

Indirectness

In Japanese communication, the onus is on the listener to understand the speaker, which is directly contrary to the Western preference for people to 'speak their minds' and make their message clear. In Japan, intelligent people are those who are adept at understanding others, and the ability to do so is called *haragei* (literally 'stomach art' and perhaps best translated as 'gut feeling'). You should only have to hint at your message for an intelligent person to understand.

This cultivation of the art of understanding means that directness is unnecessary and unseemly – hence the notorious Japanese inability to say 'no'. For example, if you ask a Japanese guest if he or she wants a drink, the reply will typically be neither 'yes' nor 'no' but an indirect response, from which you're expected to understand whether your guest wants a drink or not. Beware of asking questions such as "Don't you want a drink?" as Japanese will often reply "Yes" meaning "Yes, I don't want a drink" or "Thank you" meaning "No, thank you."

Social Obligation

The Japanese sensitivity to social obligations (*giri*) is another quality thought to stem from the rice-harvesting tradition, which necessitated maintaining good will among villagers – helping others when needed and expecting the favour to be returned. During the two-and-a-half centuries of stability under the Tokugawa *Shōgunate*, this was formalised into a moral code. In modern Japan, the concept of *giri* is expressed in the custom of offering gifts in summer and winter to those to whom you owe favours (either as a return of the favour or as an acknowledgement that you owe one), and in sending New Year's cards to everybody you know.

The concept of *giri* has even influenced the Western tradition of Valentine's Day and given it a uniquely Japanese flavour in the form of *giri-choco* (obligation chocolate). Women give chocolate not just to their beloved but also to members of the opposite sex to whom they feel a social obligation, such as a teacher, colleague or boss. In typical Japanese fashion, another date was invented when such favours could be returned in order to maintain the balance: 14th March is White Day, when men give white chocolate to the women who treated them on Valentine's Day.

Politeness & Rudeness

Centuries of living cheek by jowl have resulted in a ritualised form of communication that is often regarded by Westerners as extreme politeness. The Japanese language is full of set phrases and responses that must be used in specific circumstances, e.g. on entering and leaving a house, arriving at work in the morning, before and after eating, on leaving work or a public area such as an *onsen,* and on finishing a job.

But the Japanese aren't always polite in ways that Westerners expect. One example is their tendency to ask your age directly. Another is their reluctance to give up seats on the underground (subway) for the elderly or pregnant women, which can be explained by their fear of embarrassment due to acting as an individual, and their unwillingness to create a debt of gratitude that cannot be repaid.

A final example of what Westerners might perceive as rudeness, but what is in fact a result of cultural difference, is when a Western man, accompanied by his wife or partner or a female friend or colleague, is talking to a Japanese man and he asks the Western man about the woman instead of addressing her directly. This is because Japanese men consider it impolite to ask a woman personal questions.

Determination & Endurance

Gambaru is the quality of not only doing your best but showing a 'fighting spirit'. It's most evident in the word *gambatte!* used to encourage people in sporting events, at work and when facing examinations or moving house, and is more like 'Go for it' than merely 'Good luck'. Typical Western expressions such as 'Take it easy' and 'Don't work too hard' are rarely used in Japan.

Watching Japanese game shows may make you wonder if there's a sado-masochistic streak to the people's psyche. You may be comforted to know that such shows are in fact an expression of their admiration of

gaman or endurance – the diligence and stamina necessary to get a job done or in sporting practice and preparation. Training regimes for baseball, for example, include the *1,000 fungo* (fielding 1,000 balls in a single practice session) and having pitchers throw 200 times on their 'rest' days – hardly surprising that many promising high school pitchers are burnt out before they can turn professional.

It's no surprise either that long-distance running is a prestigious sport in Japan, where extended relay races known as *ekiden* combine the Japanese admiration for *gaman* with their preference for group activity. One of the most popular televised events of the year is the live broadcast of the Hakone Ekiden, in which university students compete in teams of ten over a 216km (134km) course – a race that lasts two days and makes the marathon look like a sprint.

> In May 2007, the All Japan High School Athletic Federation banned foreign students from running the first, and longest, leg of the All Japan High School Ekiden Championship, which is held in Kyoto in December, after the fastest Japanese participant in the 2006 event had been outpaced by four Kenyans and an *ekiden* fan complained that 'It was like an African championship.'

Attention to Detail

The Japanese obsession for detail was transferred to its renowned manufacturing industry from the tradition of craftsmanship that developed during the Edo period (1603-1867). In this time of stability, the focus shifted from the simple production of useful products to refinement in the production process, the *do*, a term which encapsulates the mental concentration required when striving for perfection and is found in many Japanese words for physical activity, religious practices or crafts. Notable among them are *bushido* ('the way of the warrior'), *sado* ('the way of the tea ceremony'), *shodo* (calligraphy) and *dotoku* (morals). The Japanese concern with precision is evident in the punctuality of trains and the meticulous planning of events.

Inscrutability

The Japanese don't smile only to express happiness. They also smile when they don't understand something or to hide embarrassment. A Western man may easily be fooled into thinking he has a rapier-like wit when a Japanese woman laughs at his jokes, but he will

Who are the Japanese?

be perturbed to discover that she will laugh at almost everything he says.

For this reason, the Japanese may smile in the face of the most terrible events. For example, after an earthquake had destroyed an elderly woman's home, she was interviewed on national TV and, with a beatific smile on her face, described how she had lost all her possessions and had no idea where she would live. Anyone who didn't understand Japanese may have thought she was talking about her grandson's birthday party.

> According to an MTV (US music network) international global survey of over 5,000 young people in 14 countries, only 43 per cent of the world's 16- to 34-year-olds are happy with their lives. In Japan, the figure was a startling 8 per cent.

HUMOUR

The Japanese aren't well known for their sense of humour, and it's a quality they place little emphasis on when asked to describe themselves. The main exception are the people of the Kansai region, which is centred around the second-largest Japanese city, Osaka. Kansai people have a reputation for being warmer and funnier than the image-obsessed Kanto (Tokyo area) people. For this reason, humour in Japan is dominated by comedians from Kansai, where many of the country's comedic traditions have developed.

Traditional Japanese humour takes two main forms: *manzai* – a repartee between a straight man and a funny guy – and *rakugo*, which consists of a person (typically a man) sitting on a cushion in traditional clothes and telling a story, changing his voice for each of the characters. Both these forms have been experiencing something of a resurgence in recent years.

The comedy seen on TV usually takes the form of a game or variety show in which minor celebrities take part. The celebrities are known as *aidoru* (a corruption of the word 'idol') and the humour is usually slapstick. For example, contestants may be asked to take part in a game of 'air hockey'. The fact that celebrities are acting foolishly is enough to make them humorous, but an important element of these shows is the most foolish participant being hit on the head. One of the most popular Japanese TV show hosts, Sanma-san, is famous for hitting his guests on the head with a foam hammer!

Verbal humour isn't widely appreciated. Punning wordplay is often dismissed as 'old man's humour', while satire and sarcasm are rare. Instead there's a brand of humour that involves creating new words, but these tend to go out of fashion very quickly, leaving only those in the know to appreciate

the joke. For example, in 2006 *makeinu* ('underdog' from the book 'Howl of the Underdog') become a popular term for unmarried women in their 30s who were enjoying a single life, and caused much amusement while it was current.

> **Many Japanese neologisms are corruptions of English, such as:**
>
> *baakooda hea* = **barcode hair**
> *rebaasu-suru* = **reversal, i.e. vomit**
> *nyuuhaafu* = **new half, i.e. a male-to-female transsexual**

Telling jokes about the Japanese royal family, homosexuality, social vices and gangsters is taboo, although recent acts, such as that of professional wrestler turned comedian Hard Gay, have started to break down the barriers.

THE CLASS SYSTEM

After the Meiji Restoration of 1869, the new rulers abolished the caste system, under which only eight social positions or roles were permitted, and reformed the education system. Japan became a meritocracy, in which education was more important than social background. After the Pacific War, most people were equally poor, and up until the collapse of the economy in 1990 the Japanese could consider their society to be almost entirely middle class.

This middle class majority is also strengthened by Japan's tax system, benefit's system and most people's preference for secure, moderately remunerated jobs over high-risk, high-reward careers. Since the crash, however, Japanese society has witnessed an increasing divide between the top and the bottom of the socio-economic heap.

There are no class distinctions in terms of accent or way of speaking, as in many other countries. Although the Japanese royal family uses a particular vocabulary and phraseology, it isn't thought of as a distinct 'class', as its numbers are so small.

In fact, a lower class has always existed in Japan. The politically correct label is *hisabetsu-buraku* (discriminated hamlet/community), but they're usually called *burakumin* (hamlet/community people). Originally these people did the jobs that were thought unclean: they were tanners, butchers, executioners and undertakers. They were separated from the rest of society into hamlets – hence their name. They still exist and, although their situation is improving, people who live in them may even today be discriminated against in the workplace or the marriage 'market'.

CHILDREN

Japan's birth rate is one of the lowest in the world and continues to fall. Partly for this reason and partly as a result of the Japanese cult of youth (see above), children are usually indulged and dressed according to the mother's ideal of cuteness. (Japanese fathers tend to be less involved in their children's upbringing than their Western counterparts, although it's changing.)

Whereas in the West discipline tends to be punishment oriented, Japanese children are taught to appreciate the impact of their behaviour on others. It appears to work, as Japanese children are well behaved by Western standards. However, when children get overexcited, a Japanese parent may let them continue whereas a Western parent would reprimand them.

> *Nanatsu made ha kami no uchi* –
> **Until the age of seven children are in the Gods' domain.**
> Japanese proverb

Japanese children typically sleep in the same space as their parents and aren't shunted off to their own room as soon as possible, as is the usual practice in Western societies. This is partly a result of the size of Japanese apartments, where the living room often doubles as a bedroom at night when futons are dragged out of cupboards. (Unlike Western imitations, Japanese futons consists only of a mattress.) Bedtimes are usually less structured than in Western households, and Japanese children soon learn the knack of being able to fall asleep at any time, anywhere. As they grow up, late bedtimes are the norm, and Japanese children often suffer a sleep deficit. It isn't surprising that many students list 'sleeping' as their favourite recreational activity.

Many Japanese children's lives are taken up with education to the exclusion of much else, and they tend to lead more sheltered lives than similarly aged children in the West. Education is always on the minds of their parents, whose responsibilities include paying for and supporting their children through university or other post-school training. (Half of Japanese children go to university and a further 25 per cent to a specialised training institute.) Getting into a top university gives you a greater likelihood of being accepted by the company you wish to join.

To give yourself the best chance of being accepted by a good university it's important to attend a good senior high school, and to get into a good senior high school a student should go to a good junior high school and before that a good elementary school. This makes exams – and particularly those at the end of high school – among the most important of life's events. To make sure they obtain good grades, many children go to a cramming school after regular school (see **Education** in Chapter 3).

ATTITUDES TO FOREIGNERS

Japanese attitudes towards foreigners operate on two levels. On the surface, the Japanese are open and friendly, welcoming of foreign tastes and fashions. For example, recent years have seen a 'Korean boom', as Korean TV dramas and films have come into vogue, and consequently Korean pop stars, food and even cosmetics, with

Japanese women extolling the beauty of Korean women's skin. Any foreign personality can become an overnight celebrity, with his image appearing everywhere on TV shows and in advertisements.

This is what happened recently to Bob Sapp, a hulking black American football player turned K1 martial arts fighter who, in a whirlwind of advertising appearances, became an omnipresent figure in the media for a couple of years, appearing in at least 23 TV commercials and 1,000 interviews, on 200 products, and as an author or subject of four books. Since then, he has completely dropped out of sight.

At a deeper level, many Japanese cling to the opinion that they are a unique and pure race which foreigners can never comprehend. The most vocal of these are ultra-patriotic right-wing groups who believe in the divinity of the emperor (and the rearming of Japan). On certain days – the emperor's birthday, for example – they can be seen with their short-cropped hair and military-style uniforms driving convoys of trucks festooned with rising-sun flags, while loudspeakers blare militaristic music interspersed with messages extolling racial purity and other chauvinistic slogans. The convoys drive at a sedate pace, ignoring traffic lights and parking restrictions, while the normally fastidious police do little to control them. In Tokyo, they make their way to the Yasukuni Shrine, which is their controversial rallying (see box). The intolerance of these groups to foreigners sometimes spills over into violence, as in 2003, when the Chinese consulate in Osaka was rammed by a truck.

> **The Yasakuni Shrine is devoted to Japan's war dead but also commemorates thousands of soldiers from countries such as Korea and Taiwan who died 'in Japan's service' – many of them having been forced to serve the Japanese. The Shrine is therefore the subject of friction between Japan and its Asian neighbours, as well as being controversial at home: in 1978, over 1,000 convicted war criminals were interred there.**

It may seem surprising that such extremists groups, which are said to have links with the *yakuza* (the Japanese mafia), are tolerated in Japanese society. However, nationalistic ideals appeal to a broad spectrum of Japanese, as can be seen by the popularity of right-wing parties, principally the Liberal Democratic Party, and politicians such as the Tokyo mayor, Shintaro Ishikawa. Ishikawa in particular is prone to expressing xenophobic opinions, such as his claim that foreigners are the cause of Tokyo's rising crime rate and would be likely to revolt in the event of a major earthquake. (Thousands of Korean immigrants were massacred after the devastating 1923 Tokyo earthquake when enraged Japanese mobs falsely accused them of poisoning water sources.) Although the Japanese rarely express their political views, their 'conservatism' is clear from the fact that politicians like Ishikawa continue to be re-elected – as he was recently for a third, four-year term.

Nevertheless, there are signs that Japan is forming a more accommodating view of the outside

Who are the Japanese?

world. On TV, foreigners used to be seen as novelties or even freaks, interesting only for their strangeness. Nowadays, they're rarely presented in this way and some foreign TV personalities have popular TV shows, while others are chosen to take part in discussion programmes, not just because they're foreign but because of their expertise and intelligence. It has to be noted, however, that 'visible' foreigners tend to be white skinned Westerners rather than people from other Asian countries, who are generally looked upon with less favour on TV and elsewhere in society.

NATIONAL ICONS

Every country has its icons – people, places, structures, symbols, flora and fauna, food and drink – which are revered or unique to that country and have special significance to its people. The following is a list of some of Japan's icons that you can expect to come across or hear reference to in one way or another.

Icons – People

Downtown – A comedy duo consisting of Masatoshi Hamada (b. 1963) and Hitoshi Matsumoto (b. 1963), who started out as a *manzai* act (see **Humour** above) and have been among the most popular comedians in Japan since 1991. They have their own television shows and feature in best-selling books and recordings.

 Geisha – Western preconceptions notwithstanding, true *geisha* are highly skilled entertainers at establishments that are so expensive as to be inaccessible to all but the seriously rich.

> If you want to praise a Japanese woman, never tell her that she looks like a *geisha*! In Japan their reputation is tarnished by the existence of those who provide less honourable forms of 'entertainment' for men – for example, *onsen geisha* at hot springs (see Chapter 8).

 Ayumi Hamasaki – Since her breakthrough hit in 1998, Hamasaki has become the top-selling female vocalist in j-pop history.

 Katsushika Hokusai (1760-1849) – One of the most venerated wood-print artists of the Edo era, Hokusai, famous for his 'wave' prints, was an important influence on the Impressionists, especially Claude Monet and Vincent Van Gogh.

 Junichiro Koizumi (b. 1942) – Japan's former prime minister (2001-06) was the second-longest serving Japanese prime minister in the post-war period, wore his hair long and was the housewives' darling. He contrasted strongly with the majority of faceless leaders who typically hold the job for a year before being forced to resign.

 Takuya Kimura (b. 1972) – Probably the most popular member of the pop band SMAP, Kimura has also had starring roles in hit TV series, variety shows and movies. He is an all-round talent whose popularity never seems to wane.

Takeshi Kitano (b. 1947) – His achievements as a film director and actor are virtually unknown in Japan, where he's a famous comedian who has been a mainstay of variety TV shows, as both host and guest.

Akira Kurosawa (1910-98) – Although Kurosawa isn't widely known in Japan, the novel directorial techniques he employed in such films as *Rashomon*, *Yojimbo* and *Hidden Fortress* are recognised as being among the most influential in cinema history.

Hibari Misora (1937-89) – A singer and actress whose songs in the *enka* (Japanese folk ballad) style of music were immensely popular in the post-war period. Misora's song *Kawa no nagare no yō ni* (*Like the Flow of a River*) was voted the best Japanese song of all time, and she was the first woman to be awarded the National Prize of Honour, although not until after her death.

Hayao Miyazaki (b. 1942) – A director of animated film, Miyazaki has been producing highly popular animated movies in Japan for years but gained worldwide attention in 1997 with *Princess Mononoke*. His next film, *Spirited Away*, broke box office records in Japan and was also successful internationally.

Ieyasu Tokugawa (1543-1616) – This warlord fought his way to the *Shōgunate* in 1603, and his descendants' rule lasted until 1869. He presided over a period of peace in Japan, which developed in almost complete isolation from the rest of the world.

Haruki Murakami (b. 1949) – A writer whose breakthrough came in 1985, when his novel *Norwegian Wood* caught the imagination of younger Japanese. Since then, Murakami has broadened his appeal in both Japan and overseas (many of his novels have been translated into English and other languages). In Japan, his writing is known for its 'Western' style.

Yoshiro Nakamatsu (b. 1928) – An inventor who has over 3,000 patents to his name, from floppy discs to love potions, springy shoes to hand-operated pumps. A true eccentric, he stood for election as mayor of Tokyo in 2007 – without success.

Hidetoshi Nakata (b. 1977) – Japan's most famous footballer took part in three World Cups and played for seven seasons in Italy's Prima Liga, winning the 2001 Italian championship with Roma. He retired after his country's final game in the 2006 World Cup.

Samurai & Ninja – The *samurai*, with their bamboo armour and long, curved swords, who lived by an almost inhuman warrior code, and the stealthy *ninja*, assassins dressed in black and waiting in ambush, are icons from Japan's past who remain cult figures in both the East and West.

Sumo Wrestlers

Although baseball and recently football have become increasingly popular, sumo is recognised as Japan's national sport. However, since one of the greatest champions, Takanohana, retired in 2001, no Japanese has made it to the top international rank, and the sport has been dominated by Mongolian wrestlers.

Masayoshi Son (b. 1957) – Coming from an immigrant Korean family proved to be no barrier to this entrepreneur, who is one of the richest men in Japan. Son made his fortune by investing in new technologies, such as broadband internet connection and, most recently, a mobile phone network, to expand his company, Softbank.

Ichiro Suzuki (b. 1973) – Always known simply by his first name and based in the US, Ichiro is Japan's most successful baseball player. In 2004, he broke George Sisler's record of 257 strikes in a season, which had stood since 1920, and in 2006 he was a key member of the Japanese team that won the World Baseball Classic.

Ryoko Tani (formerly Tamura) (b. 1975) – At just 146cm tall, judo wrestler Tani (widely known as Yawara-chan) has dominated her weight division for almost a decade, winning six World Championships and two Olympic golds. After giving birth to a daughter, she competed in the Beijing Olympics in 2008, winning a bronze medal (her 5th Olympic medal).

Osamu Tezuka (1928-89) – Known as the 'Father of Anime', Tezuka was the artist behind 'Astro Boy' and 'Kimba the White Lion,' which reached worldwide audiences, as well as many other animation hits in Japan. By the time he died in 1989, he had produced over 700 *manga* (Japanese comics), totalling an astonishing 150,000 pages.

Icons – Symbols

Chopsticks – Japanese chopsticks (*hashi*) tend to be wooden, short and tapered towards the 'eating' end. Sometimes the wood is lacquered and finely decorated with traditional pictures. Disposable wooden chopsticks (*waribashi*), which are attached in pairs, are widely used and always included with *bento* (lunch boxes) and most kinds of take-away food.

Chrysanthemum Throne – The common name given to the Imperial throne of Japan, which is the oldest monarchy in the world. The Empire of Japan was allegedly founded in 660BC by the Emperor Jimmu Tenno and his descendents continue to reign today; the current Emperor Akhito (Heisei Tenno) is the direct 125th descendant of Jimmu. Despite the fact that there has been eight Empresses, under Japanese Imperial law (promulgated by the Imperial Household Agency and the Privy Council) woman cannot reign as the sovereign. The Emperor, the *Tenno* (Heavenly sovereign), acts as a high priest in the Shinto faith, although his divine power was renounced after WWII.

Fireworks – For many Japanese, *hanabi* (literally 'fire flower') is synonymous with summer, when there are numerous opportunities to witness spectacular firework displays lasting several hours.

Gardens – Japanese gardens can be found at temples, castles and in large parks, and typically include miniature landscapes, areas of raked stones and moss in harmony with ponds, stone bridges and lanterns. A typical garden includes a small wooden building where 'tea ceremonies' may be conducted overlooking the tranquil scene.

Hello Kitty – This moon-headed cat was created by the Tokyo-based Sanrio company in 1974 and can be found adorning over 22,000 brands, as well as in cartoon series and computer games. Hello Kitty is especially popular among young Japanese women.

Hot springs – If there's an upside to being one of the most volcanic countries in the world, it's the profusion of hot springs (*onsen*) that results. Visiting an *onsen* isn't merely a relaxation but an occasion, with rites and rituals to be observed (see **Chapter 8**).

Ikebana – The Japanese art of flower arranging, *ikebana*, is also known as *kadō* (the 'way of flowers'). More than simply putting flowers in a container, *ikebana* is a disciplined art form in which nature and humanity are brought together.

Kabuki – A traditional form of Japanese theatre (though more like opera) known for stylised costumes, white make-up and strangulated voices.

Karaoke – If there's one gift to popular culture that Japan has bestowed upon the world, for better or for worse, it's *karaoke*, which literally means 'empty orchestra'. It wasn't in fact a Japanese idea – that 'honour' belongs to an American company – but Daisuke Inoue was the first to make *karaoke* machines and lease them out.

Kimono

The traditional dress of Japan is made from silk and is more usually worn by women. In summer, a less expensive, more colourful version made from cotton, called the *yukata*, is often worn when attending firework displays and festivals.

Manga & Anime – Comics and animated films are a staple of entertainment for both children and adults in Japan, and Japanese products are becoming increasingly popular in the West.

Matsuri (festivals) – Almost every neighbourhood in Japan has a festival. They sometimes involve the parading of a heavy *mikoshi* (portable shrine) through the town, dancing and processions, for which people dress in traditional costume and play traditional instruments. However, there are all manner of *matsuri*, including contests of skill and endurance, the arts and the downright bizarre.

Rising sun – The rising sun is represented in both the Japanese flag and the country's name, *Nihon* (sometimes written *Nippon*), which means 'sun's origin'.

Shinkansen (Bullet Train) – When it came into service, in time for the 1964 Tokyo Olympics, the *shinkansen* was the first high-speed train in the world. Since then, Japan's 'bullet trains' have carried some 6bn passengers and attained super-efficiency as well as high speed.

Speed & Efficiency

In 2003, Japan Rail announced that on average the arrival time of *shinkansen* was within six seconds of their scheduled time, based on 160,000 journeys and taking into account all delays through human error and accidents.

Tea Ceremony – The tea ceremony (*sadō, chadō* or *chanoyu* in Japanese) has been a Japanese tradition for over 400 years and is a ritual way of preparing and drinking (*matcha*) tea and is strongly influenced by Zen Buddhism. The tea ceremony traditionally takes place in a tea house or room (*chashitsu*) in a Chaniwa garden, designed in aesthetic simplicity according to the concepts of *sado*.

Woodblock printing – Woodblock printing (*moku hanga*) is a technique best known for its use in the ukiyo-e artistic genre (between the 17th and 20th centuries), although it had been used in China for centuries to print books, but was surprisingly only widely adopted in Japan during the Edo period (1603-1867). The technique is essentially the same as woodcut in Western printmaking.

Zen Buddhism – Although Zen Buddhism has its roots in China, it's more commonly known in the West from its practice among the Japanese and its 'embodiment' in Japanese gardens, particularly the stone garden of Ryoanji in Kyoto.

Icons – Places & Structures

Hakone – One of the most popular destinations for tourists, who go there for the forests, spectacular geothermal phenomena and views of Mount Fuji.

Hiroshima – The first city in the world to suffer a nuclear attack, at 8.15am on 6th August 1945, an event commemorated annually.

Hokkaido – The northern island of Japan wasn't brought under direct administration by the government until 1869 and is considered a play area by most Japanese. In summer it's the destination for hiking, camping and touring, while in winter it's famous for the perfect snow on its numerous ski slopes.

Ise Jingu – The most important Shinto shrine in Japan (situated in the city of Ise in Mie prefecture) is both ancient and modern. It was established over 2,000 years ago, but every 20 years the massive wooden buildings and bridge are demolished and reconstructed using the same ancient techniques – a hugely expensive process. The next rebuild will be in 2014.

Kyoto – The seat of the emperor from 794 until 1868, when it moved to Tokyo. Packed with venerable temples and immaculate gardens, Kyoto is now the centre of Japan's tourist industry.

Nara – The capital of Japan until 794 and now a peaceful provincial city. Many old temples can be found here, including the largest bronze Buddha in the country, housed in what is said to be the largest wooden building in the world.

Nikko – This fabulously decorated complex of shrines is the mausoleum of Tokugawa Leyasu, the *Shōgun* who united Japan in 1603. The shrine is part of a national park with many hot springs and some of the highest waterfalls in Japan.

Okinawa – To Japanese, Okinawa is the ultimate beach holiday destination at any time of the year. It's exotic and yet part of Japan. The food and music of Okinawa have become popular throughout Japan – as has its particularly potent form of *shochu* (see **Food & Drink** below) called *awamori*. Nevertheless, Okinawa isn't a good topic of general conversation (see **Taboos** in **Chapter 4**).

Mount Fuji

A mere 100km (62mi) from Tokyo, this towering dormant volcano, which last erupted in 1707, is for many the symbol of Japan. A magnificent sight in both summer and winter, it has been the subject of countless works of art, photographs and poems, and is of religious significance to followers of both Shinto, Japan's native religion, and Buddhism. To many Japanese, the ultimate 'nationalist experience' is to climb Mount Fuji at night in order to witness the rising of the sun from its summit.

Icons – Flora & Fauna

Bamboo – Few plants are used in as many ways as bamboo (*take*). The quickly growing evergreen has been used in construction and various arts and crafts in Japan for many centuries. Bamboo shoots (*takenoko*) are a popular spring delicacy.

Who are the Japanese?

Bobtail cat – The Japanese bobtail is a native breed of cat with an unusual 'bobbed' tail, resembling that of a rabbit. The breed has been known in Japan for centuries, and there are many stories, as well as ancient art, featuring it. Among it's strangest mutations is the odd-eyed cat, a cat with one blue eye and one green, yellow or brown eye, which is a feline form of complete heterochromia, a condition which also occurs in some other animals.

Bonsai – Literally 'tray planting', *bonsai* is the art of aesthetic miniaturisation of trees by growing them in containers. Cultivation includes techniques for shaping, watering, and re-potting in various styles of containers (see photo below).

Brown Bear – The brown bear (*higuma*) is found only on Hokkaido, where there's an estimated population of some 3,000. The severe climate and rugged terrain of Shieteko National Park is a haven for wildlife, although the brown bear is on Japan's list of endangered species.

Cherry blossom – The cherry blossom (*sakura*) is Japan's unofficial national flower and symbol. Cherry trees are planted throughout Japan and have a short but intense blossoming period of around two weeks, when flower-viewing parties (*hanami*) are popular. Disappointingly, this type of cherry tree doesn't bear fruit and most cherries in Japanese stores are imported from the US.

Chrysanthemum – Chrysanthemums (*kiku*) were cultivated in China as a flowering herb as long ago as the 15th century BC and were thought to have been introduced into Japan in the 8th century AD. In 910AD the chrysanthemum was adopted as the national flower and the Emperor's official seal, and the Japanese throne became know as the 'chrysanthemum throne'. The imperial flower is associated with longevity and is celebrated by a National Chrysanthemum Day, called the 'Festival of Happiness', on the 9th September.

Japanese carp – The Japanese carp (*koi* or *nishikigoi*, literally 'brocaded carp') is an ornamental domesticated variety of the common carp. The ornamental cultivation of carp originated in the Niigata region of Japan during the Edo period and depictions of koi with different colour variations have been found in 18th century Japanese drawings and paintings. A homophone of *koi* means 'love' or 'affection' – they are symbols of love and friendship in Japan.

Japanese Crane – The red-crowned crane (*tancho*), also called the Japanese Crane or Manchurian Crane, is a large crane and the second rarest in the world. In Japan it's a symbol of luck, longevity and fidelity, and features on the ¥1,000 banknote and in Japanese art.

Japanese Maple – The Japanese maple (*momiji*) – of which there are over 400 varieties – is the king of spectacular autumn colours (from bright yellow through orange and red) and is widely used as a decorative tree in Japanese gardens.

Japanese Plum – Blooming several weeks ahead of the cherry blossoms, plum blossoms (*ume*) are an early sign of spring. In the Tokyo area they typically flower in February and March – the event is celebrated with plum festivals (*ume matsuri*) in public parks, shrines and temples across the country.

The Jōmon Cedar – The Japanese Cedar (*sugi*) is endemic to Japan. The Jōmon Cedar, on the island of Yakushima, has a girth of 16.4m (53.8ft) and is estimated to be at least 2,000 years old.

Macaque – The macaque or snow monkey is a common red-faced monkey found in the north of Honshu, where it's often found keeping warm in the hot waters of the onsen (hot springs). The monkeys inhabit the northernmost region of Japan's main island, which is the world's coldest spot inhabited by primates (excluding humans).

Pine tree – Green throughout the year, the pine tree (*matsu*) symbolises youth and longevity in Japan. It's used as decorative plant in most Japanese gardens and is also popular for *bonsai*.

Racoon dog – The Japanese racoon dog (*tanuki*) is often mistakenly translated as raccoon or badger. It has traditionally been thought of as a weird creature with supernatural powers and has been part of Japanese folklore since ancient times.

Rhododendron – Although most of the rhododendrons grown in Japanese gardens originally came from China, they have been an integral part of Japanese landscape design for many centuries, prized for their beautiful trumpet-shaped spring flowers.

Sika – The *sika* is a member of the deer family that inhabits much of East Asia. It's found in mixed deciduous forests in the north of Japan, and mixed subtropical deciduous and evergreen forests in the south.

Tosa – The Japanese *tosa* (also called the *tosa ken*) is a breed of Japanese fighting dog, originally bred in Tosa (present day Kochi). It's popular in Japan and many other countries, although their importation and ownership is banned in some countries where they are considered a dangerous breed.

Icons – Food & Drink

Beer – Beer was introduced into Japan by the Dutch during the Edo period and today is the country's most popular alcoholic drink, accounting for some two-thirds of the 9bn litres of alcohol consumed annually. Lager-style beers (including ice beers) are the most widely drunk, although low-malt *happoushu* beers are increasingly popular, costing half the price.

Bento

A *bento* is a single-portion, take-away box of Japanese food typically consisting of rice, fish or meat and one or more pickled or cooked vegetables – all beautifully presented. The box itself is usually a disposable plastic or aluminium container, but can also be hand-crafted lacquer-ware. *Bento* are sold in convenience stores, departments stores, shopping centres and railway stations, as well as dedicated *bento* shops.

Chanko nabe – A generic term for a stew cooked in a pot for sumo wrestlers. Its ingredients vary, and the best place to sample it is at the Kokugikan, the sumo tournament stadium in Tokyo, where you can buy a cupful of *chanko nabe* for just ¥200 (US$2).

Curry rice – *Kara raisu* was introduced to Japan at the time of the Russo-Japanese War and has since become the country's most popular dish. It consists of dark brown 'gravy' (there's often little meat in it) and is bland by Indian curry standards. You can often buy a pork cutlet (*tonkatsu*) to go with it. Usually curry rice restaurants serve a range of vegetable/meat/tofu curries in mild, medium or hot (not very spicy) styles.

Dango – Dumplings, which come in many different flavours, are a popular food – characters in *anime* are often be seen eating them. They are an acquired taste for foreigners, e.g. *bocchan dango* are flavoured with sweetened red bean paste and green tea!

Fugu – *Fugu* is the Japanese word for blow- or puffer-fish, which, if prepared incorrectly, is lethally poisonous. It has become one of the most celebrated and notorious dishes in Japan, where 10,000 tons are consumed annually.

Miso – A traditional Japanese food made by fermenting rice, barley and/or soybeans with salt and *kōjikin* mould (a type of fungus also used in brewing). It's most commonly served as a soup, called *misoshiru*, a culinary staple served with most meals in Japan.

Okonomiyaki – Similar to a pancake and served with a variety of fillings. In many *okonomiyaki* restaurants, you can mix the batter yourself and cook it on a hot plate set into the table.

Onigiri – Rice balls are one of Japan's favourite snacks, sold in convenience stores in many flavours (fillings include fish and pickles). Slightly triangular in shape, *onigiri* were created before chopsticks were in use and are shaped for eating with the hands.

Ramen – Originally from China, *ramen* consists of noodles in a scalding hot soup 'traditionally' drunk to the accompaniment of loud slurping sounds. The soup is typically either soy or *miso* based, and just the thing on a cold winter's day. You can find *ramen* restaurants in every Japanese town.

Sake – Often described as 'rice wine', *sake* isn't fermented but brewed from rice, in a process similar to beer-making. Another misconception is its name: in Japanese, *sake* means alcohol, and what is known in the West as *sake* is called *nihonshu*. It's served both hot and cold, and different brands vary considerably in price.

Sashimi – Slices of raw seafood dipped in a mixture of *wasabi* (green mustard) and soy sauce.

Shochu – A spirit that can be distilled from sweet potatoes, rice or wheat, *shochu* is usually drunk on ice or with water. It usually contains 25 per cent alcohol but can be up to 40 per cent. The most famous *shochu*-producing regions are Kyushu and Okinawa, the latter being renowned for its *shochu* derivative *awamori*, made from black rice imported from Thailand. *Shochu* has recently overtaken *sake* as the second-most-consumed alcoholic drink in Japan after beer.

Soba & udon – Kinds of noodles. *Soba* is made from buckwheat while the thicker *udon* is made from wheat, and usually appears white. Both can be served hot in winter or cold in summer. *Soba* is usually served heaped on a platter with a dipping sauce and sliced spring onion on the side.

Soy sauce – A sauce made from fermented soya beans, roasted grain, water and salt, which originated in China. Japanese soy sauce is divided into a number of categories, depending on the ingredients and method of production. Some 80 per cent of all Japanese soy sauce is of the *Koikuchi* category, which originated in the Kantō region.

Takoyaki – Usually served from streetside stalls, particularly at festivals, *takoyaki* is octopus in a small batter ball. It may be cool on the outside but it shoots molten lava into your mouth when bitten. Eat with care.

Sushi

Beautifully presented small servings of raw fish, seafood, meat or vegetables (or a combination) served with rice and/or seaweed. There are two main kinds of *sushi*: *nigirizushi*, a ball of rice upon which is placed raw fish or some other topping; and *makizushi* or rolls, in which fish, meat or vegetables are coated in rice and wrapped in *nori* (seaweed).

Tempura – Introduced by the Portuguese, this consists of assorted vegetables and seafood in a light crispy batter, which is dunked in a light soup.

Teriyaki – A Japanese cooking technique in which fish and meat are marinated in sweet soy sauce (*tare*) and then broiled or grilled. The result can be served hot or cold and is commonly included in *bento* meals (see above).

Umeboshi – Although usually called plums, *umeboshi* are closer to apricots. Eaten after they've been pickled, they are extremely sour due to their high citric acid. The red, pickled fruits are often placed on top of rice to look like Hinomaru (the Japanese flag).

Unagi – Eel cooked in a sweet sauce until it's so tender it melts in your mouth, and often served on rice. *Unagi* is supposed to fortify you for the heat of summer, and is traditionally eaten on 24th July and 5th August.

Yaki-imo – Sweet potato baked in a wood-fired oven, usually mounted on the back of a small van that cruises city neighbourhoods emitting distinctive amplified wails.

Yakitori – Various parts of a chicken and/or vegetables on a skewer, grilled over charcoal embers and served with a combination of soy or sweetened sauce, fresh lemon, salt and pepper, chilli powder or green tea powder.

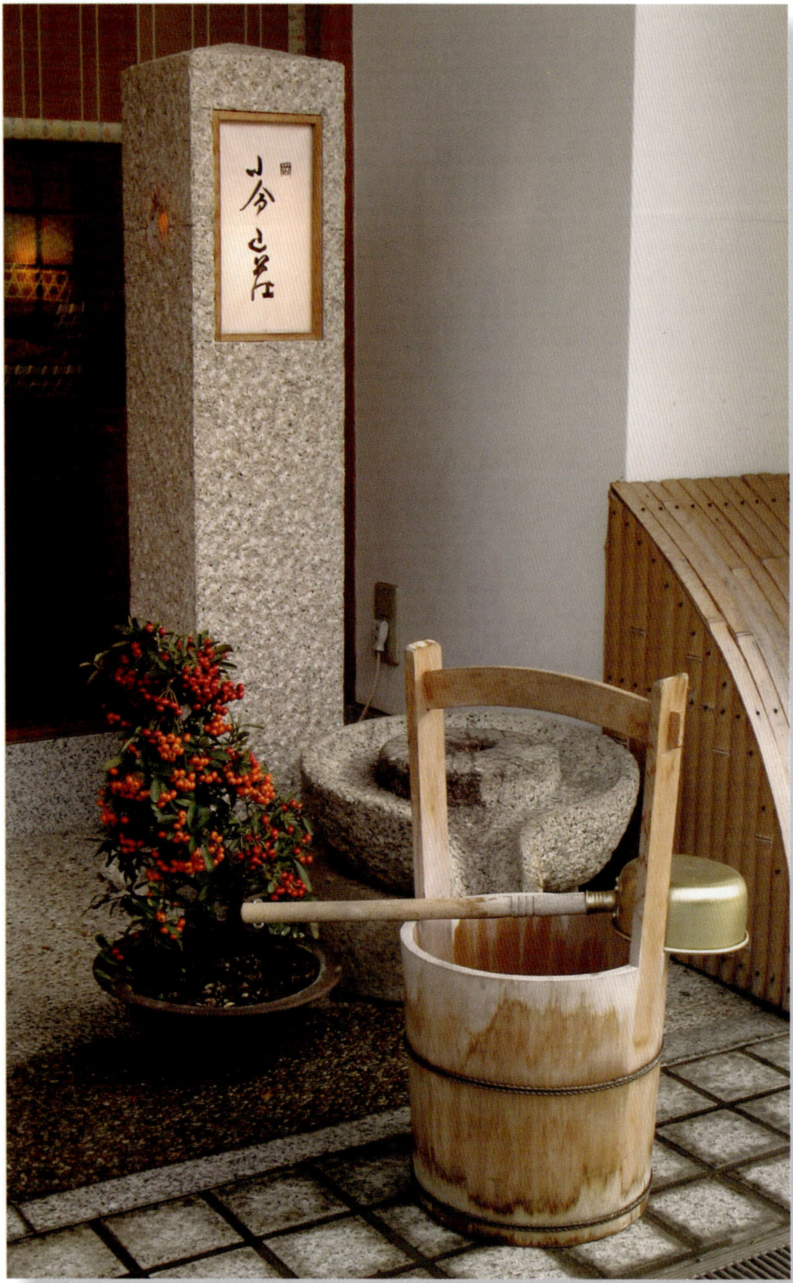

3.
GETTING STARTED

Adjusting to life in a new country can be difficult, exhausting and frustrating, especially in those first few days, when it feels as though you have a million things to do at once. If you add cultural differences to the mix, the stress can become overwhelming. This chapter will help you overcome the challenges of arriving and settling in Japan, including obtaining an alien registration card, finding accommodation, opening a bank account, finding schools for your children, getting online, and obtaining information about such things as taxes, healthcare, council services and utilities. It will also reveal much about the Japanese way of doing things.

> 'My observation is that after one hundred and twenty years of modernisation since the opening of the country to foreigners, present-day Japan is polarised.'
> Kenzaburo Oe (Japanese writer)

IMMIGRATION

When you arrive in Japan, getting through immigration, which is a department of the Ministry of Justice, is usually straightforward if you fit the following description: white, arriving from America or Europe and of 'normal' appearance – unless you've travelled via another Asian country (especially Thailand or Vietnam) on your way to Japan, in which case there's a greater chance that you'll be stopped and questioned than if you had travelled directly from your home country. If you don't fit the above description, the procedure is likely to take longer – your passport and visa will be scrutinised and your luggage may be searched. Single female visitors from other Asian countries are almost always stopped and questioned, as are both male and female visitors from Africa, South America and the Middle East.

Japanese immigration officials and customs officers are generally polite, courteous, and professional, but with the ever-present threat of terrorism and increasing drug smuggling into Japan, they're under strict orders to interrogate anyone who might be involved in either activity. It's in your interest to remain calm and civil, however long the immigration process may take.

To slow things down further, since 20th November 2007 all foreigners, including foreign residents of Japan (but excluding those under 16 and members of ethnic minorities such as Koreans and Chinese who have lived in Japan all their lives), have been required to be fingerprinted and photographed on entering the country – another US-inspired anti-terrorism measure. Anyone who refuses to cooperate is refused entry!

BUREAUCRACY

A trip to a Japanese government office is usually trouble free, but the degree of red tape you encounter depends on a number of factors: where you live, your visa status, what you need done and your nationality. Your ability to speak Japanese will also have a major influence, especially when dealing with civil servants in ward offices. If you speak little or no Japanese and you have a 'non-standard' reason for dealing with officialdom, it's advisable to take a bilingual friend or colleague with you.

Standard visits to the ward office, such as to renew your alien registration card, should be relatively smooth sailing, provided you make adequate preparation. Ensure that you have all the necessary forms, correctly completed, and the required documentation. Most Japanese civil servants don't speak English fluently, but they do provide information in English and have experience in dealing with foreigners.

Alien Registration Card

If you arrive at Narita or Kansai airport (Tokyo) on a non-tourist visa, such as a student or working visa, you'll need to go to your local ward office to apply for an alien registration card (*gaikokujin torokusho* or '*gaijin* card' as it's commonly known among foreigners). This must be done within 90 days and can take several hours, depending on how busy the office is and what time you visit (the earlier the better). Ward offices (*shiyakusho* or, in Tokyo, *kuyakusho*) are often out of the way and can be difficult to find, but there's always access by train or bus – ask someone familiar with the area or the local police.

You must take your passport, visa and two 'passport' photographs taken within the last six months, 4.5cm in length and up to 3.5cm in width, showing a frontal view of your face with no hat or other headgear. A passport photo booth is usually available nearby or in the ward office itself. After completing the necessary forms, you'll be told when to return and collect your card.

> You must carry the card and your passport at all times, as these serve as your main forms of identification for various tasks, from renting an apartment to getting a library card or obtaining a mobile phone.

Inkan or Hanko

An *inkan* or *hanko* is a stamp bearing the *kanji* or *katakana* symbol for your name. (Sometimes, certain characters aren't allowed.) You'll be asked for an *inkan/hanko* in a variety of situations: receiving packages, opening a bank account, obtaining a mobile phone or buying a vehicle. Although you can get by with just a signature in most cases (and most major city authorities accept signatures), some businesses insist on an *inkan/hanko*. If you don't have an *inkan/hanko*, you may be asked to sign in the space intended for it – usually around 1cm square. If you plan to stay in Japan for a number of years, it's wise to obtain one. You may be able to find an 'off-the-shelf' *inkan/hanko* (e.g. in a ¥100 shop – see **Chapter 9**); otherwise you must go to a specialist shop and have one made.

ACCOMMODATION

Finding suitable accommodation is one of your first and most important tasks on arrival in Japan, and the procedure is likely to be very different from what you're used to. Many foreigners are surprised by the low quality of most Japanese housing, which is generally pre-fabricated and lacking double glazing or central heating, despite the cold winters. Japan being prone to earthquakes and typhoons, the Japanese don't see a lot of point investing money and effort in buildings. The value of a property is in the land it occupies, not the building itself, and the Japanese tend to demolish buildings after around 20 years and re-build in any case.

When looking for accommodation, take note of a building's construction date, as a new building code was introduced in 1981 and anything built before this may be less earthquake-resistant.

The size of rooms is another thing that needs some getting used to, the average room being less than 10m² (108ft²). Being so confined inevitably requires changes to your way of living. For example, even a small table and chair may be too large for comfort, as are standard-size sofas. Instead, low tables are used, along with chairs without legs – the space seems larger if the furniture is nearer the ground.

However, Japanese properties aren't usually measured in square metres or square feet, but in relation to mat sizes, as follows:

- **Mats** – *Tatami* are rice-plant straw flooring mats, which in Tokyo measure 1.76m by 0.88m and in Kyoto 1.91m by 0.96m. This is important to know because all rooms are measured in terms of how many *tatami* they will accommodate – whether they actually have mats or not. In advertisements, however, the total area in square metres (m²) is also usually given.

- **Area** – A standard-size room in Japan will accommodate six *tatami* or small rooms generally four.

- **Layout** – The layout of an apartment is given in code, which appears at the top of advertisements. Typical examples are:

> **R** = room including kitchen facilities (a sink and space for a gas cooker);
>
> **K** = separate kitchen area, usually quite small;
>
> **DK** = dining kitchen, i.e. the apartment has a six-*tatami* room with kitchen facilities;
>
> **LDK** = living dining kitchen, i.e. the apartment has a larger than six-*tatami* area with kitchen facilities.

- **Rooms** – A figure precedes the above letters, representing the number of rooms. For example, a large apartment may be written as 3LDK, which means it has three rooms plus the kitchen area.

- **Flooring** – A typical home in Japan has at least one matted room, the rest being floored in linoleum or carpet (sometimes even the kitchen area is carpeted). The *tatami* are nearly always replaced for a new tenant (the money is deducted from your 'deposit' whether or not new *tatami* are necessary).

The distance of a property from the nearest station or bus stop is always prominently displayed in advertisements – not in metres or yards but the number of minutes it takes to walk it.

Rented Property

To find an apartment in Japan you must go through an estate agent; you cannot approach a landlord directly. Agencies advertise in the major English-language newspapers (see **Newspapers** below), but the apartments on offer tend to be expensive, being targeted at multi-national company executives. Alternatively, if you know where you want to live, simply go there and visit local agencies.

There are plenty of them and they're easily recognisable by the apartment plans displayed in their windows. Unfortunately, agencies tend not to be particularly foreigner-friendly – and landlords may also be reluctant to let to foreigners, especially those unable to communicate in Japanese. Stories of foreign tenants who disappear owing months of rent are common, therefore don't be surprised if you're turned down 'on sight'.

> Japanese rental properties are usually classed as either *manshon* (mansions) or *apato* (apartments). The only difference is that *manshon* are generally more solidly built.

One good thing about the long period of recession is that it has made the Japanese less fussy about who they do business with, so even if you come across a couple of agents who are uncooperative, there are plenty who are willing to help. And as landlords tend to advertise their properties with more than one agent, you're unlikely to miss out on many properties if one or two agents refuse to do business with you.

If you're looking for accommodation in a major city, you can take advantage of a number of agencies that cater specifically for foreigners. They advertise on the internet and in local magazines for foreigners, such as *Metropolis*. They have bilingual staff and offer shared and private apartments, including small apartments suitable for single people, as well as short-term contracts and low fees. They usually expect no key money (see **Deposits** below), but you may need to pay one or two months' rent as a deposit.

Some foreigner-friendly agencies offer rooms in so-called 'guest houses', which are dormitory-type dwellings with a shared kitchen and living area. If you don't require much privacy, guest houses are a great way to start a new life in Japan. Not only are they cheap and usually conveniently located, but they allow you to meet and get to know other foreigners in the same situation.

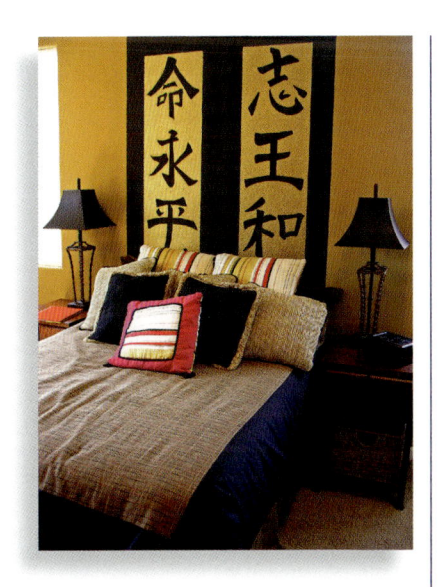

Most agents require you to provide financial background information and to have a guarantor co-sign a rental contract. A guarantor must usually be a Japanese national with a stable financial background. Most employers will act as a guarantor, but you should check before you start looking for an apartment. If your employer won't, you can hire a guarantor; willing candidates advertise at the back of English periodicals, such as *Metropolis*.

Deposits

A number of refundable and non-refundable deposits are required when renting an apartment. These usually amount to between three and five months' rent, depending on the agency, and may include the following:

- **Reservation fee** (*tetsukekin*) – payable when you apply to rent a particular apartment, but before you sign a contract, to guarantee that it won't be let to anyone else. It usually equals one month's rent (so in effect you start paying from your second month) and it's generally refundable if you decide not to rent the property.

- **Damage deposit** (*shikikin*) – to offset damage and repair costs when you move out. This can amount to several months' rent. Don't expect to get it refunded in full, even if you leave the property as you found it. Invariably the agent will pay for professional cleaning, no matter how meticulously you clean the place yourself, and the cost will be deducted from your deposit. In fact, it isn't unusual for an agency to claim they need all of it for 'damages', i.e. for renovation of the property, and you'll receive nothing back.

- **Key money** (*reikin*) – amounting to a non-refundable 'gift' to your new landlord of one or more months' rent.

- **Service fee** (*chukai tesuryo*) – one month's rent, payable to the estate agency.

An agency is likely to ask for all the above fees in cash, the last three when you sign the rental contract.

Contracts & Payment

If you find a home through a Japanese agency, you must typically sign a two-year lease. The rent cannot be increased during these two years, but when the lease expires the agency has the right to raise the rent or even terminate the contract for any reason, although the latter doesn't happen often. If you move out before the two years are up, you forfeit your deposits. If two years sounds too long for you, it's best to use the foreigner-friendly agencies mentioned above, which offer one-year or even month-by-month agreements, although these are more expensive.

Rent is paid to the agency rather than to the landlord and payments must be made by a certain date each month. Instructions are provided (in English) at most cash machines in major cities for withdrawing and depositing cash, but the procedure for transferring funds is often explained only in Japanese. If a bank is open, a clerk will usually show you how it's done, but it's more convenient to set up a direct debit (which incurs a fee).

Unlike apartments in some Western countries, Japanese apartments are let more or less bare – with fixtures such as a kitchen sink and cupboards, but without anything that's easily removable, such as a cooker and light fittings. The best way to obtain the missing items is to look in the local English-language magazines for *Sayonara* (goodbye) sales; if you're lucky, you can get things for free!

Rules & Regulations

Usually you'll have virtually no contact with your landlord but in most cases with the estate agency, which may be anything from a branch of a large nationwide company to a small family concern. Always try to maintain good relations with your agent – if you move, you may need a reference. The agency will give you a copy of the community rules and regulations for your apartment block. For example, you aren't usually permitted to sub-let, damage the walls in any way, carry out improvements or repairs, cause a nuisance to neighbours, or carry out any dangerous activity in a property.

Some apartment complexes make tenants responsible for the upkeep of

Osaka Castle

the grounds/gardens, where you either need to volunteer on certain days of the month or pay a fee in lieu.

Buying a Home

There are no legal restrictions on foreigners buying property in Japan, but approval for a home loan is often difficult to obtain, as you must usually be a 'permanent resident' (PR – an official status accorded to those who have lived in Japan for at least five years and meet certain other criteria, such as income limits and minimum length of employment) and have a guarantor, although some banks will lend to anyone with adequate security. Being married to a Japanese national helps, but even this doesn't guarantee that you'll be granted PR.

Some other factors to take into account when deciding whether to buy or rent are:

- Land values began to increase for the first time since the recession in 2007, although only in city areas, therefore now could be a good time to buy property in the expectation that the market is 'on the turn'. However, in some areas values may fall further before they start to rise.

- Interest rates in Japan have been among the lowest in the world for many years. This makes the cost of borrowing money very low. (Many foreigners earning money in Japan take out a yen loan to buy land or property in their home countries.)

- As mentioned before, the value of a property in Japan is in the land it stands on, not the building itself, which is only valuable if it's new; paying a lot for an old house isn't a good investment.

- You can expect to have to pay 20 per cent of the value of the property as a deposit.

- Purchase fees are usually a minimum 9 per cent of the value of the property.

- If you buy land in Japan, you must start building within two years (which is designed to prevent property speculation).

Buying an apartment may seem like a better deal than buying a house, but you'll be expected to pay a regular maintenance fee on top of any mortgage payments, and again, the value of the building will depreciate over its lifetime (30 years at the most). If the building is condemned while you're living in it, you'll have to pay a share of the demolition costs as well as find a new home!

BUYING OR HIRING A CAR

If you live in or close to a major city, you won't need a car, as all major cities have a reliable public transport system – besides which parking can be difficult or even impossible. However, if you live a long way from a railway station or in the country, you'll need a car or you may want one as a means of escape from the city.

There are two classes of car in Japan: those with an engine of 660cc or less (known as *kei* cars), easily recognised by their yellow number plates, and those with engines over 660cc, which have white number plates.

> **The minimum age for driving in Japan is 18.**

Car Hire

If you want to explore Japan or simply get out of town once in a while, hiring (renting) a car is worth considering. Public transport in outlying areas can be inconvenient, i.e. infrequent and, for a family or group, expensive. To hire a car in Japan you'll need a credit card and a Japanese driving licence or international driving permit (IDP). However, you can use an IDP for only a year after your arrival, after which you must obtain a Japanese licence.

Most of the major Japanese car hire companies don't provide a service in English. A notable exception is Too Coo! (🖥 www2.tocoo.jp), which probably offers the best deals of any national network. International companies such as Avis and Budget operate in Japan, but their prices are higher than those of Japanese companies. The cost of hiring a car ranges from ¥6,000 to 15,000 (US$60-150) per day, depending on the size of the vehicle and the season.

Buying a Car

Buying a new car is inexpensive in Japan, where dealers often live up to their names by offering deals and most salesmen will allow you to haggle. *Kei* cars start at less than a ¥1mn (US$10,000). As the Japanese tend to keep their cars in good condition and exchange them for newer models every five years or so, used cars are also good value – and most used car dealerships are reputable. In addition, cars in the Tokyo area are rarely used for commuting and so tend to have lower mileage than you might expect.

On the other hand, if you wish to buy a car other than a *kei*, you must prove that you have an off-road parking space and pay acquisition tax, tonnage tax and automobile tax. All cars must also undergo an inspection (*shaken*), which costs over ¥100,000 (US$1,000). Before purchasing a car, you should therefore work out whether it's worth the trouble and expense; hiring one occasionally may be a much simpler and cheaper option.

Used-car dealerships catering specifically to foreigners flourish in the major cities and have English-speaking staff who will help with every step of the buying and registration process. They advertise in periodicals such as *Metropolis* (🖥 http://metropolis.co.jp/classifieds) and on websites such as 🖥 www.gaijinpot.com/classifieds.

EMERGENCY SERVICES

Japan has efficient emergency services and, except in remote areas, and the time between call-out and arrival is usually short. However, telephone operators rarely speak English, so be prepared to explain briefly in Japanese the type of emergency and your exact location, e.g. by giving a local landmark if possible. Also, make sure that you have your address memorised or, preferably, written down near your phone. Japanese addresses tend to be long and difficult to remember, and an emergency isn't the time to have a mental block.

There are two emergency numbers: 110 for the police and 119 for an ambulance or the fire department – you'll need to be able to say which service you want. If you're using a payphone, press the red emergency button on the front of the phone and dial 110 or 119 without inserting any coins or a telephone card.

HEALTH SERVICE

Although medical services are far from perfect, the Japanese enjoy one of the longest life expectancies in the world.

Basic healthcare is guaranteed to everyone in Japan, whether rich, poor, young or old. Foreign residents living in Japan for longer than a year must contribute to a health insurance scheme (see **Health Insurance** below).

Hospitals

As well as large public hospitals (*byoin*) affiliated with universities or run by the local government, there are many small privately owned hospitals specialising in particular fields, e.g. dentistry, gynaecology and obstetrics.

In general, the larger the hospital, the better its reputation, although major hospitals often have long waiting periods: don't be surprised if you have to wait three hours for a three-minute examination. On the other hand, private hospitals often have just one examining doctor, so you may also have a long wait there. They're usually open from 8 or 9am until noon and then reopen in the afternoon from 3 to 6pm.

The word for hospital is *byoin*, but this is used to describe all doctors' offices, therefore don't be surprised if a Japanese colleague tells you he went to 'hospital' with a cold.

Emergency Treatment

All public hospitals offer emergency treatment – but not necessarily every day or at any time! If you need emergency treatment but don't require an ambulance, call 119 to find out which hospitals in your area are currently taking emergency cases. There has recently been a rise in the number of

Emergency Phrases

English	Japanese
(car) accident	(*kuruma no*) *jiko*
allergic reaction	*allerugi hannou*
attack	*busou kougeki*
bleeding	*chi ga detemasu*
broken arm	*ude wo orimashita*
broken leg	*ashi wo orimashita*
burglary	*dorobou desu*
fire	*kaji desu*
heart attack	*shinzou hossa desu*
I need an ambulance	*kyukyusha onegaishimasu*
I need a doctor	*isha o onegaishimasu*
Intruder/mugging	*goutou desu*
not breathing	*iki wo shiteimasen*
(I am) on the road to x	*x e ikutokorodesu*
unconscious	*ishiki ga arimasen*
wounded	*kega wo shiteimasu*

patients being turned away, even for emergency medical. If a hospital doesn't feel it can treat you adequately, it has the right to refuse you admission.

Accommodation

Most public hospitals have six-person, four-person and individual rooms. If a hospital is almost full, you usually have no choice of accommodation. Even if you wanted to be put in a six-person room to reduce costs, you may be placed in a four-person room and charged more. Each bed has a curtain and a TV. Bathrooms aren't usually in the room but down the hall. Towels are provided but patients are expected to take pyjamas, robes and toiletries.

Food usually consists of *okayu* (soft rice), a meat or fish dish, and other small dishes, including boiled vegetables or *tsukemono* (Japanese pickles) and *miso* soup. Some hospitals allow visitors to bring you food and drink, which can be stored in a communal refrigerator.

In general, patients stay much longer in Japanese hospitals than they would in other countries – which may be a good or bad thing, depending on your viewpoint.

Nursing Care

Japanes nurses are highly qualified professionals and often act as a buffer between you and the doctor, who has little time for 'personal' contact with his patients and may give you only a cursory examination, having gleaned all the relevant information from a nurse. Most nurses are friendly and willing to answer any questions you may have as best they can.

> Don't expect detailed information about routine procedures such as scans and blood tests. Medical staff will expect you to take them in your stride.

Childbirth

Ante-natal care is good – mothers are offered regular scans, blood tests, and check-ups – though not always free. When it comes to giving birth, you may have a choice between a large public hospital and a small private hospital that specialises in childbirth. In a large hospital, though, don't expect to be asked how you wish to give birth. In general, medical professionals are inflexible about delivery methods, birthing positions and pain relief. Partners are allowed to be present in most hospitals but not if a caesarean is required or there's a complication.

Delivery costs aren't covered by NHI (see **Health Insurance**

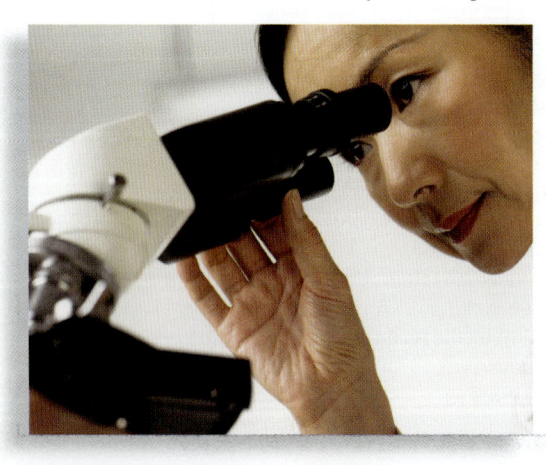

below) – although the government is considering making all childbirth-related procedures free as a way of boosting the population – and must be paid for personally. The average cost is around ¥350,000 (US$3,500) in the Tokyo area. This includes seven days of hospitalisation. However, if you contribute to the NHI you can apply for a one-time childbirth subsidy of ¥300,000 (US$3,000). Depending on where you live, other subsidies – of up to ¥500,000 (US$5,000) – may be available from local governments who are keen to encourage child birth in their area.

Doctors

Medical practitioners have traditionally been accorded the highest respect in Japan, and Japanese patients tend to be more trusting of doctors than Westerners and don't ask many questions. However, in recent years a number of malpractice suits have shaken the confidence of the Japanese public and nowadays it's more common for patients to demand information from health professionals. Nonetheless, you may find a visit to the doctor a very different experience from what you're used to; some doctors seeming to have little or no interest in your health or wellbeing and a few are downright rude.

Choosing a Doctor

The best way to find a doctor is through word of mouth. Alternatively, you can find an English-speaking doctor by contacting the AMDA International Medical Information Center (http://homepage3.nifty.com/amdack/english/E-index.html), whose service is free.

Another useful resource for choosing a doctor is the various Japanese websites that rate doctors and include comments from both satisfied and dissatisfied patients. However, these aren't available in English.

Making an Appointment

Most private and public hospitals operate on a first-come, first-served system, and appointments aren't required or possible; you simply hand in your insurance card on arrival and wait (and wait). Most doctor's surgeries open at 9am, although it's common to see a waiting room full of people at 7.30 or 8am! Needless to say, it's advisable to arrive early and avoid Mondays, which are particularly busy. Some specialists in large hospitals require an appointment to be made and some paediatricians also operate an appointment system in order to minimise the waiting time for young children.

> Even if your doctor takes appointments, you won't necessarily be examined at the specified time, as five or six other patients will usually have been given the same time! Arrive early and bring a thick book – *Shōgun* by James Clavell is recommended.

Visiting a Doctor

When you go to a doctor for the first time, you need to complete a 'first medical examination' form at reception. Although few receptionists speak English, they're usually friendly and will help as much as they can. Once you've completed the form, hand it to the receptionist with your health insurance and alien registration cards. Don't forget your insurance card or you'll be charged the full cost for the examination and must pay on the spot.

When your examination is completed you'll receive an 'examination card', which is all that's required for subsequent visits (although some hospitals require you to bring your insurance card each time): simply hand in the examination card at the reception desk, write your name on the waiting list and open your book.

You'll often feel that you're being rushed by Japanese doctors. Many have one eye on the long queue of patients outside their door and show signs of irritation when asked questions – but ask anyway!

Medicines

A visit to a Japanese doctor usually results in two or three prescriptions for potions and tablets (etc.). Traditionally, a doctor would give one medicine for every symptom the patient reported, and this is still generally the case. Rarely will you go home empty handed, even for a minor ailment. Large hospitals often have pharmacies (*yakkyoku*), where you can get a prescription filled. If not, the doctor will direct you to the nearest pharmacy – usually next door. As prices are fixed, there's no need to 'comparison shop' when it comes to getting your prescription filled in Japan.

Each medication is described in Japanese on a sheet of paper enclosed in the bag, along with the dosage instructions. Most medicines come as a powder in a square sachet. You simply empty the contents directly into your mouth and wash it down with water.

If you're enrolled in the NHI scheme, up to 70 per cent of the cost of prescribed medicines is covered, but there's no discount for purchases made without a prescription.

INSURANCE
Health Insurance

As a resident of Japan, you're required to have health insurance, whether through the National Health Insurance (NHI) scheme (*kokumin kenkohoken*), a scheme run by your employer (*kenkohoken*) or, if permitted by your employer, a private scheme. NHI contributions amount to around 8 per cent of your income. Private insurance is cheaper if you're single and may cover you overseas; some insurance companies cater specifically to expatriates. A disadvantage of private insurance is that not all medical facilities will have an agreement with your insurer and you'll have to pay expensive fees up front and then reclaim them. With the NHI or an employer-run scheme, you'll have to pay only 30 of expenses in advance. Those staying in Japan for less than a year should take out private insurance.

One advantage of the NHI scheme is that it includes dental care, whereas most private schemes don't.

Car Insurance

As in most Western countries, the minimum level of car insurance required by law is third party, but most people purchase additional insurance. Insurance documents must be carried in the car at all times and you can be fined for not having them if you're stopped by a police officer.

Household Insurance

Standard homeowner insurance policies provide cover for damage to your home or contents caused by theft, fire, storms, smoke, frozen pipes and ice or snow, as well as for liability claims, medical payments to third parties and legal costs. Standard policies cost between around ¥20,000 and 40,000 (US$200-400) for two years.

Japan is one of the most earthquake-susceptible countries in the world, and cover against earthquake and earthquake-related damage isn't included in standard insurance policies. You can take out separate earthquake insurance but it's (unsurprisingly) expensive and may not be comprehensive.

EDUCATION

Selecting the right school for your child is one of the most difficult choices you'll face if you move as a family to Japan. The decision isn't one to be taken lightly and you need to thoroughly research and consider the options. You may need to think long term beyond school, to university and work, as the type of education you choose for your children can have long-term implications.

Japanese or International School?

Japan is home to numerous international schools, although they tend to be concentrated in the Tokyo area. If you're able to choose between a Japanese and an international school (annual tuition fees for the latter are between US$10,000 and 20,000), you should weigh up the advantages and disadvantages of each.

In an international school, teaching methods and the language of instruction are likely to be familiar, so your children will probably adapt more quickly and easily than to a Japanese school. They won't be under pressure to learn Japanese quickly in order to understand the lessons. If your child is over ten and suddenly thrust into a Japanese school, he will find it difficult to keep up, especially when lessons involve reading or writing Japanese. On the other hand, your child will integrate more quickly and thoroughly into local life at a Japanese school, probably becoming bilingual in the process.

Generally, an international school is the better option if your stay is short term (say up to five years), as it's less unsettling for your children if you return to your home country or move to another country where there are international schools. If you plan to stay in Japan long term or if you're uncertain how long you'll be there, a Japanese school is likely to be preferable and will give your children better long-term education and employment prospects.

Among the most reputable international schools in and around Tokyo are the American School in Japan (http://community.asij.ac.jp), the British School in Tokyo (www.bst.ac.jp), and Yokohama International School (www.yis.ac.jp).

The Japanese Education System

Compulsory education in Japan consists of six years of elementary school (ages 6-12) and three years of junior high school (ages 12-15), although over 95 per cent of students complete a further three years at high school, as without a high school diploma job options are limited.

The phrase that defines the Japanese educational system is *minna issho* (everyone together/ the same). Unlike in the West, there's no emphasis on individual achievement. Until high school, the best students aren't streamed into a 'gifted' or 'accelerated' class, no matter how talented they may be. Every class is a mixture of talents and interests. Changes are taking place, however – some small, some radical – and the next five to ten years may prove to be a pivotal time in Japanese education history.

Below are some key aspects of the current Japanese education system:

- The national government has a strong influence on educational matters through the Ministry of Education, Sports and Culture, which establishes a uniform national curriculum and screens school textbooks.

- The school year begins in April and ends the following March, with a total of 220 school days divided into three terms. Students have spring, summer and winter holidays (vacations), summer being the longest and lasting from around 20th July to the end of August.

- Most schools have little support for non-Japanese speakers – the onus is on pupils to learn Japanese as quickly as possible.

- Although recently there has been an influx of English-speaking teachers, most Japanese teachers don't speak English. Even those who teach English often don't have much chance to practise the language and therefore may be out of touch with contemporary English.

- In almost all schools, both private and public, wearing a

uniform is compulsory, and parents must pay for it.

- A lot of learning is done by rote and students are expected to memorise huge chunks of text and facts. As a result, students tend to have excellent general knowledge.

- Many Japanese students attend an after-school *juku* (cramming school). Most go there daily to receive additional training in how to pass the strenuous entrance exams for university and/or high school and, in some cases, junior high or even primary school.

> **From the first grade, students must clean their classrooms and their school every day in teams.**

- Many public elementary schools provide hot lunches, but public junior high and high schools don't. Few private schools offer lunches. When lunch isn't provided, students usually bring their own *bento* (lunch box) or buy something in a cafeteria or shop.

- Everyone in Japan studies English from grades 7 to 12 (ages 13-18) and in their first years of university, but students don't have much opportunity to practise the language. Most English education is centred on passing the university/high school entrance exams, which require rote memorisation of grammar rules and obscure vocabulary.

- Senior high schools put a lot of effort into preparing their students for university exams – sometimes to the detriment of their education (in the true sense of the term).

Subjects

- Art is largely practical, with students working on various projects, including painting, drawing and making woodblock prints.

- Maths and science lessons are more advanced than in the UK or US.

- Children learn to read music and play the recorder and other instruments.

- A typical physical education (PE) class consists of students running or swimming and playing a team sport, such as basketball or volleyball.

- Japanese lessons focus primarily on learning and memorising *kanji,* the Japanese writing system.

- Students learn about the history of he world, not just of Japan.

Cost

Although tuition at a public (state) school is free, there are a number of costs to be taken into account, such as the uniform and fees for school trips. Fees at private Japanese schools are considerably lower than those charged by international schools.

University

Almost all Japanese students complete their degree in four years. Parents are responsible for their offspring's university education and will stump up for fees and other costs such as books. For this reason, many Japanese students live at home, particularly if their university is less than two hours away by train.

> Most Japanese agree that getting into university is the difficult part; graduating is easy.

COUNCIL SERVICES

Refuse Collection

Japan has a strict and detailed system for collecting rubbish. The onus is on you to separate your rubbish, and the precise way of doing this varies from district to district. Your landlord or city hall should provide you with an instruction booklet of about 20 pages, written in Japanese. Even though it will contain pictures and diagrams to guide you, it's worth getting a Japanese speaker to translate the salient details.

In general, Japanese rubbish is divided into four categories: *moeru gomi* (burnable items), i.e. paper, wood, clothing, and food waste; *moenai gomi* (non-burnable items), including plastic bags and containers, metal and anything that would be toxic to burn; *recycle* (recyclables), e.g. glass bottles, tin, aluminium and paper, including newspaper, magazines and cardboard (see below); and *sodaigomi* (oversized refuse – see **Other Rubbish** below). You may have to buy official bags for one or more categories.

All streets in Japan have a refuse collection site where you can find a sign detailing the collection times. It's considered bad behaviour to leave your rubbish there earlier than the night before a collection. Some *manshon* (mansions) have a place where you can deposit your rubbish at any time, and supermarkets usually have bins for plastic bottles, Styrofoam trays, batteries and milk cartons. You shouldn't throw your household rubbish in the local convenience store's rubbish bins.

Crows often attack refuse bags in search of food – use the blue netting at collection points to cover your rubbish sacks to prevent the contents from being scattered across the street.

Recycling

Japan is making a concerted effort to recycle as much waste material as possible. As stated above, recyclable refuse must be separated from non-recyclable refuse at a collection point. Certain recyclable materials, including batteries and light bulbs, can be disposed of only on certain days or at certain collection points.

Some neighbourhoods are beginning to offer a food recycling service, whereby your discarded food can be turned into mulch for gardens and lawns.

Other Rubbish

- **Electronic equipment & furniture** – Furniture and electronic equipment such as computers and televisions falls into the category of *sodaigomi* or oversized refuse. You can dispose of these items by purchasing stickers at neighbourhood shops, sticking them on the items and calling the local city office to arrange for (free) collection. Alternatively, you can try to find a recycle shop, which will collect items free of charge if they are in good condition and they can accommodate them.

- **Garden Rubbish** – In most areas, leaves, branches, soil and other refuse from your garden can be picked up free of charge if it's put in clear plastic bags.

- **Medicines** – Out-of-date or unwanted medicines should be taken to a pharmacy to ensure their safe disposal.

If you've a large amount of refuse, you can hire a truck and take it to the local refuse dump. These facilities often charge by weight.

UTILITIES

Arrangements for the connection and supply of power and other services aren't always straightforward. A summary of the main points is shown below.

Electricity

Japan's electrical system is at 110 volts, but at two frequencies: 50Hz in eastern Japan and 60Hz in the west. Many appliances sold overseas aren't compatible with Japanese standards and therefore aren't worth importing.

Attempting to use electrical appliances that operate at the wrong frequency or voltage is dangerous and likely to damage them. If you aren't sure whether an appliance is usable in Japan, ask at an electronics store, where you may be able to purchase a converter if necessary.

When you move into a property, you should locate the fuse box – usually in the entrance hall (*genkan*) or sometimes in a cupboard in the bathroom or lounge – and flip the switches to 'ON'. After making sure you have power, complete the postcard (which should be hanging in the fuse box) and send it to the electricity company. There may be an option to provide the information by telephone.

Supply Problems

Many Japanese properties don't have a sufficient supply to operate several high-wattage appliances simultaneously, and if you attempt to do so your fuse box may 'trip' off. Simply unplug a few devices and flip the switch back on. If the power doesn't come on again, contact your electricity company.

Water

As with electricity, first check that you have a water supply (by turning on a tap!) and then give the local water company your details either by phone or by completing the postcard hanging in the entrance hall or from a tap. You'll be billed every two months according to the amount of water you use and the amount of waste water and sewage you discharge.

Water heaters are usually powered by gas, not electricity, therefore you must ensure that the gas is turned on, which may need to be done each time you want hot water.

Tap water in Japan is safe to drink but has a slightly chlorinated taste, which can be eliminated by a filter.

Gas

Gas is commonly used for cooking. Electric cookers are rare, except for microwave ovens, which sometimes have a 'conventional oven' setting. Western-style ovens are rare in Japan.

Most cities and large towns have mains gas supplies; in smaller towns you may need to obtain propane (LP) gas bottles. If your home is connected to mains gas, you should contact the relevant gas company two or three days before moving in to arrange for someone to come and open the main valve, check for leaks and inspect your gas appliances.

Telephone

Telephone services in Japan are generally good and most of the country is served by landline and/or mobile phone infrastructure.

Landlines

Japan has two sysems for obtaining a fixed telephone line (landline), both of which are available only from Nippon Telegraph & Telephone (NTT). The standard system involves buying a line (or rather the 'right' to a line), which costs ¥37,800 (US$378) if you buy it direct from NTT. It's possible to buy 'second-hand' privately (the going rate is around ¥10,000/US$100), but there's no guarantee that the seller won't have outstanding charges on the line.

A new system, which NTT has recently started promoting under the brand name '*Lite*', involves paying a surcharge of ¥263 (US$2.63) per month in addition to your call charges instead of buying a line. Which is preferable depends not only on how long you plan to stay in a property, but also whether (and for how much) you can sell on a line you've bought when you move out.

Once your line is installed, you can choose from a number of telephone companies to provide your service, although NTT's free 0120 numbers will be unavailable if you use another provider. If you've chosen the *Lite* option, you must still pay the monthly surcharge to NTT.

Mobile Phones

The Japanese respect for privacy means that they would rather call a mobile than a home landline.

Many Japanese (and foreigners) have no landline but use only a mobile phone (*keitai*), although these are more often used for sending text messages and emails than for talking, which is both less expensive and less intrusive, especially when using public transport, when it's considered rude to talk on your phone. On the other hand, it's also considered impolite to use a mobile phone in company, even if only to check messages. Note that text messages can only be sent to people who subscribe to the same network as you do, but mobile phone emails can be universally received.

It can be difficult to obtain a mobile phone until you have an address and alien registration card, although some companies offer pre-pay phones on production of a foreign passport and hotel address. A useful page of links for such services can be found on the Narita airport website (💻 www.narita-airport.jp/en/guide/service/index.html).

STAYING INFORMED

Even if your knowledge of Japanese is good enough to follow Japanese media, you may occasionally (or often) hanker after some TV, radio or press in your own language. The good news is that this is fairly easy to obtain in Japan, particularly for English speakers.

Television

Japanese TV isn't renowned for its quality, although it's generally no worse than what's on offer in other countries. Programmes generally consist of game shows, films, chat shows, sports, variety shows, and what the Japanese call dramas. These are serialised programmes lasting around three months, which can be serious or comedies. Travel and food-related programmes – about either cooking or dining out – are also popular.

Japan has both private and government-owned TV networks, between them offering nine channels in the Tokyo area (fewer in more remote areas). NHK is the state network, broadcasting free-to-air programmes without advertisements, as well as several cable TV (and radio) programmes. Like the BBC, the NHK charges a licence fee – of around ¥15,000 (US$150) per year for terrestrial reception or ¥25,000 (US$250) for satellite reception – which you must pay if you can receive a signal even if you use your TV only for watching DVDs and videos.

> It's possible to buy a television with bilingual broadcast reception, which will enable you to watch films, news programmes and some sports coverage in English.

Many households in Japan have cable, satellite, or internet TV, all of which offer a number of channels in English, as well as Korean and Chinese. However, if you live in an older apartment, you may not be able to connect to cable or internet TV, only satellite.

Radio

Radio isn't a major medium in Japan, where signals are generally weak, reception can be poor and only around one in five of the population regularly tunes in. Programmes consist mainly of music, sports coverage, phone-in advice and interviews. Many television personalities, essayists and comedians have weekly or nightly radios programmes on which they discuss current topics – though nothing too controversial. The major broadcasters are limited to Tokyo, where a few stations have bilingual presenters, including J-wave 81.3 FM and InterFM 76.1-Tokyo. Most communities have a small radio station, through which you can obtain information about local events and activities.

Newspapers

The Japanese press enjoys a large and loyal readership. There are over 20 daily newspapers, several of which are published in both Japanese and English. These include the *Daily Yomiuri*, which is pro-government, and the *Asahi Evening Times* and *Mainichi Daily News*, both generally anti-government. *The Japan Times* is one of the few English-only newspapers published in Japan. Economic newspapers such as the *Asahi Wall Street Journal* and *Nikkei Weekly* are also published in English. You can purchase any of these at some convenience stores and newsstands at stations, or you can have them delivered to your home.

Many weekly English-language newspapers and magazines are published in Japan. Most contain information about local events and services and many are free. You can pick up copies at many locations in the Tokyo area, including CD shops, Irish pubs, foreign-themed restaurants, tourist information centres and most places where foreign residents congregate. The Maruzen bookshop chain often has copies. Publications include:

- *Japanzine* (www.japan-zine.com), which aims to be humorous and has the best coverage of Nagoya events;

- *Kansai Time Out* (www.japanfile.com), which concentrates on the Osaka-Kyoto area;

- *Metropolis* (www.metropolis.co.jp), which has the largest circulation;

- *Tokyo Notice Board* (www.tokyonoticeboard.co.jp), which is 80 per cent classified ads.

BANKING

Banking in Japan has improved considerably over the past decade and, although banks still lack the 24-hour convenience of those in many countries, they're convenient in other ways.

The following are some of the main characteristics of Japanese banking:

- **Opening an account:** To open a bank account in Japan, a foreign resident must usually have an alien registration card and an *inkan* or *hanko* (*kanji* stamp), although some banks will allow you to open an account without one. After you've completed the necessary forms and deposited some money in the account, you'll be given a bank account booklet, which can be used to withdraw cash at ATMs; a week or so later your bank card and your personal identification number (PIN) will arrive in the post.

- **Opening hours** – Japanese banks are usually open Mondays to Fridays from 9am to 3pm.

- **Queuing** – When you go to a bank, you must first take a number from one of the machines on the counter. Some banks have different machines for different transactions. There's usually a uniformed member of staff in the waiting area to help with any general questions.

- **Obtaining cash** – If you wish to withdraw cash from a bank counter, you must show photographic identification as well as your bank card or booklet. Japanese banks offer automatic teller machines (ATMs) at which you can withdraw and deposit money, check your balance, transfer money and pay bills, although some multi-bank machines only dispense cash. Unlike in many other countries, most machines aren't available 24 hours a day (you may find 24-hour machines in convenience stores) and you may be charged a fee to use them in the evening or at weekends.

> Most Japanese ATMs and cash machines don't accept foreign credit cards, although an increasing number (particularly in department stores and at airports) do; look for the international network symbols, such as 'Cirrus', on the side. Withdrawing cash on a Sunday night from a foreign account can be difficult – if not impossible.

- **Salary payment** – Virtually all companies pay their employees' salaries directly into their bank account. The standard payday is the 25th of each month. If this is a Saturday, Sunday or holiday, you'll be paid on the previous weekday.

- **Debit & credit card payment** – For the most part, Japan is still largely a cash-based society. Everyday payments are made in cash and a lot of businesses don't accept credit or debit cards – even some supermarkets and restaurants. To be safe, always carry sufficient cash with you to cover the cost of your purchases. If you're planning to use a credit card, ask in advance whether it will be accepted.

- **Bill payment** – Cheques aren't used in Japan. The best way to make large payments is by an account-to-account transfer (*furikomi*). This can be done at an ATM, but instructions aren't often in English, so it may be simpler to ask staff to help you. You can have most of your bills – from utilities to mobile phone – automatically paid from your bank account; this is easy to set up and saves you the worry of having your utilities cut off if you miss a payment.

- **Internet banking** – Most Japanese banks offer this facility in Japanese only, although Shinseibank (🖳 www.shinseibank.com/english) also offers an English online service. If you have a Citibank (Citigroup) account, you can bank online in English but charges are usually higher than with Japanese banks.

TAXES

Everyone living in Japan is obliged to pay Japanese taxes, irrespective of their nationality. Everyone earning a wage in Japan must pay income tax and a local resident's tax. There's also a 'consumption tax', which is equivalent to sales tax in the US or value added tax (VAT) in the UK. The current rate is 5 per cent

Some countries have mutual agreements with the Japanese government which allow their citizens an income-tax free period of two years.

Tax Avoidance

It's difficult to avoid paying taxes in Japan, although some foreign residents manage to escape paying resident's tax. This isn't wise, however, as it has been known for municipal offices to freeze a bank account until taxes are paid.

Getting Started 73

Geisha playing an Erhu

Koi nobori (carp streamers) in spring

4.
BREAKING THE ICE

One of the best ways of getting over culture shock and feeling part of life in Japan is getting acquainted with the Japanese. This chapter will help you to break down the barriers without committing social *hara-kiri*. It contains information on important aspects of Japanese society and the expatriate community, advice on how to behave in social situations, topics to steer clear of in conversation and tips on dealing with confrontation.

> Making new friends is never easy, and the language and cultural barriers in Japan make it even harder – even for the Japanese themselves.

COMMUNITY LIFE

When viewed from a distance, the urban landscape of Japan is a dense clutter of two- to four-storey housing interspaced with the odd high-rise apartment complex. Buildings are packed among narrow streets with very little space for gardens, if any. Owing to the frequency of devastating earthquakes and typhoons, most homes are cheaply built from prefabricated parts – with thin walls and floors and without such 'luxuries' as double glazing or central heating, despite the cold winters.

Fortunately, the Japanese generally make quiet and considerate neighbours. This doesn't mean, however, that they're easy to get to know. Although they're cordial enough, they will rarely introduce themselves outside of their social network. You may therefore have to make the first move with your new neighbours, but even then it's unlikely they will ever become friends, as the Japanese typically socialise away from their homes.

It's therefore around the local railway or underground (subway) station that the life of the community revolves – but mainly at weekends. During the week, the Japanese are busy working and children go straight from school to the *juku* (cramming school – see **Chapter 3**) or club activities. At the station there's often a multitude of restaurants, bars and *izakaya* (bars that serve food, usually family run rather than part of a chain), Japanese and American fast food chains, convenience stores (*combini*) and, at main stations, department stores (*depato*) and everything from gambling parlours (*pachinko*) to hairdressers' and drug stores. Major stations often incorporate several restaurants, sprawling department stores and shopping centres.

The peacefulness of weekdays is periodically broken by the amplified bawling of merchants selling their wares from vans and public announcements from the communal loudspeaker system. The most common of these is made every day at 4.30pm (in winter) or 5.30pm (in summer), telling children that it's time to stop playing and go home (which children usually ignore).

When the Japanese find some time to spend on leisure and recreation, they often do so with gusto – singing, drinking, and talking late into the night – but rarely at home. Homes are personal sanctuaries separated from work, social and recreational life.

> On moving into your new home, you should offer a small gift to your immediate neighbours (including those above and, especially, below if you're in an apartment), which will go a long way to establishing good relations. Biscuits (cookies) are usually welcome.

Community Regulations

Japanese communities have many rules, both explicit and implicit. The former can be obtained from your landlord or the local city hall or community centre. In addition, each neighbourhood has a neighbourhood association (*jichikai* or *jichitai*) that coordinates matters such as street cleaning and the resolution of minor disputes. Joining such an organisation isn't compulsory, but it's a good way of making contact with the local community and can help you avoid problems caused by ignorance or misunderstanding.

Community rules to pay particular attention to include the following:

- **Noise:** Japanese communities are extremely noise conscious – to the point that activities such as running a washing machine and vacuuming should be done only when the noise won't disturb your neighbours (bearing in mind the usually paper-thin walls of Japanese apartments).

- **Pets:** Your rental agreement will often stipulate whether pets are acceptable or not; otherwise check with your landlord before buying your children a cuddly puppy.

- **Rubbish & recycling:** Japanese communities have specific regulations regarding how rubbish should be separated and disposed of (see **Refuse Collection** in **Chapter 3**). Getting it wrong can bring complaints from your landlord and, worse, arouse the displeasure of your neighbours.

- **Laundry:** Unlike in Germany or Switzerland, there's usually no restriction on the hanging of laundry, which is often dried on balconies in full view of other residents. On sunny mornings you'll often hear the rhythmic thumping of dust being beaten from futons.

- **Parking:** In most neighbourhoods, streets are narrow and on-street parking isn't allowed. You must therefore make sure that you have a parking space before you're allowed to buy anything but a small car. Not all apartments come with parking spaces, and if they do it's likely that you'll have to pay extra for it. If your block doesn't have access to car parking, you'll have to scour the area for car parks with spare spaces. You may have to do this even for a motorcycle. Most apartments have free bicycle parking, although some require payment. Illegally or inappropriately parked vehicles attract hefty fines and can lose you licence points – or even your licence.

Allowances are usually made for foreigners who don't follow the rules immediately, but it's essential to adjust your behaviour as quickly as possible. Otherwise, not only will you perpetuate the stereotype of the inconsiderate foreigner, but your landlord could refuse to renew your rental contract – in effect evicting you.

The Japanese will normally put up with a lot before they complain, therefore if you receive a complaint from neighbours, you may already have been ostracised by your community.

SEXUAL ATTITUDES

Japan is a complicated country when it comes to sexuality. Over the last few centuries its sexual mores have been affected by often contradictory religions or beliefs. Japanese folk traditions can be permissive to an extraordinary degree, as evidenced by the penis- and vagina-worshipping festivals that still exist in various parts of the country. Visitors to Japan may be shocked by the explicit images found in cartoons for adolescents and even younger children, or the easy availability of soft pornography at convenience stores. Even within the pornography industry, the Japanese have developed a certain notoriety for deviant sexual practices.

The austerity of Confucianism and of the Christian attitudes brought in by American occupation forces at the end of the Pacific War have counteracted this licentious tendency, as can be seen, for example, in the censorship rules governing nudity in films. On a personal level, the Japanese sometimes seem curiously 'Victorian'; even your closest Japanese friends may not be comfortable discussing anything related to sex.

Men

Men in Japan are still seen as the primary income provider for a family. The typical married *salaryman* will spend ten hours or more a day at work, which leaves him little time to care for his children – if he sees them at all during the week. It's expected that businessmen should socialise with colleagues after work, which traditionally includes drinking in bars and even attending 'hostess' clubs. If a *salaryman* wants to advance in his job, he's unlikely to refuse such an invitation from his boss or colleagues.

A foreign male employee recently won a court case against his Japanese CEO for being forced to go to a strip club and participate in sexual activities against the threat of losing his job.

There are signs that this 'culture' is changing as labour shortages force companies to accept more women in the workplace and men are increasingly expected to (and indeed want to) play a wider role in the family. However, progress is slow and Japan remains near the bottom of the list of OECD countries in terms of the hours men spend doing housework and women spend working (as employees). According to Chikako Ogura of Aichi Shukutoku University, the new 'standard' for Mr Right in Japan can be summed up by 'the three Cs': comfortable (financially), communicative (emotionally) and cooperative (in housework and childcare).

Foreign women are often coveted by Japanese men for their different exoticism – their very different looks and behaviour. Those with blonde hair and blue eyes especially will turn male heads in Japan. However, Japanese men tend to be shy and don't make the first move as often as Western men will. Foreign women wishing to date Japanese men may therefore find themselves having to be more 'proactive' than they may be in their native countries. The Japanese rely on their social networks for dating and courtship, and aren't used to making direct individual approaches.

Women

Japanese women often enter the workplace alongside their male peers after university, but typically don't have the same opportunities for promotion, and are often expected to perform such menial tasks as making tea for their colleagues. Traditionally it was expected that after getting married they would stop working. Even if they wanted to continue working after marriage, Japanese companies didn't usually hold jobs open for those taking time off for childbirth, nor have facilities such as crèches or offer men parental leave. (The few companies that did offer paternal leave found that very few Japanese men took advantage of it.)

However, the economic reality of Japan's declining population is bringing a change to this depressing scenario. Women are finding an increasing number of career options open to them and sometimes even find themselves expected to take part in the drinking sessions which previously had been an exclusively male domain. Partly as a result of more women deciding to stay in the workforce and pursue a career, Japan now has the lowest birth rate (ratio of births to deaths) in the world.

Breaking the Ice

> In January 2007, the Japanese Minister of Welfare referred to women as 'baby-making machines'. Despite calls for his resignation, the Prime Minister of the time defended him and he retained his post.

Foreign men may be attracted to Japanese women because of their reputation for femininity and their acceptance of the traditional male role, but many find them excessively passive and 'remote', owing to the Japanese preference for non-verbal communication.

Conversely, the stereotype of the foreign male in Japan is that he's loud, impolite and sexually predacious. Even if they conform to this stereotype, foreign men may be regarded by Japanese women as an exotic novelty – more physically and emotionally 'available' than their Japanese counterparts. Many young Japanese women seem to find foreign men irresistible – having virility, purchasing power, and that essential quality – height!

Abuse of Women

Although the incidence of domestic abuse, sexual assault and rape is officially below or on a par with that of other developed nations, abuses are thought to be grossly under-reported due to the Japanese sense of shame and the belief that these are personal issues. However, one area of concern for all women in Japan is the prevalence of groping on public transport. The heavily crowded trains offer ideal cover for the wandering hands of a *chikan* (sexual pervert). City train operators have been introducing women-only cars during rush hours to combat this persistent problem.

Homosexuals & Transsexuals

The Japanese highly respect privacy, and homosexuals can live their private lives as they wish – as long as they present a 'normal' public face. Homosexuality has never been outlawed in Japan and indeed features prominently in Japanese art of the Edo period (1603-1867) in drama and other literary works, as well as in woodblock prints. Some examples are Saikaku Ihara's novel *The Life of An Amorous Man* (1682), Miyagawa Isshō's series of panels called *Spring Pastimes* and in the dramatic form of *Kabuki* (see **Cinema & Theatre** in **Chapter 8**).

Many cities have gay and lesbian clubs and bars, and comic books, cartoons strips and other media of a homosexual nature are routinely 'consumed'. Nonetheless, the Japanese tend to avoid exposing their private lives and foreigners are recommended to do the same.

MEETING PEOPLE

Japanese teens are the loneliest in the developed world, according to a UNICEF survey. One in three Japanese 15-year-olds feels lonely, compared with one in 20 Britons of the same age.

The Japanese aren't the most gregarious of people. Although it's easy to have cordial relations with them, it's difficult to move from acquaintanceship to friendship. Foreigners often find that Japanese acquaintances remain tied to the context in which they meet. For example, a Japanese colleague will remain a business acquaintance and is unlikely to mix with friends made under other circumstances.

This applies equally to the Japanese themselves, who often stay in touch with their classmates from elementary school, and meet them every year – but only with other classmates. For foreigners the social divisions are even harder to break down. The Japanese unconsciously assume that their culture is unique and therefore impossible for foreigners to understand, and they may mistrust foreigners who attempt to 'connect' at more than a superficial level. Though certain groups may induct you into their social circle and share more than conventional formulas, your relationship may not go as far as you think. Both male and female foreigners generally find it easier to make friends with Japanese women than men, perhaps because they're more communicative.

That said, there are many ways to meet both foreigners and Japanese, including the following:

- **At work** – Meeting colleagues for lunch or going out to an *izakaya* or *karaoke* after work is one of the preferred ways of making friends with colleagues, and such socialising is encouraged by many companies.

- **Expat networks** – Several English-language publications and websites (e.g. *Metropolis*, 🖥 www.metropolis.co.jp and *Japanzine*, 🖥 www.japanzine.co.jp) advertise events and activities, as do international online social networks such as Meetups (🖥 www.meet-up.com) and Yahoo! Groups (🖥 www.yahoo.com/groups). There are also plenty of Japanese 'social' sites (e.g. www.mixi.co.jp).

- **Language lessons & exchanges** – Whether arranged with a colleague, through a private advertisement or via an internet self-employment site (e.g. 🖥 www.findateacher.net), language lessons and exchanges can be a good way to build friendships.

- **Clubs & activities** – You can combine a Japanese cultural experience with an opportunity to meet people with similar interests by joining a local club. Local community centres may have information about such quintessentially Japanese activities as *chado* (tea ceremony), *shodo* (calligraphy), *ikebana* (flower arranging) and of course martial arts – *aikido*, *judo*, *karatedo*, *kendo*, *kyudo*, etc.

- **Gymnasiums & fitness clubs** – Private gyms are easy to find (Central Fitness, Konami Sports, Renaissance and Tipness are major chains) and may have swimming pools, golf ranges and squash courts. as well as the expected fitness equipment and aerobics, martial arts and yoga classes. However, you must usually take out (an expensive) membership. Harder to find are gyms run by local authorities, which are much cheaper and can be used casually.

- **Schools & childcare facilities** – Parents of young children have additional opportunities to meet people through schools and childcare centres. Joining a parent-teacher association can be especially beneficial.

Where & When to Meet

The usual place for people to meet is at a station (see above), but there are certain other places that have become famous as meeting spots. The Hachiko statue in Shibuya and the Studio Alta in Shinjuku are two places where there are almost always crowds of people waiting for someone.

Due to the long working hours of most Japanese, socialising is generally confined to weekends and late evenings.

> If you're staying out late, don't forget to check the time of the last train home – usually between 11pm and 1am – as late taxis are very expensive.

Paying

Small groups usually divide the bill (*betsu-betsu*) equally, irrespective of what each person ordered. If you're out with someone older than you, they may insist on paying the bill. If this happens, you should at least offer to pay for your share. If you're on a date, it's also customary to split the cost. If you want to be chivalrous and pay for everything, make sure to mention it early.

Business meetings and language exchanges are a grey area when it comes to payment, and declaring up front who you expect to pay is helpful. If your boss or manager offers to take you out, it's safe to assume that they will pay, but it's always best to check.

INVITATIONS

Receiving Invitations

As mentioned above, the Japanese rarely, if ever, have social functions at their homes. Therefore if you're invited to a Japanese home, you should consider yourself honoured. The problem is, it isn't always obvious that you've been invited. The Japanese tend to make oblique reference to activities they would like you to join them in, allowing you ample room to turn them down tactfully – often forgetting that you may not realise an invitation is being proffered!

If you receive an invitation, it's important to arrive on time. Punctuality in Japan is a must. If you're unavoidably late, give a simple explanation and apologise.

You're more likely to be invited to work parties, when alcohol plays an important role in friendship making; if you prove to be 'the life and soul of the party', you'll gain useful social status.

Dress Code

The Japanese are well known for living in their work clothes. At a typical after-work party the men will be in suits and the women in 'business' skirts. Casual smart is usually acceptable, but dressing up is rarely a bad choice – unless you're told otherwise, e.g. for a night of *karaoke* till dawn.

Gifts (Omiyage)

The Japanese have perfected the art of gift giving for almost any occasion. Traditional gift-giving occasions in Japan are *Ochugen* in mid-July and *Oseibo* in December. At *Ochugen*, which is on no particular day, gifts large and small are offered to family, friends, acquaintances, bosses and work colleagues. Suitable gifts include chocolate, Japanese desserts and teas, which are sold pre-wrapped by many shops.

Oseibo gifts should be given by 20th December and aren't Christmas gifts in the Western sense. Traditionally, *Oseibo* gifts are an appreciation of favours received during the year. The value of the gift depends on the importance of the favour (and the person). *Oseibo* gifts can also be bought pre-wrapped or ordered to be sent directly to a recipient from shops or the post office.

If you go on holiday or on a business trip, you should bring back some *omiyage* (souvenirs) for your friends or colleagues – usually something to eat or drink. The traditional gift from places within Japan is *mochi* (sweet dessert rice cake), which to Western tastes resembles uncooked cake mix; each region has its own variety of *mochi*. Other edible souvenirs include pickles and fruits. Attractively boxed souvenirs are sold at major railway stations and gift shops.

If you're visiting a Japanese home, gifts such as wine, *sake*, gourmet food, or pen and pencil sets are generally welcome. However, it pays to ask mutual friends for advice, as a substantial number of Japanese people are allergic to alcohol.

> White flowers are given only for bereavements, so don't offer them unless you're attending a funeral.

Toasts

Before a meal there will nearly always be a toast with beer, even non-drinkers having a token glass. Everyone simply raises their glass and says *kampai* (cheers). Clinking glasses isn't a traditional part of Japanese culture, but it's increasingly common. It's a faux pas to drink before the toast is made.

The Meal

If the occasion is an *enkai* (a party held by a company or organisation to celebrate a particular occasion, such as the beginning or the end of the year), the meal will be extensive – in both size and duration. It consists of an array of small dishes, e.g. of *sashimi*, *sushi*, *miso* soup, egg soup, various pickles, rice, noodles, some prepared vegetables, a salad and sometimes a few slices of meat, which will successfully fill you up by the end of the evening.

Beer, not wine, is usually drunk with the meal, and some will order *nihonshu* (*sake*) as well. Feel free to pour drinks for yourself and others, as drunkenness is encouraged. Such parties often end abruptly. Full glasses are abandoned as everyone leaves at once – perhaps to go to another party.

Whether the party is an *enkai* or at someone's house, be prepared to sit on the floor on flat cushions or low seats, as tables are usually low.

> Vegetarianism and veganism are scarcely practised and widely misunderstood in Japan. Almost all dishes contain meat of some kind, whether poultry, fish or 'red' meat. The Japanese tend not to consider fish as meat and may describe a dish as 'vegetarian' even when it includes fish.

Making Invitations

If you plan to host a party, dinner or other activity at home, bear in mind that Japanese people may feel awkward visiting your home – for the same reasons they're unlikely to invite you to theirs. On the other hand, they may feel privileged to be invited. Some Japanese are aware that foreigners tend to entertain at home and may be curious to find out what happens on such an occasion – especially if it's one not generally celebrated in Japan, such as Halloween or Christmas.

Bear in mind when making an invitation that the Japanese will shy away from declining or accepting directly, and may be so vague in their response that you think they've said 'no' when they meant 'yes' – or vice versa.

If they do come, Japanese people who have never been to a foreigner's party before are likely to be surprised that people stand up while socialising. At Japanese parties the preference is for everyone to be seated.

Providing either chopsticks or a knife, fork and spoon is acceptable, as the Japanese are generally proficient with either. Be aware, however, that the Japanese tend to use spoons, not forks, to eat rice dishes.

What to Serve

Going to somebody else's house is such a novelty for a Japanese person that it probably doesn't matter what you serve. Nonetheless, a 'foreign experience' is most likely to succeed. A huge variety of foreign foods is available at almost any supermarket or convenience store, and specialist foreign food shops can be found in most major cities. However, since the Japanese palate is more accustomed to subtle (some would say 'bland') flavours, it's probably best to stay away from spicy foods – or at least to provide alternatives. The Japanese make for conscientious guests (even if it's sometimes difficult to know what they want) and will do their best to enjoy themselves.

RESPECTING PRIVACY

The Japanese are extremely private people, sharing their innermost desires, secrets, and problems with few others, if anyone. In fact it's seen as a sign of weakness to divulge too much personal information. For similar reasons, gossip is generally avoided – although it depends on who the gossip is about. As a foreigner in a country where foreigners are few and far between, you may become the subject of gossip more often than a Japanese person would, especially in smaller communities. Some foreigners share confidences with Japanese people they consider to be friends, only to find that they've soon become common knowledge.

> If you choose to confide in a Japanese friend, make it clear that what you're telling them is confidential. Keep to neutral and general topics of conversation until you're sure you can trust someone to 'keep mum'.

As has been said, a Japanese home is a sanctum and you may never be invited to a friend's house. This isn't an affront but rather a reflection of the division between public and private life that is ever present in Japan. Never press the Japanese for an invitation to their home and don't appear unannounced on their doorstep unless it's an emergency.

TABOOS

As in any society, there are certain explicit or implicit taboos – particularly with regard to topics of conversation. This section should help you to avoid making an egregious faux pas.

Conversation

There are a number of topics that should be avoided in conversation with the Japanese, as detailed below. Note, however, that the Japanese are rarely confrontational, even when social conventions are flagrantly disregarded. You're highly unlikely to find yourself locked in a heated argument, even if you broach one of the subjects listed below. The only way you might know that you've said something offensive is to suddenly find yourself in an awkward silence.

The Pacific War

Older Japanese still feel a fair amount of resentment and shame with regard to the Pacific War, while younger Japanese are often ignorant about Japan's role in the war. 'Japanese war crimes' is, not surprisingly, a poor subject of conversation, as is the bombing of Hiroshima and Nagasaki. Japan remains the only country to have suffered bombing by nuclear weapons, which all Japanese agree was a 'bad thing' – even if they aren't fully aware of the history behind it.

The Japanese are generally bewildered when anti-Japanese feeling erupts in countries such as China over such 'issues' as Unit 731 (Japanese war crimes) or the 'rape of Nanking' and they tend to dismiss the ensuing demonstrations and rioting as pure chauvinism.

There's considerable social and professional discrimination in Japan against the *hibakusha* (A-bomb survivors) – discrimination frequently extended to their children, who may be denied employment.

Okinawa

To most Japanese people, Okinawa, with its quirky local culture and tropical climate, is the perfect place for a holiday. However, native Okinawans aren't so favourably disposed towards mainland Japan – or rather its inhabitants. Theirs was an independent kingdom until 1609, when it was invaded by the Japanese, and retained its autonomy until 1879, when it was formally annexed. They're particularly bitter about Japanese soldiers ordering them to commit suicide rather than be captured by Americans during the Pacific War. To add insult to injury, Okinawans have been forced to put up with America's armed forces occupying 20 per cent of their land, which they regard as an unfair sacrifice to make for the rest of Japan.

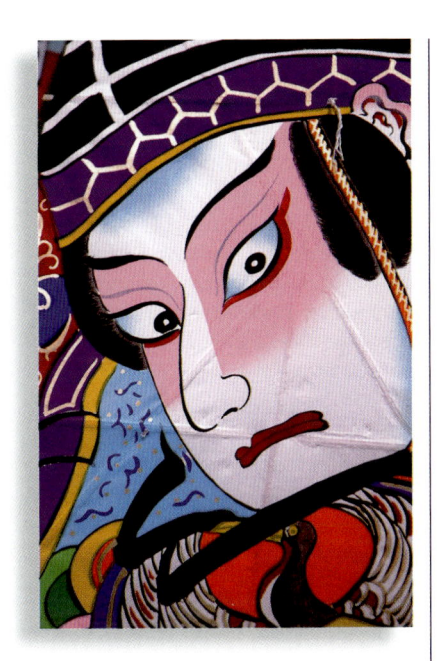

The largest ever demonstrations in Okinawa took place in September 2007, when over 110,000 people took to the streets to protest against the removal from Japanese high school textbooks of passages that explained how, during the Second World War, the Japanese army distributed hand grenades to Okinawan civilians with which to kill themselves if the Americans came. Many did.

Asian Relations

The vast majority of foreigners visiting Japan are from Korea, Taiwan, Hong Kong, China, and Thailand – in fact over 70 per cent of visitors are Asian. Yet the 20 per cent of visitors who come from English-speaking countries are far better catered for in terms of foreign-language signs and information. The explanation for this apparent contradiction is that the Japanese barely consider themselves part of Asia and hold deep-seated prejudices against other Asians, sometimes considering them 'unclean', 'rude' and 'aggressive'. Although white-skinned English speakers in Japan may not even notice this discrimination, they should realise that it's a shocking experience for those who are subjected to it – and therefore not a subject to be broached over dinner.

Any Korea-related subject is to be particularly avoided. Since the Korean boom, which started in the early 2000s, Japan's attitude to Korea has been changing positively – but there's still a long way to go. The Japanese rarely acknowledge the role that Korea has played in their history – or the role they played in Korea's. They're hesitant to admit that Buddhism, pottery, certain musical instruments and many other 'Japanese' cultural artefacts came from Korea, a country the Japanese brutally invaded twice in the 16th century and colonised from 1910 until 1945. Koreans make up Japan's largest ethnic minority and many of them become stars of the sporting and cultural worlds; as soon as they become famous, however, they're considered Japanese!

Hisabetsu-buraku

Japan's unofficial 'underclass', known as the *hisabetsu-buraku* or *burakumin* (see **The Class System** in **Chapter 2**), is a subject few Japanese have anything to say about – and therefore one to be steered clear of.

Extremists & the Mafia

Japan's ultra-patriotic right-wing groups and their supposed links with the Japanese mafia (*yakuza*) – see **Attitudes to Foreigners** in **Chapter 2** – aren't a good conversation starter. Nor are any of their proposals: that national borders should be closed to all foreigners and their influence; that atomic bomb research should be recommenced; and that the military should be strengthened.

The Emperor & Empress

The first time a common Japanese person heard an Emperor's voice was when Hirohito announced Japan's surrender to end the Pacific War. Before then he was venerated as not merely being descended from Gods, but as an actual God. These days, although you may talk about them, the Emperor and his family mustn't be objects of satire or ridicule.

Whaling

Many Japanese are puzzled by the furore that this subject raises overseas, remaining blissfully unaware of the passion behind the protests in anti-whaling countries. Generally, the Japanese think of whales primarily as a form of food, though not a delicacy. In fact, it can occasionally be bought at local supermarkets and may be cheaper than beef (so much for whaling only being carried out for 'scientific' purposes!).

Dress

Generally the smarter and neater you dress, the better the impression you'll make, and business attire is the norm. Neither men nor women reveal much flesh. Men walking around bare-chested or stripping off to sunbathe in a park are considered uncouth, and women showing ample cleavage, even in casual clothes, risk causing offence, although the boundaries of good taste are being pushed back almost daily. Dressing daringly for Japanese women means revealing some leg above the knee, belly or back.

> Sunglasses and tattoos aren't worn as often they are in Western countries and, if you do so, you might be taken for a gangster.

EXPATRIATE COMMUNITY

Although the majority of the 2mn foreigners living and working in Japan are from Asia and South America, it's unlikely you'll meet them unless you speak their language. The English-speaking expat community, although smaller, is highly visible and easy to meet. Just about every town has at least one bar or restaurant where English-speakers hang out. In larger towns and cities a range of free English publications are available from bookshops, music stores and foreign food shops. The English-speaking community in Japan is also easy to access via the internet (see **Appendix C**).

The expat community can prove an important stepping stone to integration into Japanese life – a process that can be lengthy and may never be complete, no matter how well learn you learn the language and assimilate the culture. Having other people that speak your language and understand your cultural background can increase your enjoyment of the country as well as help you cope with its challenges. Owing to the traditional reserve of the Japanese, the closest friendships you're likely to make in Japan are with other foreigners, as they too tend to be open to developing new friendships.

Beware of becoming dependent on the English expat population for friends, however. Expats tend to come and go (usually with the changing of school years), and you can easily find yourself becoming 'friendly' with people you wouldn't normally have interacted with back home (not necessarily a bad thing). Finding a balance between the expat and the native community is essential for, on the one hand, your peace of mind and, on the other, an understanding and eventual acceptance of the local culture.

Advantages

- It's easier to fit in with people of your own nationality, language and culture.

- You get the chance to relax and stop worrying about your behaviour.

- It allows you to let off steam.

Disadvantages

- Spending too much time with expats may mean you don't accept your move as definitive.

- Time spent with other expats could better be spent fitting into life with the Japanese.

- Some expatriates only complain about Japan, intensifying the symptoms of culture shock.

CONFRONTATION

The Japanese are generally polite, conciliatory, and apologetic, even in the face of a confrontation or dispute. Although it isn't unheard of for Japanese to fly into a rage, anger is generally frowned upon. As has been seen, the Japanese also tend to avoid conversing about politics, religion, sex and other 'sensitive' subjects with anyone but their most trusted friends – and sometimes not even them. This can be frustrating for foreigners who relish heated discussion.

The Japanese may react to confrontation in 'subtle' ways. The stereotype of the underhand Japanese isn't always inaccurate. If a Japanese person is displeased with you at work or in your social circle, he will usually remain polite and cordial to your face and with your peers, but he may bad mouth you to your colleagues and superiors when you aren't around or simply 'overlook' you in the future – and you may never find out. The situation will rarely escalate beyond this, however, and in time such disputes can usually be settled.

The way most Japanese people deal with conflict, though, is through simple, sincere apology. If you knowingly or unknowingly cause a problem, apologising will often defuse the situation.

It's best to remain calm in all matters in Japan. This will earn you respect, whereas blowing your top will merely confirm the Japanese prejudice that foreigners are unable to control themselves.

DEALING WITH OFFICIALS

Japan has a long tradition of officious bureaucracy. Police and government officials are orderly and thorough to the point of obsessiveness, requiring an implausible number of copies of every document. Dealing with the Immigration Office over matters relating to a visa or passport, with local government regarding registration or residence, and with the police on any subject can be a severe test of your patience.

In all such dealings, it's best to remain calm and quietly cheerful. Civil servants, even in departments that deal with foreigners, may not have been chosen for their language skills, so use the best Japanese you know or the most basic English you can think of to express yourself, and if you have a non-standard question or problem, bring a friend to translate.

Here are some tips for dealing with Japanese officials:

- Dress smartly.

- Use the most polite form (honorific) of Japanese verbs (see **Chapter 5**).

- Always be polite, and never lose your temper.

- Thank the official and bow (see **Greetings** in **Chapter 5**) at the end of each meeting.

Police

Police in Japan are generally friendly and helpful – and plentiful in urban areas, where the local police are never far from stations and major intersections. (Given Japan's tortuous address system, it isn't surprising that one of their main functions is to help those who have lost their way.)

There's a general perception in Japan that foreigners are responsible for a disproportionate amount of crime. Although unsupported by statistics, this has led to tighter immigration controls and more frequent police questioning of foreigners – both during investigations and on the street.

> A *koban* is a police box manned by two or three police officers. They can be found in front of most railway stations (though at large stations the *koban* may be inside), indicated by a red light hanging above the doorway.

Foreigners are expected to carry identification at all times: either a valid passport and visa (if necessary) or an alien registration card. Police may stop you merely to check whether you have identification. If you don't, you can be taken to a police station, where you must write a letter of apology while somebody else goes to your home to collect an identity document and bring it to the station.

Civil Servants

Interaction with Japanese civil servants is inevitable for residents, as they handle the issue of residence and work permits, foreigner registration and various other administrative functions. While many speak some English, you shouldn't rely on it. Even for a routine matter, you should make a note of the key words in Japanese or take a Japanese-speaking person with you.

Teachers

Most teachers in Japan are employed by the local government and are highly constrained in what they can teach and what they may do other than teaching. Many teachers follow the Japanese work ethic of arriving early and leaving late, although they rarely provide after-school tutoring – that's the job of the cramming schools (*juku*) that many Japanese students attend (see **Education** in **Chapter 3**).

In your dealings with teachers and school administrators, it's polite to ask if they speak English rather than starting a conversation in English – even when talking to English teachers, who may not be confident of their ability to speak the language they teach! You may be able to get interpreting help from English teachers and assistants in junior and senior high schools, but don't bank on it.

一	二	三	四	五	六	七	八	九	十	KANJI				
ONE	TWO	THREE	FOUR	FIVE	SIX	SEVEN	EIGHT	NINE	TEN					
図	族	人	行	事	後	先	答	品	秋	悪	前	始	大	鳥	黒
DRAWING	FAMILY	PERSON	ACT	AFFAIR	AFTER	AHEAD	ANSWER	ARTICLE	AUTUMN	BAD	BEFORE	BEGIN	BIG	BIRD	BLACK
青	台	体	本	借	域	明	建	館	買	運	因	字	長	子	漢
BLUE	BOARD	BODY	BOOK	BORROW	BOUNDED	BRIGHT	BUILD	BUILDING	BUY	CARRY	CAUSE	CHARACTER	CHIEF	CHILD	CHINESE
衣	服	雲	集	来	委	社	写	国	工	習	切	暗	曜	度	死
CLOTHES	CLOTHING	CLOUD	COLLECT	COME	COMMIT	COMPANY	COPY	COUNTRY	CRAFT	CUSTOM	CUT	DARK	DAY	DEGREE	DIE
方	医	犬	下	引	画	飲	早	東	食	電	終	勉	入	用	永
DIRECTION	DOCTOR	DOG	DOWN	DRAW	DRAWING	DRINK	EARLY	EAST	EAT	ELECTRICITY	END	ENDEAVOUR	ENTER	ERRAND	ETERNAL
夕	毎	高	目	家	父	羽	料	野	火	肉	花	足	友	以	栄
EVENING	EVERY	EXPENSIVE	EYE	FAMILY	FATHER	FEATHER	FEE	FIELD	FIRE	FLESH	FLOWER	FOOT	FRIEND	FROM	GLORY
午	金	地	半	堂	手	有	聞	心	天	重	持	屋	百	病	中
GO	GOLD	GROUND	HALF	HALL	HAND	HAVE	HEAR	HEART	HEAVENS	HEAVY	HOLD	HOUSE	HUNDRED	ILLNESS	IN
院	間	知	語	学	出	左	貸	文	生	少	住	愛	主	作	男
INSTITUTION	INTERVAL	KNOW	LANGUAGE	LEARN	LEAVE	LEFT	LEND	LETTER	LIFE	LITTLE	LIVE	LOVE	MAIN	MAKE	MAN
営	多	印	飯	員	意	分	口	山	月	朝	母	動	名	新	夜
MANAGE	MANY	MARK	MEAL	MEMBER	MIND	MINUTE	MOUTH	MOUNTAIN	MOON	MORNING	MOTHER	MOVE	NAME	NEW	NIGHT
北	不	洋	古	兄	姉	開	元	外	紙	親	通	色	道	安	世
NORTH	NOT	OCEAN	OLD	OLDER BRO.	OLDER SIS.	OPEN	ORIGIN	OUTSIDE	PAPER	PARENT	PASS	PASSION	PATH	PEACEFUL	PERIOD
者	場	計	楽	位	注	力	圧	代	私	質	問	雨	育	読	理
PERSON	PLACE	PLAN	PLEASURE	POSITION	POUR	POWER	PRESSURE	PRICE	PRIVATE	QUALITY	QUESTION	RAIN	RAISE	READ	REASON
赤	映	研	休	帰	田	正	起	川	室	走	同	校	海	見	自
RED	REFLECT	RESEARCH	REST	RETURN	RICE FIELD	RIGHT	RISE	RIVER	ROOM	RUN	SAME	SCHOOL	SEA	SEE	SELF
売	送	話	別	仕	鋭	店	風	小	会	土	歌	音	南	言	気
SELL	SEND	SPEAK	SEPARATE	SERVE	SHARP	SHOP	WIND	SMALL	SOCIETY	SOIL	SONG	SOUND	SOUTH	SPEECH	SPIRIT
春	立	発	駅	止	究	服	夏	日	英	泳	味	茶	万	験	物
SPRING	STAND	START	STATION	STOP	STUDY	SUBMIT	SUMMER	SUN	SUPERB	SWIM	TASTE	TEA	TEN THOUSAND	TEST	THING
考	今	千	時	題	右	思	町	旅	木	真	試	転	宇	上	使
THINK	THIS	THOUSAND	TIME	TITLE	RIGHT	THINK	TOWN	TRAVEL	TREE	TRUE	TRY	TURN	UNIVERSE	UP	USE
車	待	歩	水	着	週	西	何	白	広	冬	界	年	円	弟	妹
VEHICLE	WAIT	WALK	WATER	WEAR	WEEK	WEST	WHAT	WHITE	WIDE	WINTER	WORLD	YEAR	YEN	YOUNGER BRO.	Y. SIS.

5.
THE LANGUAGE BARRIER

Being able to communicate with the Japanese, and knowing what to say (and what not to say) when you meet them in a particular situation, are priorities when you move to Japan. In a country whose people value 'face' – a complex combination of reputation, dignity and honour – as much as the Japanese, it should come as no surprise that a great deal of importance is ascribed to communication, both verbal and non-verbal, and that both are highly formalised.

> 'A different language is a different vision of life.'
> Federico Fellini
> (Italian film maker)

Learning to speak a foreign language is never easy and full of potential pitfalls – all expats have stories to tell of when they said 'the wrong thing', often with embarrassing consequences. The added challenge for most foreigners in Japan is that Japanese bears little or no relation to Western languages, in particular using a completely different writing system.

To help you get to grips with the language and keep your collection of 'amusing' anecdotes as small as possible, this chapter offers tips on learning Japanese, insights into regional languages, and explanations of body language and gestures (and their importance in communication), forms of address and greetings, and telephone and letter etiquette.

LEARNING JAPANESE

Relocation and culture shock experts generally agree that one of the best ways of settling into a foreign country where your language isn't spoken is to learn the local language as soon as possible. Even a basic knowledge of a few key phrases when you arrive will help you feel more in control (or less out of control) of your new situation.

In fact, you'll probably be surprised by Japanese people's low expectations of your learning any Japanese – let alone mastering its subtleties and nuances – and any Japanese you manage to utter will most likely be greeted with genuine admiration.

Many basic tasks and transactions in Japan can be completed with little or no Japanese. Your success in carrying out more complicated tasks will depend largely on your location. In the major cities, it usually isn't difficult to find someone who can speak English and help you out. Unfortunately, the same cannot be said for rural areas, where it can be quite a challenge to find an English speaker (or someone willing to use the little English he has).

But living in a foreign country isn't just about 'getting by'. Having little or no Japanese proficiency will greatly limit your experiences in Japan – the more Japanese you learn, the richer they will be. Expats with no language knowledge tend to feel frustrated and cut off when all they can do is nod and gesture. An inability to express even the simplest of needs and messages can be aggravating and lead to a sense of isolation. The benefits of mastering the basics are enormous and it will do wonders for your self-esteem and sense of achievement if you can understand and be understood when you first set foot in Japan.

Yes or No?

If you assume that the direct style of communication used in many Western countries is the norm throughout the world, you'll be in for another surprise in Japan, where there's often a gap – not to say a gulf – between what is said and what is meant. Perhaps nowhere is this more apparent than when a request is being refused. Because of Japanese people's desire to maintain harmony and avoid disrespect, they have a general disinclination to say 'no'. Instead, a question or request might be met with 'maybe', 'perhaps' or 'it will be difficult', with little follow-up. Usually such responses can be interpreted as a refusal. Sometimes, however, a 'maybe' actually means maybe and 'it will be difficult' may imply a 'but we can do it'.

Similarly, if a Japanese person nods at what you're saying, it isn't necessarily an indication that he's agreeing with you; very often it means only that he's listening and understanding. And if you finish speaking and are met with silence, don't be alarmed. Japanese people have a much higher tolerance for silence than Westerners. Silence usually just means they're thinking; when they're ready to speak they will speak.

Instruction on how to pick up on the implicit signals and read between the lines when communicating in Japan is beyond the scope of this book, which can provide only a few general pointers. However, the longer you stay in Japan and the more people you talk to, the easier you'll find it. As is the case with any cross-cultural communication, the best advice is to be patient and not to jump to conclusions.

Writing Systems

The Japanese writing system is arguably the most complicated in the world, consisting in fact of three distinct but related systems: *kanji*, *hiragana* and *katakana*.

- *Kanji* – *Kanji* are characters originally borrowed from Chinese and used to represent the main words in the language: nouns, verbs and adjectives. It's believed that learning the 1,945 *joyo kanji* (the most commonly used *kanji*, according to the Japanese government) is sufficient to be able to read a Japanese newspaper.

- *Hiragana* – *Kanji* are supplemented by *hiragana*, which is a phonetic alphabet consisting of 47 characters used to indicate grammatical functions.

- *Katakana* – another alphabet of 47 different (but similar!) phonetic characters used to spell loanwords, the names of plants and animals, and onomatopoeic words. Many restaurant menus, especially where non-Japanese food is served, use a lot of *katakana* and poring over them is an excellent way to improve your *katakana* comprehension.

Loanwords

Not surprisingly, most loanwords derive from English, and many Japanese use them with foreigners, assuming that they will easily understand them. However, not only does their pronunciation usually make them unrecognisable, but the form or meaning of the words has often changed – or they come from a language other than English – as in the following examples:

Anime – animation (an abbreviation – a common Japanese linguistic device)

Arubaito (from the German *Arbeit* meaning work) – part time or temporary job

Cunningu – cheat

Pan – bread (from Portuguese)

Sabisu – free (from the English 'service')

Sandouichhi – sandwich

Sarada – salad

Shoku – disbelief (from 'shock')

Some Japanese words are written using English letters. *Romaji*, as it's called, is commonly seen on street and subway signs.

Spoken Japanese

The good news is that spoken Japanese is considerably less complicated than the written language, and attempts to use it are rewarded with encouragement and praise. There are no articles ('a', 'the', etc.) or plurals, and verbs aren't conjugated for person or gender. Very often the subject of a sentence is left unspoken if it's obvious from the context.

One key difference between Japanese and English is the ordering of words in a sentence. Whereas English generally uses a subject-verb-object structure, Japanese uses subject-object-verb. For example, a literal translation of *Watashi wa sumo wo mimasu* is "I sumo watch."

Pronunciation is straightforward, especially for English-speakers, there being only one sound that differs from English (the 'r' sound is pronounced like a soft 'd'), and it's easy to build up a repertoire of words and phrases.

The Language Barrier

> Approximately 128mn people speak Japanese, making it the ninth most commonly spoken first language in the world. Substantial communities of Japanese people live in 26 countries.

Why Japanese is Essential

- In an accident or emergency, knowing what to say in Japanese could save your (or someone else's) life.

- Your chance of finding a job or making a success of being self-employed increases dramatically.

- You save time and money when interacting with Japanese people and don't have to rely on others to help you.

- The sense of being a stranger diminishes.

- The Japanese will greatly appreciate your efforts, which will help you integrate.

- Your understanding and appreciation of Japanese culture will increase with your Japanese proficiency.

- Your circle of friends will be widened beyond other English-speaking expats.

- Doors that are often closed to non-Japanese speakers will be opened, particularly in rural parts of Japan.

- Joining a language class is an excellent way of meeting people.

Know Before You Go

On the surface, it would seem that living in Japan would offer limitless opportunities for learning and practising Japanese. Ironically, this isn't always the case, particularly for beginners. Although you'll be surrounded by native speakers of Japanese, expectations that you'll be able to 'pick it up' when you get to Japan are probably unrealistic, as you'll be faced with the more pressing tasks of getting settled into your new home, finding your way around, adjusting to your new job, and dealing with all the other logistical minutiae that go along with relocating to a new country. It's therefore likely that you'll put learning Japanese on the back burner for a few weeks – or a few months.

Once you begin putting it off, however, it's all too easy to go on doing so. It's therefore recommended that you learn at least a little Japanese before your arrival in Japan. A few basic phrases, the ability to count, a rudimentary grasp of pronunciation, the hiragana and katakana alphabets – anything you can get to grips with will be a considerable boon. Online podcasts such as those offered by 🖥 www.japanesepod101.com offer free language classes (from beginner to advanced).

Once in Japan

Once you arrive in Japan it's best to enrol in a formal Japanese class, rather than rely on 'acquiring' the language as you go along. Although informal practice is extremely helpful, it's no substitute for a structured teaching programme and the guidance of trained professionals.

Many universities and private language schools offer Japanese lessons for foreigners, which are listed on the websites 🖥 http://murasakishikibu.co.jp/jls and www.

languageschoolsguide.com. If most cities there's an International Center run by the local government, possibly in association with private organisations. They are often located at the town hall and offer free or subsidised language lessons and opportunities to mix with internationally-minded Japanese. They are excellent information sources for both residents and visitors, with libraries containing books about Japan, foreign newspapers, access to foreign news media such as the BBC and CNN, and internet access. Some also provide free legal advice.

In addition to formal instruction, finding a language exchange partner is highly beneficial. In the large cities, there's no shortage of Japanese people eager to help you learn Japanese in exchange for English practice. Look for advertisements (or place one yourself) in *Metropolis* (🖳 www.metropolis.co.jp), a free magazine that caters to Tokyo's expat community, *Kansai Time Out* (🖳 www.japanfile.com) if you're in the Kansai area, or *Japanzine* (🖳 www.japan-zine.com) elsewhere.

If, like most foreigners in Japan, you simply don't have the time to take a language course, you could try the three-part *Japanese for Busy People* (Kodansha International), the standard self-study textbook, used by many language schools.

Tips for Learning Japanese

- **Learn *hiragana* & *katakana*:** See how many advertisement hoardings (billboards), signs and notices you can read on your daily commute.

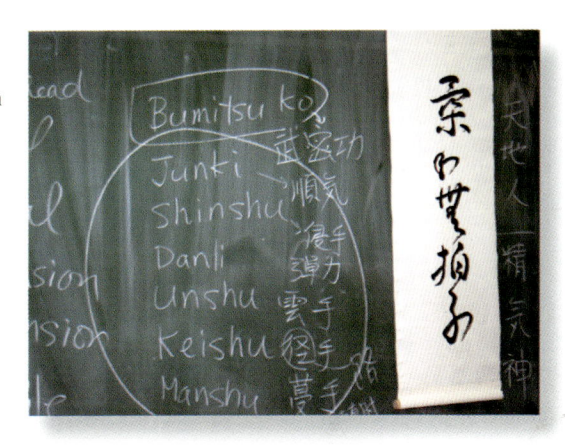

- **Learn *kanji*:** even if you think you only need to know how to speak the language;

- **Be patient:** Early in your language learning, your progress will be obvious and seem rapid; as you move on, your progress may feel slower, but that isn't necessarily the case. It's just that it's harder to assess.

- **Practise every day:** Even if you work on it for only five minutes a day, making Japanese a part of your daily schedule will make it feel more natural.

- **Don't hesitate:** Ask people questions in Japanese even if you already know the answers. It's a good way to practise both speaking and understanding the language.

- **Learn at least ten new words a week.**

- **Laugh at your mistakes:** The more you speak, the more mistakes you'll make and the faster you'll learn.

- **Take pride in your progress:** Pat yourself on the back when you manage to communicate something successfully.
- **Persevere:** Practice makes perfect and, even if you make a mess of your carefully prepared sentence, the Japanese are usually patient and forgiving of mistakes made by foreigners.

Children

If you're relocating as a family to Japan, your children will also need to learn Japanese. Although children tend to learn quickly when they're 'immersed' in a foreign language, it's highly recommended that you enrol them in a Japanese class before leaving your home country. The concept of 'special needs students' isn't as familiar in Japan as it is in Western countries, and public (state) schools are unlikely to offer extra classes in Japanese.

This isn't to say that school officials will be unwilling to help you. On the contrary, principals and teachers at the vast majority of Japanese schools will readily do whatever they can to attempt to accommodate your child, including monitoring his progress and finding a tutor.

Naturally, a Western child in a Japanese school will stand out and get a lot of attention – both negative as well as positive. If he's lucky, your child will enjoy a 'honeymoon' period of celebrity followed by acceptance into a peer group. If he's unlucky, he'll be targeted by bullies and remain an outsider. In both situations, the more Japanese he knows, the better off he'll be.

Another option, particularly in a large city, is to enrol your children in an international school, although the fees at these schools can be high (see **Education** in **Chapter 3**).

> All children should learn to say their telephone number and address in Japanese as soon as possible.

OTHER LANGUAGES

In addition to Japanese, a group of six languages (known as the Ryukyuan languages) is spoken in and around Okinawa and the other Ryukyu Islands in southernmost Japan. Each of these languages is quite different from standard Japanese – and indeed from the other five. In most cases, however, people in these areas also speak standard Japanese – at least in professional settings. In Hokkaido, the Ainu people also have their own language, which is unrelated to Japanese.

The largest ethnic populations (Koreans and Chinese) often use their

The Language Barrier

own language at home and in certain districts in the larger cities.

However, the most important second language in Japan is English. School children and many adults learn it, and there are sizeable English-speaking expatriate communities in all the large cities.

Dialects & Accents

There's considerable regional variation in Japanese – with local dialects as well as various ways of pronouncing standard (Tokyo) Japanese. Some dialects are all but incomprehensible to speakers of standard Japanese.

The principal difference between dialects is often the pronunciation of verbs. For example, 'I don't understand' is *wakarimasen* in standard Japanese, but *wakarahen* in Kansai-ben. The Japanese are fascinated by such regional variations and enjoy discussing those they've come across.

Different dialects and accents carry with them stereotypes of the people who use them. The most obvious example is the accent of the Kansai region, which has become 'the language of comedy'. Those from Tohoku in the north aren't so fortunate, their way of speaking being considered slow and clumsy, while it's said that Hiroshima speakers sound 'manly'.

Fortunately, almost everyone in Japan can speak and understand the standard Japanese that is used on TV and in business. If you're studying Japanese before arriving in Japan, it's invariably standard Japanese that you'll learn.

SLANG & SWEARING

In many countries, profanities are among the first words a learner of the language acquires, but you can live in Japan a long time without hearing swearing of any kind. Quite simply, the Japanese rarely swear. (The Japanese equivalent of 'f*** off' is *zakkennayo*, a shortened form of *fuzakeru nai yo*, which means merely "don't joke around with me", but even this is hardly ever heard.) This is largely due to their sense of propriety and respect. You should therefore follow suit and avoid swearing – even in your own language.

Japanese 'slang' is also pretty tame. Most of what counts as slang is simply the use of 'plain' rather than polite forms of words, e.g. *miru* for 'see' as opposed to *mimasu*. There are, however, some 'genuine' slang expressions, such as *mecha* (very), *nampa suru* (to pick up a member of the opposite sex) and *maguro* (literally meaning a cut of tuna found in *sashimi* but slang for a woman who is passive in bed).

Another form of Japanese slang is the shortening of common words: for example, *boro boro* (old or worn out), might be shortened to *boroi*, *hazukashi* (embarrassed) to *hazui* and *omoshiroi* (interesting/amusing) to *oroi*. *Ossu* is used as an informal greeting – the equivalent of 'hi'.

The Language Barrier

> English words are in common use, and not merely as slang, but some are more often used by adolescents, such as *choberigu*, a corruption of 'so very good'.

Japanese has few adjectives, but as if to make up for that it has a rich stock of onomatopoeic words. These are generally used in informal situations in place of more formal, *kanji*-derived words, and some of them are much more slangy than others. A few examples are *gan gan* (a pounding headache), *guu guu* (fast asleep) and *peko peko* (hungry).

BODY & SIGN LANGUAGE

Like the Italians, although in a very different sense, the Japanese are world-famous for their body language. Not only bowing, facial expressions and eye contact, but also the way you stand and sit and your respect for others' personal space all play an important part in establishing your position and role in the social structure.

It's unrealistic to expect to become a master of non-verbal communication in Japan within a few weeks or even months, but the following basics – along with the reassurance that the Japanese are generally forgiving of foreigners' mistakes – will get you started.

Bowing

Introducing yourself in Japanese can be an extremely formal affair involving the exchange of name cards, different degrees of bowing, and a highly nuanced, almost subliminal system of etiquette – none of which foreigners are expected to be au fait with.

As a general rule, however, when you meet someone for the first time, say your surname followed by "*desu*" ("I am Smith") and then "*Hajimemashite*." (It is nice to meet you.) "*Douzo yoroshuiko onegai shimasu.*" ("Please bestow your favour on me.") This should be accompanied by a bow from the hips, the depth of which depends on the age and seniority of the person you're meeting.

When you enter a shop or restaurant, you can expect to be regaled by everyone who works there with a gracious bow and an almost disconcertingly enthusiastic "*Iirashemase*!" (Welcome!). When you leave a restaurant, you'll also be welcomed to come again, and it's polite to say "*Gochisosamma deshita*" ("That was delicious!") as you leave.

Gestures

When it comes to gesticulation, the Japanese are closer to the reserved

British than to the exuberant Italians, though you'll certainly witness some unfamiliar gestures. Although you may not feel comfortable using these yourself – at least until you're proficient in the spoken language – you may find it helpful to know what they mean.

- **Holding your hand palm down and waggling your fingers back and forth towards you** – Come here.
- **Pointing to your nose** – Who, me?
- **Making a circle with your thumb and index finger** – Money.
- **Making an X with your hands** – No, forbidden or sold out.

If someone sticks a thumb or little finger out when talking on the telephone, this indicates that he or she is speaking to a boyfriend or girlfriend respectively.

If you encounter someone in a crowded area making a chopping motion with his hand, he isn't trying to say anything; he's merely forcing his way through.

> If you see a group of Japanese people making a V-sign, the chances are they're having their picture taken. The V or peace sign is probably more common than a smile in Japanese photographs. A smile doesn't necessarily indicate happiness, but can mean that you're confused, angry, apologetic or embarrassed.

Personal Space

The Japanese are used to being close to each other and you may find the lack of 'personal space' constricting. It can take some getting used to. Nevertheless, the Japanese desire for order and harmony means that they make every effort not to encroach on the space of others – and you should do likewise.

For example, you should sit upright on public transport, and if you want to sleep do so with your head bowed forward, not thrown back or lolling against the person next to you. Having a loud conversation or speaking on your mobile phone on a train is extremely bad manners. If you must join a queue, maintain orderly single file, and before crossing the street wait patiently for the light to change.

FORMS OF ADDRESS

The Japanese place a high value on courtesy, respect and status. This is reflected in their language, which has informal, polite and honorific forms for everything from greetings to verb endings to basic vocabulary. No form is simpler or more difficult than another to learn; the tricky part is working out when to use which. Using an informal form when a polite form is in order can indicate a lack of respect, while using a polite form when the more informal form is called for can give the impression that you're cold and distant.

Even native speakers sometimes get it wrong (a common complaint among the Japanese themselves is that many youngsters don't know – or know when to use – the honorific forms), and the more skilled you become at Japanese the more you'll be expected to get it right – and the more offensive it will appear if you don't. While it's obvious that you're learning the language, Japanese people will be tolerant of your gaffes, but it's worth making the effort to use the appropriate forms of address. You should at least know the informal and polite forms; a smattering of knowledge of honorific forms is desirable.

You're likely to learn the polite forms first, especially if you attend Japanese classes, and then hear the familiar forms being used between those of equal status, such as friends and work colleagues. Husbands may call their wives *omae* or just *oi!* (impolite). Wives often call husbands *anata* (you), not their name.

> When meeting someone for the first time and when addressing someone who is older than you or in a higher position, use the polite form.

Names & Titles

In many aspects of life in Japan, the group takes precedence over the individual – and names are no exception. As a reflection of the family being more important than any particular member of it, a person's surname comes first and their 'Christian' name second. Therefore, the actor known in the West as Ken Watanabe is, to the Japanese, Watanabe Ken.

In almost all professional relationships and many casual relationships in Japan, people go by their surnames rather than their given names. From time to time, you'll meet people who have lived overseas and wish to be addressed by their first name. However, unless your Japanese counterparts specifically invite you to use their first names, address them by their surname followed by *san or samma* (even more respectful), irrespective of their sex. Never use 'san' with your own name or your spouse's, as it's impolite to elevate yourself or your family.

In a professional situation, it's advisable to 'do as the Romans do' and go by your surname preceded by Mr or Ms, etc. Your Japanese colleagues and counterparts will feel more at ease than if you ask them to call you 'Bill' or 'Joan'. Adhering to Japanese norms and respecting their social hierarchies will go a long way towards generating goodwill with your Japanese associates.

The Japanese often resolve their confusion in addressing foreigners who prefer to go by their first name by adding *san* to it, even though they themselves they you should only use san with a first name when addressing close friends. Never use *san* with a first name yourself unless invited to do so.

People's status and position within an organisation are of paramount importance in Japanese professional relationships. The length of time someone has worked for a company, his seniority and his position dictate the amount of respect and deference he must be afforded. Among the ways that this respect manifests itself is in job titles, which are often used instead of names in professional settings.

Some of the titles you're likely to encounter are:

kaicho – chairman

shacho – president

fuku-shacho – vice-president

bucho – department manager

kakari-cho – supervisor

Children

It's normal to address children by their given (Christian) names rather than their surnames, sometimes followed by *chan* (for girls) or *kun* (for boys). These suffixes are also often used when addressing pets and those of lower seniority (close female friends may also address each other as *chan*). During their school years, children generally call each other by their first names; however, once they graduate and enter the working world, most switch to surnames.

Western children will usually be forgiven if they call a Japanese adult by his given name; however, it's much better manners for them to use surnames when talking to grown-ups.

Traditionally many Japanese boys' names ended with 'ro', which means son or bright. Many girls' names ended in 'ko', which means child, or 'mi', which means beauty. However, in recent years Japanese parents have become more adventurous and young people now have a much greater variety of names.

GREETINGS

Introducing yourself in Japanese can be a highly formal affair involving the exchange of business cards, various degrees of bowing and the utterance of set – but subtly nuanced – expressions. However, by learning a few key phrases and gestures, you can make a favourable first impression.

In a professional context – as well as many personal contexts – meeting people for the first time involves an exchange of business cards (see **Business Cards** in **Chapter 6**). As you do so, say your surname followed by '*desu. Hajimemashite. Douzo yoroshuiko onegai shimasu*' ('I am _____. It is nice to meet you. Please bestow your favour on me'), simultaneously executing a bow from the hips, the depth of which will depend on the relative age and seniority of the person you're addressing. Practise it at home first.

Greetings - Useful Phrases

My name is ____	____ *desu* (more formally *Watashi no namae wa ____ desu*)
Good morning	*Ohayo gozaimasu*
Good day	*Konnichiwa*
Good evening	*Konbanwa*
What is your name?	*O-namae wa (nan desuka)?*
How are you?	*O-genki desu ka?*
I'm fine (informal)	*Genki desu*
I'm fine (polite)	*Okagesama de*
Good night (when leaving work)	*Osaki ni*
Good night (to someone leaving work)	*Otsuka re sama deshita*
Good night (when going to bed)	*Oyasuminasai*

TELEPHONE, EMAIL & LETTERS

For someone who is learning a language, having to talk on the telephone can be a daunting prospect. You can't use body language, writing or drawing to compensate for any language gaps, and not being able to see the person you're speaking to makes it harder to understand.

Practising what you need to say before you make a call can make it go smoother. However, most company receptionists speak at least a little English. If you're unlucky enough to find one who doesn't, you could try calling the person's mobile instead of the switchboard.

When sending an email in English to a Japanese person, use simple, straightforward sentences and try to avoid slang and idioms in order to reduce the chance of misunderstanding. Use the same form of address that you would if you were talking to him.

You can send and receive letters using addresses written in English, although it's advisable to write them as clearly as possible in capitals. A Japanese address should be written as follows:

> Person's name
>
> (Business name)
>
> Sub-area, block number, apartment name and number
>
> City, village or ward name
>
> Prefecture and seven-digit post code
>
> Japan

If you're writing the address in *kanji*, the name of the person will be beneath the address.

Japanese envelopes are often in 'portrait' rather than 'landscape' format, with a row of seven boxes at the top in which to put the post code. The addressee's name should be put at the bottom.

The Language Barrier

Umeda Sky Building, Osaka

6.
THE JAPANESE AT WORK

Expecting Japan's working world to operate in the same way as in your native country is a mistake that's often made by foreigners. It takes time and patience to grow accustomed to the Japanese working environment, and there are psychological, social and structural – as well as linguistic – differences to be overcome if you want to succeed in business in Japan. This chapter offers essential information on working for a Japanese employer, starting your own business and business etiquette.

> In 2007, the Ministry of Health, Labour and Welfare proposed exempting white-collar workers from overtime pay – a move which in any other country would have provoked riots.

WORK ETHIC

In Japan it's generally thought that almost any job with a large corporation is superior to any job with a smaller firm. There's a fairly well known hierarchy of companies, and if you're employed by one of the major companies you'll earn respect, irrespective of your position. Wherever you work, however, you'll be expected to value the company more than your individual needs.

Japanese employees are accustomed to working long hours: they work an average of 55 hours a week, and staying on long past 7pm is common. (Workers sleeping on trains are an everyday sight.) Although a typical 'official' workday is from 9am to 6pm, your boss may ask you to work late or to work at the weekend – a request you cannot refuse if you wish to retain your job. Family time, holidays and weekends are often sacrificed to work or unpaid training.

Theoretically, hourly-paid employees must be given 125 per cent of their normal pay in overtime for each hour worked over 40 hours. However, it's usual for Japanese workers to do overtime without claiming extra pay. Official figures indicate that the average Japanese works 1,780 hours a year, compared with 1,800 worked by Americans and 1,440 by Germans. But these statistics don't include 'free overtime', and unofficial figures show that a third of males aged between 30 and 40 work over 60 hours a week, half of them without overtime pay. However, the lowest paid workers are part-time workers, most of whom are women.

Similarly, leaving work before your boss may be considered rude; in many companies, employees are afraid to leave work before their boss and would rather sit at their desk twiddling their thumbs until he goes home. And to refuse an invitation for after-work drinks or a *karaoke* session by company superiors is unheard of.

Some large companies have traditions that seem strange to Westerners. At Mitsubishi, for example, inductees must be at work before their superiors to welcome them when they arrive each day. As a foreigner, however, you may not be expected to know or follow company tradition.

Women used to be able to avoid going out for drinks more easily than male employees, but as gender differences start to blur, career-minded women may also be expected to unwind at the end of the day with colleagues and bosses if they want to be promoted. Workers often stop at an *izakaya* (a bar serving alcohol and small plates of food) on their way home. Sometimes a drink turns into a party, which may end up in a *karaoke* bar.

Despite the expectation (and reality) of company loyalty, a 'job for life' is no longer guaranteed to Japanese workers – if it ever was (this idea is largely an exported myth) – who can be laid off at any time for any reason.

Fortunately, the work ethic in Japan is slowly evolving in a more employee-friendly direction. Since the economic bubble burst in the '90s, employees have been demanding shorter working hours and more paid holidays, and the number of hours worked per month is declining by around 2 per cent each year.

> IBM decided to have some parts manufactured in Japan as a trial project. In the specifications, they set out that they would accept three defective parts per 10,000. When the delivery came in there was an accompanying letter. "We Japanese people have a difficult time understanding North American business practices. But the three defective parts per 10,000 have been separately manufactured and have been included in the consignment. Hope this pleases you."

HOLIDAYS & LEAVE

In their first year of employment with a company, you're entitled to ten days' paid holiday (vacation), which can be taken consecutively or non-consecutively. This is increased by one day for every subsequent year worked. Holidays must be requested in writing

The Japanese at Work 107

Public Holidays

Date	Holiday
First week of January	New Year Holiday (*Shogatsu/Oshogatsu*)
Second Monday in January	Coming of Age Day (*Seijin no hi*)
11th February	National Foundation Day (*Kenkoku kinen no hi*)
3rd March	Girls' Holiday (*Hinamatsuri*)
Around 21st March	Vernal Equinox (*Shunbun no hi*)
29th April	Showa Day (*Showa no hi*)
3rd May	Constitution Memorial Day (*Kenpo kinenbi*)
4th May	Greenery Day (*Midori no hi*)
5th May	Children's Day (*Kodomo no hi*)
Third Monday in July	Marine Day (*Umi no hi*)
mid-July or mid-August	*Obon* Festival
Third Monday in September	Respect for the Aged Day (*Keiro no hi*)
23rd September	Autumnal Equinox (*Shubun no hi*)
Second Monday in October	Health and Sports Day (*Taiiku no hi*)
3rd November	Culture Day (*Bunka no hi*)
23rd November	Labour Thanksgiving Day (*Kinro kansha no hi*)
23rd December	The Emperor's Birthday (*Tenno tanjobi*)

at least a month in advance, but requests can be rejected (or even approved and then cancelled) by the company if normal business will be hindered by your absence.

According to a report by The Japan Institute of Labour, employees take an average of only half the number of paid holidays that they're entitled to.

Public Holidays

Japan has many national public 'holidays' (see table), but employers aren't required to give staff time off, although many businesses close during Golden Week, for *Obon* and at New Year (see below). Most shops stay open on public holidays, but schools and government offices are generally closed. When a holiday falls on a Saturday or Sunday, a day off during the week isn't granted in lieu.

Golden Week

Golden Week comprises three holidays: Showa Day on 29th April, Constitution Memorial Day on 3rd May and Greenery Day on 4th May. Some businesses, especially small and family-owned companies, close for the whole week, while others close on 3rd and 4th May only. Schools and government offices are generally closed only on 3rd and 4th May.

The Japanese at Work

Obon

A Buddhist festival to honour one's ancestors, *Obon* is celebrated in mid-July or mid-August, depending on the region. It's a popular event, when people hang lanterns outside their homes and there are festivals with traditional entertainment. Many businesses and small restaurants shut during *Obon*, although you can expect large supermarkets and chain restaurants to remain open.

Christmas & New Year

Christmas isn't a holiday in Japan (though a time for shopping), therefore you can expect to have to work irrespective of your religion or nationality. The 'New Year', on the other hand, is a family holiday of between 6 and 12 days. Most businesses close on 27th December and reopen on the Monday after 1st January; universities normally close for two weeks. New Year's eve, though, isn't as widely celebrated as New Year's Day (see **Chapter 8**).

Leave

Although Japanese law provides for up to a year's (unpaid) parental leave, only some 20 per cent of Japanese women return to their jobs after giving birth, the common practice being for them to resign and take up full-time motherhood. It's even rarer for Japanese men to take parental leave: a mere one in 200 fathers do so.

FINDING A JOB

Because of the lack of skilled, English-speaking employees in the finance, education, import/export and electronics sectors, openings are available for appropriately qualified foreigners – especially as an increasing number of foreign companies are opening offices in Japan.

The ability to speak Japanese will make you stand out against most other foreign job applicants, although it depends on how many Japanese employees are working in a company. Whatever the company, however, a deciding factor in your success will be your ability to develop business relationships.

English-teaching jobs are in ample supply in Japan and offer an easy way in to the Japanese employment market. English teaching companies are called *eikawa* (literally 'English conversation'), and there's at least one in almost every neighbourhood. Even if you don't want to teach long term, you can take a job with an *eikawa* in order to obtain a working visa (see **Permits & Paperwork** below), then look for another job in Japan.

Small language schools tend to pay slightly more

than the large chains and provide a more personal work environment, and you usually have greater freedom in terms of teaching methods. However, whereas the chains hold interviews in English-speaking countries, smaller schools interview only in Japan.

> Aeon, Berlitz, Gaba and Geos are among the best known English-teaching schools in Japan. Nova was the largest until October 2007, when the company filed for bankruptcy, leaving over 5,000 English teachers unemployed. G Communications has since bought Nova and re-employed many of its teachers.

Teaching isn't the only English-related job you can do in Japan. Editing, rewriting and transcribing are also popular occupations among foreign employees.

Permits & Paperwork

To work in Japan, you must initially obtain a one-year 'non-permanent resident work visa' (hereinafter referred to simply as a 'work visa'), which requires a Japanese company to 'sponsor' you, i.e. confirm that it has offered you a job. Thanks to the Japanese love of red tape, the application process can take as long as three months, but once you have a visa, you can extend it or change companies simply by taking your employment contract (and your tax records – to prove that you've been working legally in Japan) to the immigration office.

Work visas are available for a wide variety of employees including teachers, artists, journalists, business investors, engineers and skilled jobs, among others. This type of visa can be issued for one to three-year stays. Many foreigners get a one-year work visa as a Specialist in Humanities/International Studies because it encompasses a wide range of jobs from editor to tour guide. Changing the job status on your visa is simply resolved by completing a 'Status Change' form at the immigration office.

Even if you're on a visa that doesn't allow you to work or restricts job movement, you can change your visa status or obtain a different type of visa without leaving Japan – although you must, of course, meet the criteria for the new visa. You'll need to submit a diploma and work references to prove that you're suitably qualified and capable of carrying out the job.

Six-month working holiday visas are available to citizens and residents of Australia, Canada and New Zealand, who can extend them for a further six months while in Japan. Legal residents of Denmark, France, Germany, Ireland, the Republic of Korea and the UK are entitled to a one-year working holiday visa, but cannot renew it. Working holiday visa holders, who must be aged between 18 and 30, may work full or part time – but not in a nightclub – in order to earn money for travelling in Japan.

Obtaining permission to establish a business is a little harder – and most of the necessary forms are available in Japanese only.

Educational qualifications and work experience earned in most countries are recognised in Japan, but almost all work visas require a university degree or ten years' relevant work experience.

Speaking Japanese

Unless teaching English (or another language) is your only job prospect, the ability to speak Japanese will give you a distinct advantage, even if a company doesn't explicitly require Japanese language skills. Many companies require a score of at least 60 (known as the 'passing score') in a recognised Japanese language proficiency test (JLPT) – *Nouryoku Shiken* is the most widely known.

This test has four levels, Level 4 is a rudimentary level, Level 3 is suitable for everyday interactions, including essential *kanji* characters, Level 2 is sufficient for basic business interaction and Level 1 is necessary if you want to take up a course at a Japanese university. The test can be taken only once a year, in December, and applications must be submitted by September.

Other assessment systems include the Japan External Trade Organisation (JETRO)'s business Japanese test, the Nihon Kanji Proficiency Test and the Japanese Communication Ability Test (JCAT).

If a foreign employee wants to be promoted within a Japanese company, it's usually essential for him to be proficient in the language.

Discrimination

Discrimination in the workplace is prohibited by Article 3 of Japan's Labour Standards Law, which states: 'An employer shall not engage in discriminatory treatment with respect to wages, working hours or other working conditions by reason of nationality, creed or social status of any worker.' In practice, however, discrimination in recruitment and promotion is widespread – particularly against women (see below). Other groups that may experience discrimination in Japan are ethnic Koreans and Chinese (even if they've lived in Japan all their lives).

Any foreigners other than the blond, blue-eyed and white skinned may also find it difficult to gain employment, and blacks in particular may be subject to the kind of racism that results from ignorance, although the popularity of black personalities (most notably the K1 fighter Bob Sapp) and black urban culture (hip hop, rap, etc.) has done much to break down negative attitudes (amongst younger Japanese at least).

Women

The trend used to be that women would join companies as 'office ladies' to find husbands, then retire from work to start a family. Nowadays, many women re-enter the workforce later in life or remaining in employment after marriage. An increasing number of women are joining the Japanese workforce and almost 50 per cent of women aged 15 or over now work, comprising around 40 per cent of the workforce.

However, as in other countries, female employment is largely limited to certain sectors of the economy. The industries that employ the most women – and in which they outnumber men – are the wholesale and retail trades, followed by the medical, healthcare and welfare industries. Women also tend to work shorter hours: over 50 per cent are part-time or temporary staff, compared with less than 20 per cent of men. Not surprisingly this results in a huge disparity in earning power.

> While 60 per cent of men earn ¥3mn to ¥7mn (US$30,000-70,000) per year, only a third of women fall into the same income bracket. And a mere 3 per cent of women compared with over 20 per cent of men earn over ¥7mn (US$70,000).

The Equal Employment Opportunity Law for Men and Women was revised in 1997, removing clauses applying specifically to women that prohibited working late in the evening, during holidays and at other 'abnormal' times. This helped to reduce discrimination in recruitment, but complaints from women at not being paid as much or promoted as quickly as their male counterparts, or not being given meaningful or challenging work remain common. And, according to the statistics, women are still discriminated against when applying for jobs.

In a poll conducted by Pasona Inc., a temporary-staff recruitment agency, over 40 per cent of women claimed that they were discriminated against when interviewed for jobs – although, of course, such discrimination is almost impossible to prove. Many companies, especially those with more 'conservative' executives, operate on the assumption that women will work only until they find a husband, therefore training them or giving them opportunities to play a more important role in the company is futile.

The same applies to foreign women wishing to work in Japan. Male English teachers, for example, are often hired in preference to females for business English teaching positions, and they are often paid more. They also tend to be preferred by female students and a certain amount of flirting between teacher and student is *de rigeur* in Japan. On the other hand, foreign women are more often hired to teach children. In general, it's easier for a foreigner who conforms to the Japanese idea of an 'ideal Westerner', i.e. blond hair and blue eyes, to obtain an English-teaching job, especially with children, and most difficult for a foreigner of Asian or African descent.

As Japan's population continues to decline, however, female employees are becoming increasingly important to the economic wellbeing of the country – and such inequalities are gradually disappearing.

EMPLOYMENT AGENCIES

Most recruitment for full-time jobs is done by the companies concerned, which expend considerable resources in finding the right person for a job – and for the company. Companies compete for the 'bright young sparks' leaving university, who will start work on 1st April after graduation, but the recruitment process begins much earlier. Students usually start applying for graduate positions from midway through their third (penultimate) year of studies and aim to have found their ideal job some time in the middle of the first term of their last year. The final year and a half of university for most students is devoted to the job hunt, with studies taking a back seat. It isn't unheard of for the best students to start work before they graduate.

Some specialist businesses with particular needs, such as those in the entertainment and IT sectors, use recruitment agencies. The Tokyo Employment Service Center for Foreigners in Tokyo and Osaka (💻 www.tfemploy.go.jp/en/info/info_1.html) is, as its name suggests, geared towards foreigners, but mostly helps international students find jobs to support their studies.

In recent years, Japanese companies have been increasingly relying on temporary agencies to fill low-ranking positions once occupied by full-time employees. However, the vast majority of workers in Japan would rather have a full-time job, and the government has campaigned to encourage companies to make their temps full-time employees.

Applications & Interviews

Many Japanese companies require job applicants to handwrite their qualifications and work experience on a standardised form.

When applying for jobs in Japan, you should be aware that assertiveness isn't always considered a virtue and you should try to strike a balance between humility, when speaking about your experience, and pride, in describing your accomplishments.

Selection & Probation

Candidate selection in a Japanese company may involve two or even three interviews. If Japanese language skills are required, you must submit your *Nouryoku Shiken* test score or equivalent (see **Speaking Japanese** above) and may also have to take a test in *kanji* that's particular to the job that you're applying for. The latter is standard for native Japanese speakers as well as foreign applicants.

The usual probationary period is 90 days, but it's mainly for the benefit of the employee, since Japanese companies can fire any employee at any time for any reason (see **Contracts** below).

SALARY

Salaries in Japan are roughly the same as in the US. The average wage of full-time employees and self-employed workers is around ¥320,000 (US$32,000). The cost of living is higher in Tokyo and Osaka, however, than in almost any other cities in the world, therefore by the time you've paid for rent, transportation and food, you won't have much money left.

> Some companies include your expected overtime pay in the salary they quote you when you apply for a job.

In addition to salary, most companies pay employees a biannual bonus, usually in June and December. The size of the bonus varies depending on the company you work for and your position, as well as your perceived contribution to profits for the year and the number of people in your team who gain promotion. Bonuses can be as little as one month's pay and as much as four months'. Bonuses may not be offered to foreign employees, however, so it's advisable to check if a bonus isn't mentioned in your contract.

All employees in Japan are reimbursed for the cost of travelling to and from work, but many companies have a limit on the amount they'll reimburse. Check whether there's a 'cap' before deciding where to live.

Salary Payments

Salaries are usually paid directly into your bank account, generally towards the end of the month. You're given a monthly pay slip (in Japanese) detailing gross pay, income tax, insurance and other deductions, overtime worked, and sick leave and personal holidays taken.

CONTRACTS

Employment contracts usually lack the detail found in Western contracts. This is true even in the largest companies, which hire graduates and then decide where to place them in the company. Often the most important details are specified orally, which is sufficient for the Japanese – and the only type of 'agreement' you may be given – although your contract should specify the regulations relating to such formalities as punctuality and sickness. In some Japanese companies you can be fined for being late or going off sick. (After all, the trains are always on time, so it's naturally assumed if you're late that you've been irresponsible.) The major language schools are especially keen on deducting fines from employees' pay cheques.

If your train is even a few minutes late (which happens only in exceptional circumstances), you can pick up a *shoumeisho* from the station, which is a late train confirmation. This is the only thing that will prevent your getting dirty looks from colleagues and being punished by the boss.

Generally, foreign employees are contracted to work for a year, but you can terminate your employment earlier by giving two to four weeks' notice, depending on your contract.

Firing employees is easy for Japanese companies and all is required is to give one month's written notice or one month's salary in lieu of notice. No reason needs to be specified.

STARTING OR BUYING A BUSINESS

Of the 42 countries surveyed in 2006 by Global Entrepreneurship Monitor (GEM), Japan ranks lowest in entrepreneurial activity. One reason for this is that most employees are paid according to seniority rather than on performance. Another reason is simply that there's a lack of venture capitalists (or 'angels') willing to invest in new businesses in Japan. An additional obstacle for foreigners wishing to run a business in Japan is, of course, the language.

Administratively, however, setting up shop in Japan isn't as difficult as it used to be and can be done in as little as a month (between one and three months is usual) and at next to no cost. Limited liability partnerships (LLP), limited liability companies (LLC) and joint stock companies can be established for ¥2 or less. The regulations are less complex than in many other countries and you usually need only complete the relevant forms. Whether your business is a success or not is another matter!

The most popular business structure is the LLP, as there's no need to notify the Bank of Japan and the paperwork is less complex. For details about business start-ups see the Japan External Trade Organisation's (JETRO, 🖥 www.jetro.org) website. JETRO is a government-funded body that promotes trade and investment in Japan and provides free business advice, lists of prospective partners, and free office space for up to three months in the main cities.

Loans & Grants

Before they will grant a loan, banks in Japan require personal guarantors that have no stakes in the company and assets equal to the amount loaned. The National Life Finance Corporation (NLFC) provides loans to small businesses with a guarantor, irrespective of the owner's personal assets.

> Often, banks don't put a limit on how long your guarantor must be liable for the business's financial failure.

Japanese and foreign government grants are available to entrepreneurs with innovative ideas. The Japan Social Development Fund, the World Bank, the UK's Department of Institutional Development and the Inter-American Development Bank are among the organisations offering grants.

Premises

Most business premises are rented (or leased – the terms are used synonymously in Japan), rather than purchased, due to the high price of property. Renting business premises involves a similar process to renting an apartment, a number of fees needing to be paid before the space becomes yours. These may include the following:

- *chukai tesuryo*: a 'management' fee paid to the agency and normally equivalent to one month's rent;

- *reikin*: 'key money', a non-refundable deposit given to the landlord at the beginning of the rental period or when it's renewed and usually equal to one or two months' rent, but sometimes more;

- *shikikin*: a damage deposit, also payable to the landlord and also typically one or two months' rent, refunded when you vacate the premises minus the cost of repairing any damage to the property and possibly professional cleaning.

Working from Home

Many foreigners and native Japanese (especially women) work from home, in fields ranging from piano and yoga teaching to writing and teaching English. Tax deductions are available if you (legally) use your home for business purposes, but some apartment rental contracts forbid business use, therefore it's important to check before signing if you plan to work from home.

Self-employment

Self-employment isn't popular with the Japanese. Indeed, Japan ranks near the bottom of the list of OECD countries in terms of the percentage of self-employed workers. For foreigners, however, it can be a viable option, particularly for those in the field of language education. Being a self-employed teacher is legally possible, but you must prove that you can maintain an adequate income – allowing for taxes and social security contributions – to retain your work visa.

Several websites – in English for teachers and Japanese for students – provide a simple way to find customers. Two of the most prominent are 🖥 www.findateacher.net and 🖥 www.labochi.com, both of which are free to teachers. You complete a 'profile' specifying the area you'll cover, the times at which you're available, your charges, and the methods you use or subject areas you specialise in.

The advantages of teaching private students are that it's more personal, it's flexible and, depending on your scruples, you can 'hide' at least some of your income from the taxman (see **Black Economy** below). The negative side is that the students can (and frequently do) cancel, therefore the pay isn't as reliable as with employment at a school.

Marketing

The internet and word of mouth are effective marketing tools anywhere in the world, and Japan is no exception.

However, in Japan it's especially important to maintain high standards. It's possible to gear your business specifically towards the English-speaking community, which may be less demanding, but this is a miniscule market. If you want your business to do well, attracting Japanese customers is vital – and to appeal to the notoriously fussy Japanese, a reputation for quality and service is essential.

BUSINESS ETIQUETTE

As in every country, there are rules in the Japanese workplace that must be adhered to in order to maintain order and maximise efficiency. To most Westerners, Japanese business etiquette seems rigid – bowing and not speaking to a superior until he has spoken to you are among the conventions – but the rules can be picked up quite easily if you're observant.

One important custom to observe is to not speak in a direct manner to your superiors – or even to your colleagues unless you have a relationship in which speaking frankly has been established as acceptable. An indirect approach – beating about the bush – is expected in business as in most social situations. If there's an emergency or an urgent problem to be dealt with, you can bypass this requirement, but otherwise speaking 'in black and white' will merely reinforce the stereotype that Japanese have of foreigners as complaining, brash and over-confident.

> The Japanese are famously incapable of saying 'no', but they will indicate that your idea, suggestion or proposal doesn't meet with their approval by a sharp intake of breath and telling you that 'it's difficult' (*muzukashii*). This doesn't necessarily mean that you should abandon your idea altogether, but you may need to change your approach to getting it adopted.

Dress

The Japanese leave home every morning impeccably dressed for work, including matching jewellery, shoes and handbags or briefcases. For the Japanese salaryman, the navy blue suit, white shirt and a tie still reign supreme. Many office workers, especially secretaries, must wear a standard uniform.

Normal attire is relaxed in summer, when 'Cool Biz' is in effect – a Ministry of the Environment campaign launched in 2005 to encourage businesses to set their thermostats as high as 28°C (82°F) from 1st June, thereby saving energy and carbon dioxide emissions, and allow workers to remove their jackets and ties. Department stores capitalised on the idea by introducing 'Cool Biz' sections selling clothing designed to keep the body temperature down.

An equivalent 'Warm Biz' campaign has been proposed for the winter, whereby companies would be encouraged to keep indoor temperatures at 20°C (68°F) instead of heating them to at least 25°C (77°F), but it hasn't been endorsed by the government and the majority of companies are against the idea.

Language

English isn't widely spoken in Japan, and you mustn't assume that people in your company speak English. Although everybody in Japan has studied English for at least six years in junior and senior high school, they can often understand no more than simple greetings and phrases relating to food and drink. Nonetheless, they will probably try to communicate in English to make you feel more comfortable – even if your Japanese is better than their English.

> Yoroshiku onegai-shimasu (literally 'Please be happy with me') is a formal phrase used when arriving at work and after speaking to executives. Another important phrase is Otsukaresama deshita (literally 'Honoured tired one'), which is what you should say on leaving work – unless, of course, you're going to a karaoke bar with your workmates.

Appointments

Spontaneity is virtually unheard of in Japan. You must make an appointment to speak to anyone business related, pick up paperwork from government offices or go for coffee with Japanese friends. If you cannot make an appointment, you should phone to warn the person that you're coming.

Timekeeping

Punctuality is of great importance in Japan. Appointment times aren't the time at which you're asked to sit and read a magazine by a receptionist but the time at which you'll be received by your manager, interviewer or whoever you've arranged to meet. If you're likely to be even a couple of minutes late, it's imperative to let the person know. Being more than five minutes late requires an explanation and an apology.

Business Cards

Business cards (meishi) are essential in Japan. You should have yours printed in English on one side and Japanese on the other. Meishi tend to be simple: black type on a white or beige card.

Cards are exchanged at the beginning of a any meeting, formal or otherwise, and knowing the correct way to handle them is essential. When presenting your card to someone, use both hands and hold it so that the relevant language faces the person receiving it – and is the right way up.

> When you're given a business card, you should look at it for a few seconds, then put it in your wallet or card holder respectfully. It's disrespectful to put it in your back pocket, as this means you'll end up sitting on it.

Meetings

Forming a relationship with a future employee or business partner is important in Japan. First meetings are generally to learn about each other's families, background, travel experience and interests. Talking about business during the first meeting is generally considered bad manners and should be avoided unless a business topic is raised by a superior or prospective client.

Intra-company meetings are held quite frequently in Japan but are often used for announcements, not as forums in which to share ideas. Many employees have meetings every day, lasting from 15 minutes to two or more hours. You're generally expected only to listen to the information you're given.

Wait for others to sit down or to be told where to sit in order to avoid inadvertently sitting in the wrong place. It's customary, for example, for the person with the highest rank or an honoured guest to sit furthest from the door.

There's usually a printed agenda, which is closely followed.

Negotiating

Negotiating with the Japanese requires patience and reserve. Here are some tips:

- Bring lots of data and background information. Thorough research and careful preparation are highly regarded in Japanese business.

- The Japanese aren't impressed by boasting about achievements – whether yours or your company's.

- Don't fill silence by chatting. Most Japanese don't feel the need to fill every available second with talk. Silence is used for thinking about and gauging a situation. Babbling irrelevantly will make you seem unprepared or nervous.

- A decision is unlikely to be reached at a meeting. After collecting the information from you, your counterparts will discuss your proposal or offer among themselves before making a decision.

- Don't try to pressurise anyone into making a decision, as this is usually counterproductive.

- Contracts have been used since Japan entered the global market, but oral agreements, 'sealed' with a bow, are still usual – and are considered asbinding as a written contract.

Business Gifts

Business in Japan is about building relationships and trust. Japanese companies are devoutly loyal to those companies they have regular dealings with, which is one of the reasons why new companies, particularly foreign ones, find it difficult to break into the market (and why Japan ranks so low in the field of entrepreneurship). Gift giving is a way for companies to express their appreciation of an existing or prospective relationship and is an accepted part of business custom. It's therefore not only common, but expected – in a variety of situations:

The Japanese at Work

- Small gifts, especially Japanese pastries, are often given to employees by customers or superiors to show their appreciation and respect.

- When you meet representatives of another company to negotiate a deal, you should take gifts – and should spend up to ¥10,000 (US$100). The usual gifts are a bottle of Japanese *sake* or a luxury office product but, as a foreigner, you may be expected to give items from your home country.

- If you go on a business trip or even a holiday, you're expected to bring back some form of edible souvenir (*omiyage*) to share with your colleagues. You can find boxes of these in plentiful supply at railway stations and souvenir shops at tourist spots.

- Colleagues, superiors, clients and business partners should be offered gifts at *Ochugen* in mid-July and *Oseibo* in December (see **Gifts** in **Chapter 4**).

Regional Differences

Nagoya, Osaka, Tokyo and Yokohama have the highest concentration of businesses in Japan as well as the largest numbers of foreigners. Companies in these four cities are therefore accustomed to foreign employees and business partners. The same may not be true in other parts of the country.

There's considerable rivalry between Osaka and Tokyo, the latter being said to be the administrative centre of Japan, the former the merchants' capital. Business people in Osaka have a reputation for their mercantile instincts and the emphasis they place on making money. A common greeting in Osaka is '*Moukari makka?*' ('Are you making money?').

> 'Between Tokyoites and Osakans the major difference is the attitude toward money. The former put priority on money for appearance's sake, whereas the latter regard it in terms of material gain. These attributes are clear-cut customs that go back a long way.'
>
> Shinichi Yano, head of the Number One Strategy Research Institute

EMPLOYING PEOPLE

If you're contemplating setting up a business requiring staff, you couldn't choose a better place than Japan. Japanese employees are among the most dedicated in the world. Only the threat of a typhoon or an earthquake will keep them away from work. They will work long hours and give up weekends for the good of the company, and are always well dressed and smiling.

Certain regulations apply, of course. There's a minimum wage, which varies by region – the minimum in Osaka and

Tokyo is currently ¥739 (US$7.39) an hour – and you must give employees at least ten days' annual holiday (increasing by one day fore each year of service). Although you aren't required by law to grant public holidays (see above), most employees expect to have Golden Week off in May and several days around New Year.

Contracts

As noted above, contracts in Japan tend to be vague, and employees can generally be fired with a month's notice for any reason, although you can, if you're magnanimous, specify conditions in which you'll dismiss your workers, such as persistent lateness, bad behaviour or inefficiency. Contracts usually also stipulate that employees must apply to take their holiday entitlement at least a month in advance.

> Every employee must be allowed a break of 45 minutes a day, but this time doesn't have to be paid.

Tax & Social Security

Japanese companies pay between 22 and 41 per cent tax on turnover, according to various factors. Business taxes include corporate tax (up to 30 per cent), inhabitant tax and enterprise tax. Enterprise tax is a deductible expense, whereas corporate and inhabitant tax aren't.

Twelve per cent of an employee's salary must be deducted for social security contributions (for the national healthcare system, pension payments and unemployment benefits) and a further 12.9 per cent for tax.

TRADE UNIONS

Japanese trade unions are organised in a three-tier hierarchy: enterprise-based unions at the bottom, industrial unions, and the Japanese Trade Union Confederation (known as JTUC-RENGO) at the top. JTUC-RENGO (www.jtuc-rengo.org, also in English) is the largest union, with 6mn members, and is responsible for negotiating social security contribution levels, the national minimum wage, taxes and labour standards with the national government. It also represents many smaller unions, which otherwise negotiate working conditions and wages. Since foreign employees have the same rights as Japanese employees, trade unions also negotiate on their behalf.

Employees aren't required to join a union but can benefit from general legal advice and translation and interpreting services by joining the General Union (www.generalunion.org), which is open to workers in any field and of any nationality, although most of its members are foreigners teaching at language schools, colleges and universities. Membership costs ¥2,000 (US$20) per month.

For general questions or to make complaints about contract violations or unfair treatment, contact the Labour Administration office in your nearest major city. These have designated times when assistance is given in foreign languages, including English.

The Japanese at Work

Shinkansen 'bullet train'

7.
ON THE MOVE

Japan has an extensive public transport system within cities and excellent nationwide bus, train and airline services that are safe to use at any time. It's possible to travel almost anywhere in the country on public transport – given sufficient time and a not inconsiderable amount of money.

Motoring – whether in a hired (rented) or private car – is also an expensive proposition in Japan. Unless you buy a tiny car, you must pay for an off-road parking space and pay acquisition tax, tonnage tax and automobile tax. All cars must also undergo an inspection (*shaken*), which costs over ¥100,000 (US$1,000). And thanks to high taxes, petrol is expensive and there are tolls on motorways, which makes them as expensive as using a bullet train. Avoiding toll roads can save you money but, as the speed limit on most other roads is 50kph or less (in urban areas it's as low as 40kph; only on toll roads are you permitted to drive at 80kph), it's hardly an option for long-distance travel.

Given the cost of motoring, the frequency of traffic jams and the near impossibility of parking, it's hardly surprising that many Japanese city dwellers don't own a car; if they do, they don't use it for commuting. Outside the cities, a car makes more sense as public transport offers fewer services at less convenient times.

This chapter gives an overview of the transport options available and tips on how to make the most of them.

It may come as a surprise to newcomers that the Japanese drive on the left.

DRIVING

Outside the cities and off the beaten track, driving in Japan can be a pleasure. The Japanese government speeds a lot of money on the upkeep of roads even in the remotest regions of the country, so there are plenty of well maintained roads wending their way through the mountains on which you'll rarely see another vehicle. The problem is that you have to slog your way through an inflexible traffic light system and masses of other cars on narrow roads to get to the mountains – and at peak holiday times motorways can be jammed for kilometres.

Japanese Drivers

Narrow streets, heavy traffic and national characteristics have combined to make the Japanese cautious, considerate, patient and polite drivers. In Japan, drivers who are held up by an obstruction are more likely to wait patiently than blast their horn.

While this makes a welcome change from most other countries (including some other Asian nations), it can lead to frustration – as when the driver in front of you decides to stop to let an oncoming car turn right (the Japanese, like the British, drive on the left), causing everybody behind to come to an abrupt and unexpected halt.

> Hazard warning lights are most often used to say 'thank you' to the person you push in front of.

Japanese motorists do have their foibles, however, as anyone trying to cross a road will soon discover: drivers routinely ignore pedestrian crossings. They often wait until just before turning before signalling, and they have a tendency to queue across streets and entrances for car parks and petrol stations – to the annoyance of drivers waiting to exit from them.

And despite their prevailing caution, speeding is a common habit. Japanese drivers tend to go as fast as conditions allow, irrespective of the speed limit. Late at night on major roads in the middle of a city, speeds of 80kph in a 50kph zone are common.

Japanese Roads

Although even the most far flung places have well surfaced roads, they tend to be narrow. Main routes will usually have four lanes – two in each direction – but on some intercity toll roads there are just two lanes. There are no roundabouts (traffic circles) in Japan.

Many residential areas in large cities have narrow lanes with mirrors placed at intersections to enable you to see oncoming traffic – take care.

Traffic Jams

Japan's narrow city streets are frequently jammed, especially at rush hours – from 7.30 to 8.45am and after 6.30pm. Queues often build up at railway crossings, which seem to close an inordinately long time before a train actually passes. The start and end of holiday periods in particular are times to avoid using a car if possible, as jams can extend for kilometres on major expressways and at their entrances and exits.

Road Rules

The *Japanese Road Code* (¥1,100/ US$11) can be purchased at Japan Automobile Federation offices – below are some of its most salient points:

- In Japan you must drive on the left.

- A red-bordered inverted triangle at junctions (intersections) doesn't mean 'give way' but 'stop'. If the police catch you merely slowing down, you'll be fined. According to the *Road Code*, 'give way' signs do exist, but nobody has ever seen one.

- A blue circular sign with a white arrow means that you must travel in that direction only. These signs are used instead of 'no right/left turn' signs at junctions.

- The signs to major destinations are in roman script as well as Japanese characters. However, other signs are usually only in Japanese, so being familiar with the characters representing the name of your destination is highly advisable.

- A broken white line in the middle of the road means that you may overtake. You may also cross a solid white line, but if you cause a crash you're likely to be in big trouble. You may not cross a solid yellow line unless there's a white line on your side. No overtaking is allowed in tunnels.

- The fine for using a mobile phone while driving – even with a 'hands-free' system – is ¥50,000 (US$500).

- The drink-driving limit is among the lowest in the world. If you're caught driving with as little as 0.15mg of alcohol per litre of air in your lungs – equivalent to less than one standard drink – you'll be fined ¥300,000 (US$3,000) and have your licence suspended for 30 days.

> In Japan there are two classes of car: those with engines of 600cc or smaller, which are given yellow number plates and those with larger engines, which have white number plates; yellow-plated cars cost less in terms of tax, tolls and parking (see Buying or Hiring a Car in Chapter 3).

Licences

Japan is a signatory to the Geneva Convention on driving licences, which means that licences from other convention countries, as well as international driving permits (IDPs), are valid for a year. Holders of licences from other countries must obtain an authorised translation of their licence, which is also valid for a year. After that, you must obtain a Japanese licence, for which the procedure varies according to your country of origin. If you're lucky you'll 'only' have to spend the best part of a day completing paperwork in a Japanese licence centre; if not, you must pass written and practical driving tests – an expensive and time-consuming process.

If you have a driving licence from one of the following countries, you don't need to take a driving test to obtain a Japanese licence: Austria, Australia, Belgium, Canada, Denmark, Finland, France, Germany, Greece, Iceland, Ireland, Italy, Luxembourg, the Netherlands, New Zealand, Norway, Portugal, South Korea Spain, Sweden, Switzerland and the United Kingdom. However, you must take a routine sight test.

Points System

In additional to fines and (in extreme cases) jail sentences, you incur 'points' on your licence for traffic violations. If you accumulate three points in any

Licence Points

Points	Reason
1	failure to use headlights, parking in a 'no parking' zone, making an illegal turn at a junction or tailgating;
2	illegal overtaking or excessive noise (e.g. a faulty silencer);
3	driving at between 25 and 40kph over the limit or parking in a 'no stopping' zone;
4	having over 25mg of alcohol per 100ml of air in your lungs, failing to stop at a 'stop' sign or a red light, throwing rubbish out of your car or dangerous overtaking;
6	driving at between 40 and 50kph over the limit, driving with over 30mg alcohol per 100ml*, driving without insurance or driving an unregistered car;
12	driving at more than 50kph over the limit;
13	driving with over 50mg alcohol per 100ml* or causing an accident while 'driving with fatigue' (the interpretation of which is presumably open);
19	driving without a licence.

* may incur an extra 25-point penalty at the discretion of police

12-month period, you must report to the nearest traffic licensing office for a day of lectures and an hour controlling a pedestrian crossing with flags – a clever way of making you lose 'face'. If you receive six penalty points, your licence is suspended for a month; the suspension becomes progressively longer the more points you receive.

Points are allocated as shown in the table above.

Finding Your Way

Being lost is a familiar experience to both foreigners and natives in Japan, where there are no street numbers and most roads have no names. If a road does have a name, it isn't included in the addresses of buildings along it. Instead, addresses are broken down into districts, neighbourhoods and finally blocks – but the relative position of blocks isn't always as you might expect. It's likely that Block 3 is somewhere near Block 4, but don't be surprised if you come across Block 12 next to either.

With such an inconvenient system it's a wonder anybody ever finds where they want to go, but there are several ways of getting help, which are listed below in order of reliability:

1. Ask at a *koban* (police box). These are everywhere and policemen are usually happy to help you, with the

aid of the detailed map books kept inside each box.

2. If you can't find a *koban*, try a policeman on a bicycle or on foot, who carry local maps inside their caps.

3. If there isn't a policeman in sight, look for a neighbourhood map on a notice board. Some just have block numbers on them, while others include the names of everybody living on each block.

4. If all else fails, ask at a petrol station or convenience store. Staff will usually go out of their way to point you in the right direction, taking you out on to the street and enthusiastically waving their hands in order to get their meaning across. Be warned though: some people will try to help you even if they haven't understood where you want to go.

Technology is coming to the aid of those who always have difficulty finding their way around (which is everyone at one time or another). As well as ever-cheaper satellite navigation systems for cars, there are now mobile phones that will guide you to your destination.

Parking

Parking in Japanese cities is expensive and spaces are usually difficult to find. Large department stores have their own car parks and may provide free parking if you buy something (check whether you need to get your receipt stamped before leaving the store). There are also automatic parking buildings, in which your car is drawn into the building at the bottom and stacked neatly inside like a rotisserie chicken.

'No parking' and 'no stopping' signs, and accompanying kerb markings, are similar to those found in the West, but illegal parking is less common. Some drivers park in narrow streets with hazard lights flashing while they 'pop' into a shop or a bank, causing traffic to back up, but wardens are primed to prosecute drivers for this, especially in Tokyo.

Petrol

Plenty of petrol stations (*gasu stando*) are open during the day, but those not on main roads may close overnight. In quieter areas they're usually manned, while in city areas and late at night they're more likely to be partially or entirely self-service.

The service at a manned station is spectacular by Western standards. Staff will bow as your car pulls in, quickly give your windscreen a wash, give you a packet of paper handkerchiefs then hold the traffic up so that you can exit. You don't need to tip anybody, even if your tyre pressures are checked.

The procedure at self-service stations (indicated by the sign '*selfu*' in Japanese or English) is often complicated and explained entirely in Japanese. Be sure to learn the *katakana* for the type of fuel you need.

Petrol stations in Japan often don't have much in the way of amenities beyond a toilet and a vending machine selling drinks. If you're hungry, you would do better to stop at a convenience store.

In 1974 the Japanese government imposed a provisional fuel tax of ¥25.1 per litre to fund road building. Although it was supposed to be temporary, successive governments found the revenue useful, and continued to renew it. This went on until 2008, when, as a result of political deadlock in parliament, the ruling party couldn't pass the renewal bill, and the tax expired. On 1st April 2008, in the midst of a global rise in fuel costs, the price of petrol in Japan dropped by 17 per cent, causing a stampede to fill up. On 1st May prices returned to their former level.

Motorcyclists & Cyclists

In many ways, Japan is a motorcyclist's heaven. Car drivers are generally more 'bike aware' than in most other countries, while motorcyclists themselves are less prone to suicidal manoeuvres. Motorcyclists to be wary of, however, are the *bousozoku*: youth gangs whose bikes are modified so that they make as much noise as possible, and who tend to ride either extremely slowly or extremely fast and generally make a nuisance of themselves.

Fortunately, since a law limiting riding in groups was introduced, the number of gangs has been declining.

> Watch out for bicycles! They're everywhere and follow no rules but their own. Cyclists will ride on either side of a street, while using a mobile phone or, if it's raining, brandishing an umbrella.

First-time visitors to Japan are usually surprised at the number of bicycles that clog the streets. The typical Japanese bike looks as if it was designed at the turn of the century – the 20th – with a basket on the front and no gears, but they're the usual way of travelling between home and the station.

Some stations have bicycle parking buildings nearby, which may feature double-decker cycle parking racks, and the world's first fully automated bicycle parking building recently opened its doors in Tokyo. Others have parking 'attendants', where you pay ¥100-300 (US$1-3) to leave your bicycle. Sometimes no bicycle parking is allowed, but this doesn't stop the Japanese from leaving their bikes – in row upon row.

Usually they get away with it, but every so often the local government collects all illegally parked bikes and deposits them at a kind of 'pound'. Because all bicycles in Japan must be registered, the owners eventually receive a letter informing them that their cycle has been impounded and that they must pay between ¥5,000 and ¥8,000 (US$50-80) to retrieve it. Because it takes so long (up to a month) for the notification to arrive and a bicycle is an indispensable part of life, most Japanese who have their bikes impounded simply buy a new one, leaving local authorities with a lot of used bicycles on their hands.

Impounded bikes that are unclaimed may be auctioned off, sold to bicycle stores (the second-hand market in Japan is small) or donated as a form of aid to countries that need them. Since 1980 the Japanese Organization for International Cooperation in Family Planning has been refurbishing unclaimed bikes and sending them to Third World countries, particularly in Africa. To date, over 55,000 have been sent to 89 countries around the world.

PUBLIC TRANSPORT

Public transport in Japanese cities is generally excellent and nationally Japan has an extensive network of fast trains, buses and airline services.

General Information

The following points apply to Japanese public transport in general:

- **Beggars** – As in many other countries, train and bus stations are populated by homeless people, who occasionally ask for money.

- **Fares** – There's no such thing as a return fare; unless you've no intention of coming back, you must buy two one-way tickets.

- **Food & drink** – You can buy beer at station kiosks and good quality *bento* (lunch boxes) are usually available inside stations.

- **Thieves** – You may see signs warning of pickpockets in the major cities, but such crime is rare.

Trains

The first thing to be aware of when travelling by train in Japan is that there are two types of service: those operated by Japan Rail (JR) and those operated by other companies. (In fact, JR now consists of seven companies, but all their trains bear the JR logo and services are seamlessly integrated.) There are 16 major rail operators, apart from JR, and almost 100 smaller ones, some with only a single line – each with a different logo.

To further complicate matters, JR operates several types of train, for which the charges vary: a basic fare allows you to travel on local (*futsu*), express, semi-express and commuter express trains. 'Limited express' (*tokyu*) and 'bullet' (*shinkansen*) trains, which are faster, require a surcharge of between 40 and 100 per cent, depending on the facilities provided.

Other operators have different systems: some make no extra charge for 'limited express' trains, while others do. If you're unsure whether an extra charge applies, there are several clues. First, a named service (e.g. Keisei's 'Skyliner' service from Narita airport to Tokyo centre) usually attracts a surcharge. Second, if a train consists entirely of two-by-two seating, rather than a single bench seat running the length of each carriage or a mixture of bench and two-by-two seating, you're likely to have to pay a surcharge.

If you get on a surcharged service by mistake, and the ticket inspector catches up with you, you won't be fined, but you must pay the appropriate surcharge.

If you aren't sure how much you should pay for a journey, buy the cheapest ticket and jump on the train. Once you're on board you can either find a ticket inspector, who will charge you any extra you owe, or use a ticket adjustment machine. Simply feed your ticket into the machine and it will tell you how much more you owe. There's no penalty for not having a valid train ticket in Japan.

> You can check your route on online websites available in English, such as 🖥 http://grace.hyperdia.com/cgi-english/hyperWeb.cgi. However, it's best to use these sites in conjunction with a map, as they don't always pick the best route.

Train Services

If you're planning to travel by train in Japan, also bear in the mind the following:

- For *shinkansen* services you have a choice between 'unreserved' and 'reserved' tickets, both of which can be bought in advance. The more expensive reserved tickets guarantee you a seat; those with unreserved tickets can take spare seats on a first-come-first served basis (you may have to queue early on the platform to get one) and if none are available you'll have to stand in the aisles. On the fastest *shinkansen* services there are no unreserved tickets.

- If you're travelling at peak times (especially New Year, *Obon* or Golden Week), book well in advance at JR offices in major stations (small stations don't have ticket offices) or using a ticket machine; otherwise, you're unlikely to get a seat. Surprisingly, there's no online booking facility for Japanese trains.

- During university holiday periods you can buy a s*eishun juhachi kippu* (a 'youth ticket', but in fact anyone can buy them), which allows you five days' unlimited travel for ¥11,500 (US$115) on local and non-surcharge express trains, but not limited express trains or *shinkansen*.

- The last trains in cities are usually between 11pm and 1am and are invariably packed. If you have a backpack you should put it on the floor to avoid inconveniencing other passengers.

- You'll hear an announcement in Japanese and a signal warning you that the doors are about to close. Don't attempt to enter a train after this. When a crowded train stops at a major station that isn't your stop, it's often a good idea to let the crowd carry you outside and then get back on – before the warning signal.

- There's usually a smoking car on *shinkansen*. If you're a non-smoker, It's wise to avoid even the adjoining carriages, as the smoke often spreads. At stations there are smoking areas at the end of each platform.

- Women are often the target of wandering hands on packed commuter trains, which is why many city trains have women-only carriages during rush hours. These are usually at each end – look for the pink signs (in English).

Buses

Local Buses

Buses are typically operated by local municipalities in Japan. Bus stops can be found everywhere and services are generally frequent and reliable. Regular routes often start early in the morning but may finish before 10pm.

> Be sure to check the time of the last bus if you depend on it. Except for intercity travel (see below), night bus services don't exist in Japan.

Each bus stop has times and destinations printed on it, but almost always entirely in *kanji*, which makes them difficult for non-Japanese-speaking visitors to read. Bus routes are identified by a number, and the destination of a bus is indicated on the front by a large sign in *kanji* and a smaller sign in *romaji*. Inside the bus there are usually recorded announcements or a digital signboard that gives the name of each stop (and sometimes both), but this isn't often in English or *romaji*. However, some municipalities have made an effort to make their bus services foreigner-friendly. Kyoto's service stands out in this regard, with maps available in different languages.

The method of payment for bus services differs according to where you are. In Tokyo, you pay a flat fee of Ys210 (US2) as you enter the bus.

You can pay in cash or use a prepaid or rechargeable transport card. In most other parts of the country you pick up a ticket with a number on it as you enter (via the rear doors). The number shows the stop at which you got on, and an electronic board at the front of the bus displays the cost of each journey for your number. You pay when you leave through the front door by putting the correct amount of cash into a box located next to the driver. There's also a change machine at the front of the bus.

Local buses are nearly always more expensive than a comparable trip by train.

Intercity Buses

Intercity buses are run by numerous private companies in Japan and are a less expensive way of travelling long distance than *shinkansen*, but much slower; longer distances involve an overnight trip.

Intercity buses are modern, with reclining seats and a toilet. On busy routes, competition has reduced fares, but on less popular routes companies work together and have similar prices. For example, a one-way ticket on the competitive Tokyo–Kyoto route, a journey of 500km (310mi) that takes almost eight hours, can cost as little as ¥6,000 (US$60), while a bus from Tokyo to Fukui (530km away) costs ¥8,300 (US$83). In comparison, a regular train to Kyoto costs at least ¥8,000 (US$80) and can take over eight hours, while the fastest *shinkansen* does the journey in 2 hours 18 minutes but costs ¥13,000 (US$130) or more.

You need to reserve a seat at the bus ticket office or by telephone. It's advisable to do this at least several days before you travel or earlier for holiday periods.

The website 🖳 www.bus.or.jp/kousoku_e/index.html provides details of a number of company's services in English.

Underground (Subway)

The cities with the most extensive underground (subway) networks are Nagoya, Osaka and Tokyo, while Fukuoka, Kobe, Kyoto, Sapporo, Sendai and Yokohama each have between one and three underground lines.

Getting around Japan's cities has recently become much easier with the introduction of rechargeable travel cards that can be used for any bus, underground or overground train, and can even be used in some convenience stores. Typically, each city's card has a name, as follows:

Card Name	City	Date of Introduction
Icoca	Hiroshima/Okayama/Osaka	2007
Kitaca	Sapporo	2008
Sugoca	Fukuoka	2010
Suica	Nigata/Sendai/Tokyo,	2007
Toica	Nagoya/Shizuoka	2008

On the Move

Trains generally start around 5am and run until midnight at the latest, and ticket prices range from ¥100 (US$1) in Fukuoka to ¥200 (US$2) on most other networks. Day passes can save you money if you're sightseeing and often include bus travel. The most complex system is (predictably) Tokyo's, which has 13 lines run by two companies.

Trams

Over a dozen city transport systems include trams, the largest being in Hiroshima. Tokyo used to have an extensive system, but now only one line remains.

Taxis

It's rarely difficult to find a taxi in Japan. You'll usually see them queuing for kilometres outside railway stations, although you must go to the designated pick-up spot just outside the station.

You're expected to sit in the rear of a Japanese taxi and don't have to open the door – the driver controls it.

Taxis are expensive, particularly for long trips, unless there's a group. Tokyo taxis are especially pricey, fares starting between ¥640 and 710 (US$6-7) for the first 2km and increasing by ¥100 (US$1) every 500m thereafter. All taxis are metered and licensed; there's no haggling over the fare and it isn't necessary to tip the driver.

Air

Domestic air travel in Japan is increasingly competitive and it's worth comparing prices with *shinkansen* fares.

Tokyo has two airports: Haneda, the main domestic airport, with some international flights to a handful of Asian cities, and Narita, the main international airport, which is a long way from Tokyo. The cheapest way to travel between Tokyo and Narita is by train on the Keisei line, which terminates at Ueno station, four stations to the north of Tokyo station. The 'Skyliner' is the premium service (taking 56 minutes and costing ¥2,000/US$20), but if you can afford 15 minutes travelling time, the Limited Express will cost you only half as much.

Buses are also available to Shinjuku and Tokyo stations (80-110 minute, ¥3,000/US$30) as well as from most major hotels.

> Narita Airport has two terminals, therefore when departing you should check which terminal you're flying from.

ON FOOT

Finally a couple of notes on being a pedestrian in Japan – should you decide to take the risk. The lack of footpaths on many streets and the constant danger of being run over by a bicycle make Japan a hazardous place to walk, as pedestrians are expected to share the footpaths with bikes in many cities. Indeed, the number of accidents involving pedestrians has been increasing in the past decade – a statistic doubtless not unrelated to the increase in the use of mobile phones, mp3 players and portable game stations over the same period.

- **Crossings** – The law states that pedestrians have the right of way over motorists, but you wouldn't know it if you attempt to use a pedestrian crossing, as drivers won't stop to let you cross. It's advisable to signal with a hand to indicate that you're planning to cross.

- **Drains** – Japanese roads have to deal with typhoon deluges, therefore drains are often deep and, in some rural areas, uncovered – or covered by rickety concrete slabs. It's advisable not to step on them.

- **Hitchhiking** – Although legal and safer than in almost any other country, hitchhiking is almost unheard of, especially among the Japanese themselves, and it can be difficult to find suitable spots to hitch a ride.

- **Jaywalking** – Drivers in Japan are unused to jaywalkers as the Japanese tend to wait patiently for the pedestrian light to turn green before crossing the road. It's advisable to do likewise.

- **Pavements** – There are no footpaths (sidewalks) on many secondary streets in residential areas, and even where there's a pavement it's likely to be used by *kamikaze* cyclists.

Wish doll (Daruma)

On the Move 135

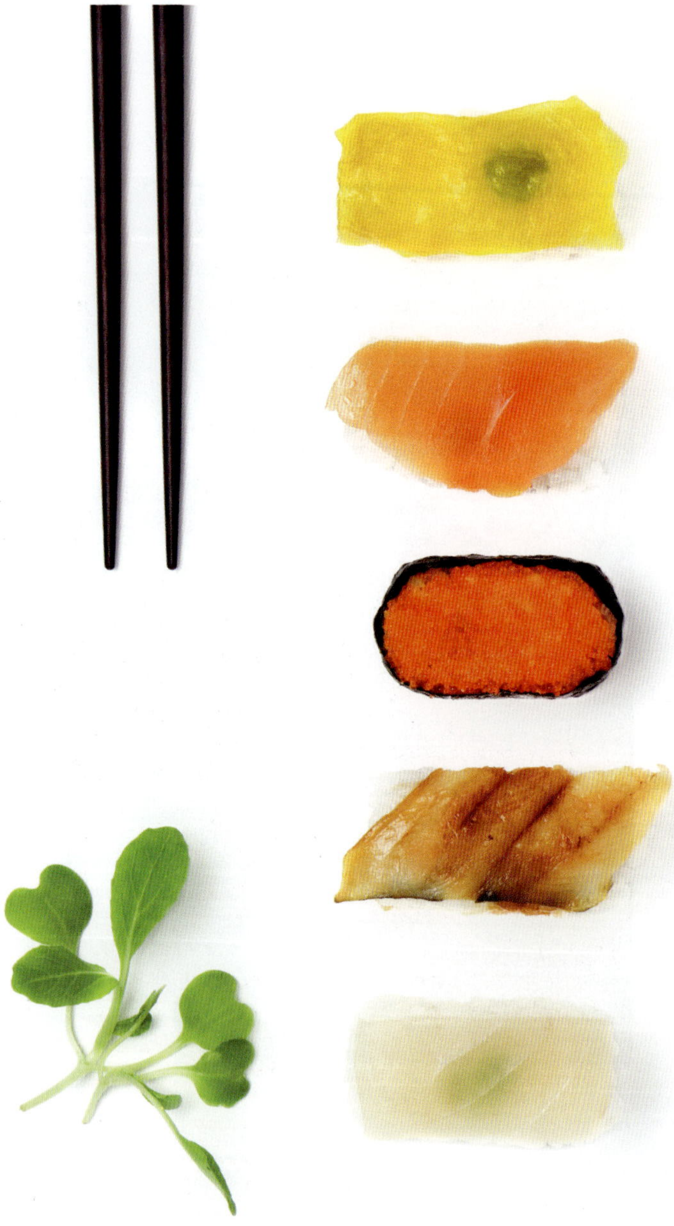

8.
THE JAPANESE AT PLAY

The Japanese have a highly refined sense of the appropriate behaviour for every situation and, while they're readily forgiving of foreigners' lapses, the onus is on you to develop a sense of the social mores – which will make your Japanese acquaintances and colleagues much more comfortable around you. It's unlikely that even a Japanese friend will correct your behaviour, therefore you'll need to be constantly alert to clues as to what you should and, more importantly, shouldn't do.

> The Japanese have a bizarre sense of humour, which involves making fun of people being subjected to sadistic and humiliating deeds.

This chapter contains essential information on what to expect, how to dress and how to behave in everyday social situations.

DRESS CODE

Generally the Japanese dress smartly, even when at play, and by American and European standards they may seem over-dressed. Although there's a trend towards being more casual, both at work and at rest, the Japanese are ever conscious of the appropriateness of their attire – of 'dressing for the occasion'. As well as being a status symbol, wearing the right clothes is as important in showing respect for others as knowing how to act and speak.

At Home

Japanese families do, however, dress casually at home, where jeans, sweatshirts, tracksuits, 'summer pyjamas' (*jimbe*) and other simple, comfortable clothes are the norm, but such things aren't worn in public – except perhaps, on the way to a public bath. During festivals and on special occasions, Japanese women – and sometimes men – may don a kimono (in winter) or a *yukata* (in summer).

The kimono is the traditional garment of Japan. It means simply 'something one wears'. Formal kimono have many layers, and the belt or sash that ties them together is called an *obi*. A festival called *shichi-go-san* marks important stages of growing up – the ages of three, five and seven, when children are dressed in kimonos and taken to a shrine to receive blessings for a healthy, happy life (see **Family Celebrations** below). When a Japanese person turns 60 or retires, his grandchildren give him an *akai chanchanko*, a red kimono set, to celebrate the beginning of a new stage in his life.

Places of Worship

Most Japanese people visit Shinto shrines and Buddhist temples in business or other smart clothes. Foreigners visiting shrines – especially during holiday seasons such as the New Year period – should dress respectfully, although it's unlikely you'll be refused entry even in casual wear.

EATING

Traditional Japanese food is varied, interesting and healthy. Rice is the basis of most meals; indeed a meal isn't considered complete unless rice is served. Japan is known worldwide for its seafood, famously eaten raw, but it also has a tradition of making chicken dishes (particularly *brochettes*) and stews, served in pots on gas burners.

Meals

Breakfast

A traditional breakfast in Japan consists of steamed rice, *miso* (soy bean paste) soup, grilled or dried fish, *tamagoyaki* (omelette), pickled vegetables, dried seaweed, *natto* (fermented soy beans) and green salad. Many foreigners find a traditional Japanese breakfast something of a shock (to put it mildly!), but with its focus on vegetables and protein it's a healthy way to start a day.

For a quick breakfast the Japanese will grab a thick round of heavily buttered toast and perhaps a coffee. Cereals are usually considered to be only for children, and in many Japanese supermarkets the only variety to be found is sweetened cornflakes. Weetabix is unheard of and muesli or granola can be difficult to find, though there's one Japanese manufacturer which makes a high-quality toasted granola, which can be purchased in the larger supermarkets.

Lunch

Lunches in restaurants and company or school cafeterias often consist of a set menu (*teishoku*), which is reasonably priced. Even non-Japanese restaurants offer a *teishoku* at lunchtime. This usually includes some sort of soup, a salad, a main dish and a drink (hot or iced tea or coffee). Noodles and rice dishes are popular.

If you don't have time to sit down, a *bento* (lunch box) can be bought at a convenience store or a specialist outlet. *Bento* contain a balanced meal with rice, pickles, an assortment of meats and vegetables, sauces and *waribashi* (disposable chopsticks).

Traditionally, a Japanese wife rises early to prepare *bento* for her husband and children to take to work/school for lunch, in addition to fixing breakfast.

People who take packed lunches to school or work also use *bento*, which come in various designs. In a 'stacking' *bento*, the bottom layer contains the rice, the next the main course, and on top are the vegetables or salad.

A typical home lunch consists of curry rice, *sukiyaki* (fried beef) and *nabe* (stew).

Dinner

Dinner at home is a family meal and is often cooked at the table – for example, *sukiyaki* is cooked in a shallow frying pan (usually electric) and *nabe* in a deep pot heated by a gas stove. Again rice is ubiquitous, although sometimes it may be replaced by a noodle dish such as *soba* or *udon*.

Many Japanese families (and workers) eat out in the evenings, especially in the larger urban areas, and most entertaining is done in restaurants rather than at home, where there often isn't room to accommodate even a few guests.

Formal Dining

Eating formally often means a stylised *kaiseki* banquet. Originally *kaiseki* was a Zen Buddhist vegetarian meal served after a tea ceremony presided over by monks. But the term has evolved to describe a meal – though it's more a culinary art form – that balances taste, texture and appearance, and is a form of celebration of the current season. *Kaiseki* courses are usually quite small and each is carefully presented on colourful plates that reinforce the seasonal theme. Garnishes usually include leaves, flowers and other items typical of the region.

There's a prescribed order to a *kaiseki* meal (as show below), although every course won't necessarily be included:

Kaiseki Meal

Japanese	Description
Sakizuke	an appetiser similar to French *amuse-bouche*
Hassun	sets the seasonal theme and usually includes one kind of sushi and several smaller side dishes
Mukozuke	seasonal *sashimi*, slices of raw fish dipped into a mixture of *wasabi* (green mustard) and soy sauce
Takiawase	vegetables served with meat, fish or tofu, having been simmered separately to keep their individual flavours distinct
Futamono	a 'lidded dish', typically a soup or egg custard
Yakimono	broiled fish
Su-zakana	a small dish used to 'clean the palate', such as pickled vegetables
Hiyashi-bachi	(only in summer) chilled, blanched vegetables
Naka-choko	another palate-cleanser, a very small portion of a simple soup often with a citrus base
Shiizakana	a substantial dish, such as a hot pot, stew or heavier broth
Gohan	a rice dish with seasonal ingredients
Ko no mono	pickled vegetables
Tome-wan	a *miso*-based or vegetable soup served with rice
Mizumono	a seasonal dessert, often fruit, sometimes ice cream or cake

Informal Dining

Informal dining with friends and family usually involves serving yourself from communal serving plates to smaller individual plates. Dishes include bowls of stew, platters of sushi or *sashimi*, roasted or grilled fish and meats. Even in an informal setting it's a sign of respect to serve your guests first and pour alcohol for others.

Seating

The seating arrangement is important when it's a formal or business occasion. The general rule of thumb is that the guest of honour or highest ranking member of the group will be seated farthest from the exit/door, the host of the event will be closest to the door and elders or those of high status will sit near one or the other. Status, which is determined by age and company rank, is more important than gender in seating arrangements, so there's no alternation of couples as is common in the West. At work-related informal gatherings where spouses are included, it's common for the men to sit together in one place and the women to sit together in another.

The Japanese tend to be punctual, so usually everyone arrives at more or less the same time. If you arrive early, there may be nowhere to wait, so you must sit where you think is appropriate or, preferably, ask where you should sit. If you're unable to get up when other guests arrive, a deep nod of the head held for a second or more (depending on the importance of the person) is usually sufficient by way of a greeting.

At traditional-styled low tables, men sit cross-legged while women are expected to kneel and sit on their heels. When removing shoes before entering a *tatami* room at a restaurant, you should upturn the shoes to face outward in preparation for using the bathroom or leaving. At a host's home, slippers will always be provided – never walk around in bare feet or socks – and a separate pair of slippers may reside outside the bathroom for in-bathroom use.

Cutlery

Wooden chopsticks (*hashi*) are the main form of utensil in Japan, being either disposable (*waribashi*) or reusable. Western food, however, is often eaten with forks, knives and spoons, but foreign rice dishes such as curry and fried rice are eaten with a spoon rather than a fork, and soup may be drunk from the bowl (depending on the type of bowl). As ever, follow your hosts' lead.

Grace

Meals in Japan begin not with a prayer but by saying '*itadakimasu*' (literally 'I receive' and equivalent to '*bon appétit*'). This custom has its origins in Shinto and Buddhism and is said to be an expression of gratitude to everyone who had a part in preparing the food. When they've finished eating, the Japanese say '*gochisōsama deshita*' ('thank you for the feast').

When to Start

If the meal consists of separate courses, each person being served a plate of food, it's considered polite to wait until everyone has been served before starting. If, however, everyone is serving themselves from communal dishes, you can dig in as soon as everyone is seated, the last dish has been put on the table and everyone has said '*itadakimasu*'.

Toasts

You shouldn't start drinking until everybody at the table is served and the glasses are raised for a toast, which is usually simply the word *kampai*, meaning 'dry glass'. This doesn't mean that you should empty your glass at a draught, which is invited by the word *iki* ('one breath').

> The English word 'cheers' is acceptable, but avoid saying 'chin chin', as this is a Japanese slang term for male genitalia!

A dinner organised by a company or association may end with a *banzai* cheer. The senior members will stand at the front and lead a sequence of rhythmic clapping, after which everyone shouts '*banzai*' (meaning '10,000 years' or 'long life') three times, raising their hands at the same time. Another customary ending to a party or festival is called *ipponjime*, when the leader says '*yo*' and everyone claps their hands once, which is supposed to bring good luck.

Noises

In contrast to many other countries, where people are often taught not to make slurping noises when eating, it's considered normal in Japan to do so when eating noodles – though not other foods. Burping and, especially, blowing your nose at the table are considered rude, but the Japanese have a much higher tolerance for sniffing than most Westerners, and it's common for them to keep sniffing rather than go outside to blow their nose.

Table Manners

Don't fill your mouth or open it while chewing. It's considered polite to empty your plate. If you're given a second helping, e.g. a bowl of rice, accept it with both hands. Don't mix food from one plate/dish with another. To drink soup containing large pieces of food, first eat the food with your chopsticks, then drink the soup from the bowl.

There are certain rules to observe when using chopsticks:

- Separate large pieces of food with your chopsticks and then eat the smaller pieces.

- Never pass food from your chopsticks directly to someone else's chopsticks.

- When getting food from a shared serving plate, reverse your chopsticks so that you don't use the end you're eating from.

- When not using your chopsticks, don't stick them vertically into your bowl of rice or food, but place them on the rest provided.

- It's considered rude to play with your chopsticks.

Using your chopsticks to pass food and sticking them vertically into your food are believed to bring bad luck due to their association with funeral rites.

Bread

Bread (*pan*) is available throughout Japan and is usually of high quality. Until recently, only white bread was sold, but nowadays you can often find 'wholemeal' bread in bakeries and supermarkets. However, there may be only a couple of loaves and they can be suspiciously similar to white bread, only darker. In the major cities it's possible to find specialist bakeries that offer a better choice, including heavier breads such as rye bread.

Bread and sandwiches can be bought in convenience stores, but the latter won't contain butter. Popular fillings include tuna, egg salad and minced meat, but although such sandwiches may look familiar, they may taste quite different from what you're used to.

Department stores such as Takashimaya and Matsuzakaya often have a basement floor dedicated to bread and pastries and their selection of French and German-inspired patisserie is excellent (samplings are usually available). When considering traditional Japanese baked products, be wary of buns containing sweet fillings, particularly the ubiquitous *anpan*. Many an unwary foreigner has bought what he thought was plain bread only to find that it was sweet and filled with a strange substance such as chestnut or *anko* (sweet red bean paste). (Anpan man is an animated children's super-hero whose head is a made of an *anpan* filled with *anko*. The *manga* stories, written by Takashi Yanase, have collectively sold over 50mn copies in Japan, and the TV show is one of the most popular in Japan, having been broadcast continuously since 1968.)

Conversation

Appropriate topics of conversation while eating will naturally depend on how friendly you are with your hosts or guests and the environment, and it's always a good idea to let the Japanese lead the conversation. Neutral topics, such as the weather, food, places to visit in Japan and local events can safely be discussed (see **Taboos** in **Chapter 4**). If your host doesn't know you well, expect to be questioned about your home town, your family and your opinion of Japan. Make these positive, be polite and, if you've been invited, be sure to compliment your hosts on the food.

Bear in mind that the Japanese have a higher tolerance for silence than most Westerners. You don't need to fill every gap in the conversation with small talk.

DRINKING

> The legal age for purchasing and consuming alcohol (and tobacco products) is 20.

Drinking plays an important role in Japanese society and is a common activity for strengthening social and business ties; among work colleagues it's considered as a team-building exercise. Even those who are allergic to alcohol often take part in a toast,

The Japanese at Play

Some drinks can catch you out. What the Japanese call *cider* is more like British lemonade and definitely not made from apples. Similarly, when you order a beer, you may be served *happoshu*, which is a beer-like substance made with low malt in order to beat Japanese tax laws and something of an acquired taste. Should you acquire it, you'll be pleased to learn that *happoshu* is cheaper than beer. Restaurants usually serve 'real' beer.

pretending to take a sip of beer at the appropriate moment – although they sometimes order *oolong* tea, which is the same colour as beer.

Alcoholic drinks are sold in supermarkets, department stores, convenience stores and liquor stores, and from vending machines (though they are switched off at 11pm). A variety of alcoholic drinks is usually available in bars and restaurants, including:

- **beer** – which is draught (*nama beeru*) or bottled, typically costing between ¥500 and 900 (US$5-9) per pint, depending on the establishment;

- *nihonshu* – known as *sake* in English (though *sake* in Japanese means 'alcohol');

- *shochu* – a spirit distilled from potato, grain or rice which is usually around 25 per cent alcohol and is drunk on the rocks or with water. Many Japanese women drink *chuhai*, which is a *shochu*-based fruit drink.

- **whisky** – and other spirits;

- **wine** – imported red or white wine may be ordered by the glass or bottle.

While it's considered bad manners to become obviously drunk in a formal restaurant, the same isn't true in other places, such as *izakaya*, as long as you don't bother other guests. There is generally a high tolerance of drunken behaviour in Japan, even of unsavoury behaviour such as urinating in the street.

The Japanese consume some 9bn litres of alcoholic drinks every year, 38 per cent of it beer, 19 per cent *happoshu*, 11 per cent *shochu*, 8 per cent *sake*, 6 per cent liqueurs and a mere 3 per cent wine.

CAFES, BARS & RESTAURANTS

Japan has a bewildering variety of places to dine and entertain friends, from the intimate to the rowdy. This section is a brief guide to the main kinds of dining establishments.

Cafés

The traditional Japanese café *kissaten* was a smoky coffee shop frequented by businessmen and used for meetings or simply for reading newspapers and comic books. However, this is now giving way to bright, airy European-style establishments – many modelled on the largest café chain in the world, Starbucks – serving a variety of teas and coffees and healthy snacks. Famously, when Starbucks opened in Japan in 1997, all its cafés were non-smoking, which came as a surprise to most Japanese. The new type of café attracts more women and young people, but they're still usually open only during business hours – i.e. including the evenings – and close before the last trains.

It's easy to get a coffee fix in Japan, without even having to go into a café: 200ml cans of coffee – 'hot' and cold – are available from vending machines just about everywhere. Usually it's sweet, but it's possible to find unsweetened coffee. Iced coffee is popular in the summer but decaffeinated coffee is almost non-existent.

Bars

Traditionally, Japanese bars had provided table service and customers paid when they left. While this is still the rule, some bars have changed to the Western system of ordering at the bar – but with a traditional twist, whereby customers are trusted to pay as they leave. At least, Japanese customers are trusted; foreigners may be discriminated against and be asked to pay for each drink.

There are various kinds of bar in Japan:

- **Snack bars** – These are frequented by Japanese *salarymen* and are usually tiny, with seating for a dozen at the most. The (usually) genial proprietor will bring you a small dish of snacks, such as nuts or preserved fish or even fruit, for which you'll be charged at least ¥300 (US$3) – and sometimes a lot more – even if you don't eat it. In effect, this is a service or cover charge, which you have no choice but to pay. It's advisable to check the charge before you sit down. Snack bars usually have regulars, and the owner may discourage others, especially foreigners, from entering and taking the seats of customers they're expecting – either by setting a high cover charge or by simply telling you that you aren't welcome. Fortunately, however, most snack bars are keen to attract new customers, and you can expect to be well received.

- **Stand bars** – In large cities, where space is at a premium, 'stand bars' have become popular and are another favourite haunt of *salarymen* at the end of the working day. As the name suggests, these places have no seats – just a counter to prop yourself up against with a drink and a bite to eat.

- **Theme bars** – Japanese theme bars aren't merely decorated in a particular way, as in other countries, but animated by the proprietor according to his hobby or interest. The theme is often a musical one and you can 'order' your music at the same time as you order your drinks. Theme bars aren't the place to go for an amorous tête-à-tête, as you'll be expected to talk 'shop' with the owner. Theme bars come and go like fads. Recently 'darts bars' have become popular. With the development of electronic darts boards, the game suddenly become a craze, and bar owners cashed in.

> **Smoking**
>
> Very few restaurants, bars or cafés are non-smoking or even have non-smoking sections, although this is slowing changing. Some restaurants even sell cigarettes. When making a booking at a restaurant, you can ask if they have non-smoking (*kien-seki*) tables.

- **Pubs** – English- and Irish-style pubs have spread across Japan, where several chains operate in the larger cities (in Tokyo the largest is The Hub). There's no cover charge and you pay as you drink, as in England and Ireland. You can even order fish and chips.

- **Karaoke bars** – Some snack bars and other types of bar have a *karaoke* machine and a song list, but the usual way of enjoying this activity – if indeed you do enjoy *karaoke* – is in a *karaoke* room, which is part of a dedicated *karaoke* establishment. Rooms are rented out by the hour or (sometimes) half hour and you're shut in, communicating with staff by telephone to order food, drinks and – if you're unable to drag yourself away – a time extension. *Karaoke* rooms are often open all night. There's comfortable accommodation and maybe a disco ball and tambourines as well as the *karaoke* equipment itself. Huge books list the thousands of songs available, and there's normally at least one page of English songs (often at the back) – sometimes an entire section.

- **Izakaya** – A kind of bar catering to groups which serves a variety of food, including both Japanese and Western dishes, such as *sushi*, *tempura*, fried chicken, small pizzas and salads, substantial enough for people to go there just to eat. Often they're decorated in traditional Japanese style with low tables, at which you sit on the floor, although they may have tables with chairs or a mixture of the two or an ingenious hybrid system that combines a low table with a well allowing customers to sit normally. In addition there are usually stools at the bar. The atmosphere is lively with a loud '*irrashaimase*' (literally 'come in') greeting each customer and orders and instructions shouted across the room. Some *izakaya* are themed, serving, for example, Okinawa-style food and alcohol. There's often an interesting variety of alcohol available as well, usually including various *nihonshu* and *shochu* as well as beers and spirits. *Izakaya* cover the whole price range, from cheap and cheerful to upmarket and expensive, although prices are generally moderate.

Restaurants

In large cities, especially Tokyo, you can find restaurants serving food from every corner of the world. In the first *Michelin Guide* to Tokyo (published in 2007), the city was awarded more stars than any other major urban area and was described as one of the best cities in the world for gourmet dining.

- **Opening hours** – Restaurants are generally open from before noon to early afternoon, and then from around 5pm until the final train, or later. *Ramen* (noodle restaurants) often stay open into the early hours of the morning. Most restaurants are open seven days a week; those that have a day off usually close on a Monday.

- **Booking** – Some restaurants take bookings, others don't – and many Japanese are prepared to wait hours to eat at their favourite restaurant rather than book a time somewhere else.

- **Seating** – When you enter a restaurant you'll be greeted by the word '*irrashaimase*', sometimes in an undertone, sometimes boisterously, and a waiter or waitress will take you to a table. If there's a choice, you'll be asked whether you want to sit in a smoking or non-smoking area.

- **Table settings** – Many restaurants have a box of chopsticks on the table, from which you help yourself, while others bring chopsticks to the table when you order. If you aren't confident of your chopstick-wielding skills, you can ask for a knife and fork.

- **Menu** – Many restaurants and most *izakaya* have menus with colour pictures, which make 'point-and-shoot' ordering possible. Some have an English menu, but outside most restaurants there are plastic models of the food on offer, allowing linguistically challenged customers to work out what they want to order. It isn't unknown for foreigners to drag a waiter outside and point at the desired dish if they cannot find it on the menu. If the menu is entirely in Japanese, staff will do their best to help you, but it's wise to take along a knowledgeable friend or a menu translator.

- **Water** – Customers are always offered a hot or cold towel and a glass of water, for which there's no charge.

- **Service** – Waiting is usually done by young part-timers in Japan, but what they may lack in experience they usually make up for in enthusiasm and dedication. Even if you don't get what you think you ordered the first time, it will invariably arrive promptly at the second attempt.

- **The bill** – Your bill is usually left on the table when you've made your initial order and updated as you order more items. When you're ready to pay, simply take the bill to the cashier. If the bill hasn't been left on the table, catch the waiter's or waitress's eye and say '*Reshiito wo kudasai*'.

- **Tipping** – No tips are necessary in Japan. They aren't expected and, if you leave one, it's likely that a waiter will run after you to give you your money back, thinking you left it behind my mistake.

NIGHTLIFE

Dancing

When it comes to dancing, the Japanese tend to be 'all or nothing'. Either they barely dance at all or they've obviously been to dancing classes and are fully kitted out in accordance with the type of dance they've learned. Sometimes it seems as if the whole dance class has turned up and is putting on a show.

Whereas the major cities offer a choice of dance clubs, bars, pubs, *karaoke* rooms and late night *izakaya*, many small towns and cities in Japan lack nightlife due to the ageing population and the draw of the major cities for younger people. However, even in towns with a population of around 100,000 you can find snack bars, *izakaya* or *karaoke* rooms that are open most of the night. These are typically concentrated in a street near the railway station or on the main road that bypasses the station. Often such towns have one or two bars that are frequented by foreigners (invariably including English teachers), which are referred to as the 'local *gaijin* bar'. In a city of 200,000 or more there may also be a disco or two and some 'live houses' (see **Popular Music** below).

The following information will help you get into the groove of Japan's clubbing scene:

- **Opening hours** – Pubs and bars tend to either close before the last train out of the local station or stay open until the first train of the morning. As in most other countries, although nightclubs start opening between 8 and 11pm, they don't start hopping until at least midnight and keep on going until five or six in the morning.

- **Age** – You should be over 20, but few clubs check the age of customers – even fewer the age of foreigners. If you're aged over 30, however, you may feel like a pensioner in a youth club.

- **Dress code** – Casual dress is the norm for most nightclubs, although some don't allow jeans. However, foreigners can get away with almost any kind of dress in most nightclubs.

- **Bouncers** – Door staff at Japanese nightclubs have one of the world's cushiest jobs. The Japanese may get drunk, but they invariably remain well mannered and rarely become aggressive or violent. The people mostly likely to cause trouble are foreigners.

- **Drinks** – Clubs serve all types of alcoholic and non-alcoholic drinks with the exception of hot drinks; few venues serve coffee. Entrance fees can be high – up to ¥4,000 (US$40), which usually includes at least one drink. Beers cost at least ¥800 (US$8), cocktails generally between ¥1,000 and 1,500 (US$10-15), but sometimes more.

- **Paying** – In Western-style nightclubs, which are in the majority, there are few tables and customers pay for drinks at the bar. In older, Japanese-style nightclubs, tables are arranged in front of a stage, on which there's a dance show, and you order food and drinks from a menu at your table and pay afterwards.

There are, of course, other kinds of 'nightlife' available in Japan, and areas where *karaoke* rooms proliferate often also offer hostess bars and 'love hotels'. In the former, you pay by the hour for the pleasure of having an attractive woman – perhaps from Russia or the Philippines – pour you drinks and flirt with you. Hostess bars are easily recognised by the posters of women and the scrawny doormen outside. Generally, however, foreigners aren't welcome and will be turned away. At a love hotel, you can pay for a 'rest' of two and half hours or an entire night.

There are alternatives to taking the last train home (and missing the action) or trying to stay awake all night. You can grab a few hours' sleep in a capsule hotel, where for ¥2,000-3,000 (US$20-30) you get a space as large as a bed with a TV and DVD player and the use of a washroom. Or you can try a *manga* café. These are like internet cafés, but they have individual rooms containing cushioned seating, which can be laid flat; be warned, however, that the walls are thin and some couples use these as 'love hotels'.

FAMILY CELEBRATIONS

Traditional family celebrations are central to Japanese culture. Although there are still many families in which several generations live under the same roof, the nuclear family is becoming more common and on major holidays such as *Obon* and New Year, people travel great distances to be with their family.

Birthdays

Birthdays are generally celebrated with less fanfare than in the West, although present-giving, birthday cakes and parties (none of them Japanese traditions) are becoming more common, especially among the young. However, certain ages are considered worthy of special celebration. Most of these occur in childhood. On the weekend nearest to 15th November – a day known as *shichi-go-san* – all children turning three, five and seven that year dress up, go to the local shrine and receive a blessing for a healthy, happy life.

> *Chitoseame* or 'thousand year candy' is given to children on *shichi-go-san*. This is a long, thin red-and-white candy, which symbolises healthy growth and longevity. It's traditionally given in a bag with a crane and a turtle on it, which also represent long life.

Another special birthday is the 20th. A public holiday called *Seijin no hi* (Coming of Age day), on the second Monday in January, is dedicated to those in their 20th year, who go to their hometown, dress up in their best suit or kimono and take part in a ceremony presided over by the mayor of the town or a local dignitary.

Engagement Parties

The Japanese have an elaborate ritual called *Yui-no* for celebrating a couple's engagement. It's a part of a traditional Japanese wedding (see below). Once the two families have agreed to the couple being married, they meet at a formal dinner on an 'auspicious' day in the Japanese calendar and exchange gifts. The main gift for a bride-to-be is an *obi* (a kimono sash), representing female virtues, while a *hakama* robe, representing fidelity, is given to the groom-to-be.

In addition to the *obi* and *hakama*, there may be gifts symbolising happiness and good fortune, such as the following:

- ***Katsuo-bushi*** (dried bonito fish) – to wish the couple a long marriage;

- ***Konbu*** (a kind of seaweed that propagates quickly) – to wish the couple healthy children;

- ***Shiraga*** (hemp) – its strong fibres symbolising strong family ties;

- ***Suehiro*** (a folding fan) – given as a wish for happiness and a prosperous future;

- ***Surume*** (dried squid) – to wish the couple a lasting marriage;

- ***Yanagi-daru*** (a cask filled with *sake*) – meant to symbolise obedience andgentleness in marriage.

Christmas & New Year

Christmas isn't a traditional Japanese celebration, although in recent years more people have been at least adopting the 'trappings' and indulging in the commercial aspects of

Christmas. When it comes to Christmas decorations, for example, there are no half measures: it's either nothing at all or gaudy flashing lights strung across roofs, complete with illuminated windmills and Arcs de Triomphe (though what either has to do with Christmas is anybody's guess) and plastic Santas caught in the act of climbing up or down.

Shopping districts spend fortunes on illuminations which they hope will entice customers. Christmas presents, however, are given only to children. By the time a child reaches senior high school, the presents have dried up. Christmas Day isn't a public holiday, and banks and businesses are open during normal hours on 24th and 25th December.

> Christmas Eve is often celebrated by young couples in somewhat the same way as Valentine's Day in the UK or US. Expensive restaurants and love hotels (see above) do a roaring trade.

The most important family holiday of the year is New Year (*Shogatsu*), when most Japanese eat cold food (*osetchi ryori*) – a practice deriving from the tradition of not working over the New Year period: by preparing *osetchi ryori* in advance, the wife (who's invariably the cook) can enjoy a much-needed break. Typical foods vary from region to region but usually include cold seafood, beans and vegetables – all artfully prepared and beautifully presented, although not particularly tasty – and long *soba* noodles, which symbolise long life and good health. These days, department stores and other shops sell pre-packed *osetchi ryori*, which mean even less work for mum.

Another New Year tradition is *O-soji* (literally 'honourable cleaning'). Homes and offices are all vigorously scrubbed, bills are paid and debts are cleared in the hope of starting the new year with a clean slate.

Weddings

Weddings are big business in Japan. In some regions, such as Nagoya, elaborate and expensive ceremonies are common and most brides celebrate with a mix of Japanese and Western traditions. 'Church' weddings (or rather ceremonies in the 'chapel' of specially designed wedding buildings) are common – whether the couple is among the 3 per cent of the population that practises Christianity or not: to many, the symbolism of the bride in the white dress being led down a vaulted aisle in front of a 'priest' (often a moonlighting English teacher) is irresistible.

However, Shinto and, less commonly, Buddhist weddings in traditional kimonos are making a comeback. The bride and groom are blessed by a Shinto priest (or Buddhist monk) in an intimate ceremony which involves immediate family only. Following this is a lavish and formal Western-style reception with a sit-down dinner for family, friends and work colleagues. These two ceremonies are sometimes combined and can either or both be known as *hiroen* in Japanese. Speeches play an important part in the wedding; those that are given by the couple's senior acquaintances are considered the most important.

The wedding is not complete however without the *nijikai* or second party, a more casual affair in which the couple can relax and really celebrate with their friends. It takes place immediately after the first, with just enough time in between for the couple to change into more casual clothes. Honeymoons are also popular, a favourite destination being Hawaii.

Increasingly some couples, especially those who've been married before, will skip a large ceremony and party and simply register their marriage, before escaping on their honeymoon.

Invitations

Sometimes the couple will call friends before they send out official invitations. Even if you've already said 'yes', you're expected to respond to the written invitation as soon as possible.

Gifts

A big difference between weddings in the West and weddings in Japan is that Japanese guests give a present of money to the couple rather than a gift. The payment, which is presented in a fancy wedding envelope called a *goshugi*, should be between ¥20,000 and 100,000 (US$200-1,000), according to your relationship with the couple (the closer the relationship, the more you should pay) and therefore your 'status' as a guest, though since the economic recession a ¥20,000 (US$200) gift has become generally acceptable. However, the amount shouldn't be an even number – especially not the unlucky number four. The envelope isn't given directly to the couple but handed in at the door when you arrive – a practice that would hardly persist in the West.

At the end of the reception the married couple stand behind a golden screen, personally thank all attendees and offer them a small gift (*hikidemono*) or a catalogue from which to choose something later.

Dress

If a Japanese ceremony is staged, the couple will wear traditional wedding kimonos. The bride will wear a white over-kimono (*shiro-maku*, meaning literally 'white wrap') for the ceremony, removing it for the reception to reveal a sumptuous kimono in bright colours, often with gold and silver embroidery. Her hair will be elaborately decorated and she will carry some items for luck, including a *kaiken* (a dagger worn in her belt) and a *hakoseko* (a small case carried in the sleeve of the kimono).

A Shinto ceremony takes place at a Shinto shrine and is conducted by a Shinto priest. The ceremony begins with the 'purification' of the couple. After the purification vows have been recited, the bride and groom exchange cups of *sake*, which symbolises not only their own union but also the coming together of their families. To close the ceremony, an offering of tree twigs called *sakaki* is made to the God of the shrine.

Western-style ceremonies feature

the usual bridal gown, bridesmaids' dresses and, for the men, dinner jackets (tuxedos) or formal suits. The couple arrive at the party in their wedding clothes and change later to semi-formal attire, such as a cocktail dress and suit.

Guests are expected to dress formally for both the wedding and the party.

> Female guests at a Japanese wedding shouldn't wear white – in order not to be confused with the bride.

Key Players

Apart from the bride and bridegroom, the following are the principal players at a Japanese wedding:

- **Master of ceremonies** – often a hired professional, who officiates the service, letting guests know who's speaking and what they should do at each stage;

- **Senior acquaintances** – These can be the couple's bosses or a favourite teacher or anyone they hold in high regard. They will give a speech about the bride or groom and wish them well on behalf of their guests. Other speeches are usually given by best friends and older family members.

- **Best friends** – The *nijikai* party after the main function (see above) will be organised by a friend or group of friends, who plan the activities and speeches.

FUNERALS

Most Japanese funeral services are Buddhist. There are many variations but the general procedure involves the corpse being dressed in a suit (men) or kimono (men or women) and laid in a cask along with anything combustible that he or she was fond of, e.g. cigarettes. Money may also be put in the cask to pay for the deceased's journey across the River of Three Hells (a Buddhist belief). The cask is then placed in front of the mortuary or family altar (if the wake is to take place at home), and friends, acquaintances and relatives come and pay their respects.

Mourners may be asked to sign a registry and pay condolence money, which is presented in a special envelope with a thin black and white ribbon around it. The amount, usually between ¥5,000 and 30,000 (US$50-300) depending on how close to the deceased the mourner was, is written on the outside. Incense is kept burning as guests kneel on a cushion in front of the altar to pay their respects. Meanwhile a Buddhist priest may chant *sutras*. Mourners then go to another room, where food is served.

The funeral itself is usually held the following day in a temple. Again there will be incense burning and a priest chanting *sutras*, and there's also the custom of the corpse being given a new name. The purpose of this is to prevent the dead person returning to life if his or her old name is used. Temples charge for this 'service' according to the length and 'prestige' of the name, the most highly prized names costing up to ¥1mn (US$10,000).

When the ceremony is over the body is taken to a crematorium, where the family witnesses its cremation. The remains are spread on a kind of trolley or gurney, and family members pick out the bones with chopsticks and pass them around before depositing them in an urn (this is why it's a *faux pas* to pass food from one person to another using chopsticks in Japan). The urn may remain at the family's house for a few days or may be taken directly to a cemetery. Japanese cemeteries consist of stone headstones, under each of which is a small crypt containing the urns of family members.

The Japanese visit their ancestors' graves often, especially during the *Obon* holiday week in summer and on the anniversary of their deaths.

Dress

Although in former times mourners wore white, now the custom is to wear black: men a black suit and black tie, and women a black dress or kimono. Low collars or necklines and short sleeves are unacceptable, as are decorative jewellery or other accessories.

Make sure your black socks or stockings don't have holes in them when you attend a Japanese funeral, as the ceremony is conducted in a temple, where you must remove your shoes.

CLUBS

The Japanese don't usually engage in a range of sports or activities but commit to one and devote a great deal of time to practising or participating in it, sometimes throughout their lives. This usually involves joining a club. Common clubs for women include flower arranging (*ikebana*) and traditional tea-making, although these activities are declining in popularity and many young Japanese are now creating and joining clubs and classes involving 'Western' pursuits. Dancing, including hula, salsa, and flamenco, have become popular with women, while golf, tennis and martial arts are popular with men, as are hobby clubs such as *manga* (comic book) 'appreciation', professional clubs and business networking organisations.

If you join a Japanese club or sporting team, a high level of commitment is expected and a long or strenuous practice schedule will be mapped out. Missing meetings or practice sessions is regarded as letting down the other members of the group.

POPULAR CULTURE

Certain aspects of Japanese popular culture, such as animation, computer games, J-pop music and *manga* (comics), have become world famous. Young Japanese people pride themselves on being up on the latest trends and technologies. However, there's a lot more to popular culture in Japan than ephemera, as illustrated in this section.

Festivals & Fairs

Japan boasts a wide range of traditional festivals (*matsuri*) as well as many world-class exhibitions. Almost every neighbourhood in Japan has a *matsuri*, which typically features crowds of Japanese wearing a *happi* (short jacket with the name of the district emblazoned on the back) and perhaps a *fundoshi* (loin cloth) and *tabi* (traditional cloth boots, with the big toes separated from the others). They take it in turns to carry a heavy *mikoshi* (portable shrine) around the streets so that its God can bless the town. There may also be a procession of people in traditional costume and floats carrying drummers and flautists.

Some of the major *matsuri* in Japan are:

- **Hamamatsu matsuri** (Hamamatsu, early May) – By day this is a spectacular kite-fighting festival, each neighbourhood fielding a team with a huge (3-5m) kite with which they try to knock the opposing kites out of the sky. There can be as many as 150 kites in the sky at one time in a great confusion of strings and torn paper. At night there's a procession of beautifully decorated *danjiri* (wheeled shrines).

- **Sanja matsuri** (Tokyo, May) – Held at Asakusa shrine, this is the wildest of Tokyo's festivals. It has recently become notorious for the local *yakuza* showing off their ornately tattooed bodies, sometimes while riding on the *mikoshi* (shrine), despite attempts to ban the practice. Over 2mn people attend every year.

- **Sanja matsuri** (Osaka, July) – This is Osaka's main summer event, which includes processions of some 3,000 people in period costume through the old neighbourhoods on foot and by boat.

- **Gion matsuri** (Kyoto, mid-July) – Lasting three days, this festival features a huge procession of *mikoshi* and floats. There are hundreds of stands selling traditional foods, and some of the old houses in the merchants' district are open to visitors.

- **Nebuta matsuri** (Aomori, August) – This festival has incredibly ornate and impressively massive paper lanterns in the shape of characters from Japan's history and folklore.

- There are thousands of smaller *matsuri* which are worth visiting, some of which are quite bizarre (even by Japanese standards), including the following:

- **Kanamara matsuri** (in Kawasaki) – This is a fertility festival held in early April in which the *mikoshi* have a large, detailed steel or wooden phallus mounted on them. There's also a huge pink papier-mâché one, carried by transvestites who chant rhythmically "*rekai mara, rekai mara*" (big penis, big penis).

- **Waraji matsuri** (in Daio-Nakiri Shima) – Held in a small fishing village in Mie-ken, this festival requires participants to make a large *waraji* (a straw sandal-cum-slipper), measuring some 2.5m by 1.8m, and launch it into the sea. The origin of this festival is a myth concerning a one-eyed giant who terrorised the village but was intimidated by the sight of the huge *waraji*.

- **Imari Ton-Ten-Ton matsuri** (in Imari, a town in the Saga prefecture) – This is one of the 'three great fighting festivals' of Japan (see **Hamamatsu matsuri** above); in this one *mikoshi*-carrying teams crash into each other violently as they compete in a race. Every year there are injuries, some of them serious.

Festival listings for the Tokyo area can be found at 🖳 www.japantimes.co.jp/entertainment/festivals.html and for the whole of Japan from the Japan National Tourist Organization website (🖳 www.jnto.go.jp/eng/indepth/history/traditionalevents/index.html).

Smoker's Paradise?

Unlike in most Western countries, smoking is permitted in most cafés, bars, restaurants and other public places, but not in the streets. Many urban streets have designated smoking areas and walking-and-smoking bans, but not for the sake of public health. Rather it's to avoid litter and 'walk-by' cigarette burns.

Popular Music

A peculiarity of Japanese culture is the 'live house'. It's unusual in Japan for bars to have a band, as for example in the UK, so if you want to experience live music you need to find the local live house. These establishments operate by renting out their space to bands, who are responsible for selling tickets. Tickets are often expensive (as high as ¥4,000/US$400) and you'll usually be asked which band(s) you came to see so your entry fee can be allocated accordingly. There may be a line-up of four or more unknown bands, or there may be only one well known band, which may play for up to three hours. Usually the style of music is heavy rock and, while the quality of musicianship is invariably high, there's often a lack of originality. 'Gigs' start and finish early, and the crowd tends to be young university students dressed in black.

Gambling

Legally, gambling in Japan is restricted to the national lottery and licensed premises, but it goes on everywhere under the flimsy cover of *pachinko* parlours, which originated in Nagoya. These noisy, garishly lit buildings can be found in the smallest towns and the largest cities. They're filled with small, upright pinball-type machines, but with no paddles at the bottom. Players feed hundreds of small steel balls in at the top, controlling only their speed. As the balls fall, some are caught in pins, releasing more balls. Any 'winnings' are exchanged for prizes, which are then taken to a small shop around the corner and 'sold' for cash. *Pachinko* addiction is a serious problem in Japan.

Many *pachinko* parlours are owned by ethnic North Koreans, who illegally send home an estimated ¥5bn (US$50m) each year to help prop up the impoverished regime.

The Japanese also gamble on horse-racing, sprint cycling and jet boat racing, among other pursuits.

Spectator Sports

The Japanese make great supporters and bring a unique atmosphere to a major sporting event. The culture of 'supporting' is fostered from early school days and can be seen at its most fervent at the national high school baseball tournament held every year at the Koshien stadium near Kobe. Japanese fans are never negative – booing or jeering is unknown – and they're tidy and pick up their litter when they leave.

Sumo

Japan's national sport has a major tournament (*basho*) every two months. These are always televised live on NHK 1 and, with English commentary, on NHK BS2. Every second tournament is held in Tokyo, the remaining tournaments taking place in Kyushu, Nagoya and Osaka. Between these *basho* are one-day events in smaller cities. The *basho* lasts for 15 days, the champion being the wrestler with the most wins over this period, rather than the winner of a knock-out competition.

Sumo is currently dominated by foreign wrestlers, mostly from Mongolia, and (partly for this reason) is in something of a decline. Apparently, Japanese high school boys are reluctant to don what looks like a huge nappy and submit to rigorous training regimes.

Baseball

Baseball is the king of spectator sports in Japan, and going to a game provides a fascinating insight into Japanese group mentality. Supporters all cheer together, at the same time, at the appropriate time – which is to support their team when it's batting. When the opposition is batting they will fall silent and let the opposing supporters do the cheering, which is often directed at a particular player and is always supportive, no matter how badly the team is doing.

Japan's top professional teams compete in two leagues of six teams: the Pacific League and the Central League.

Traditionally the Central League has been the stronger and more popular of the two, especially because the Yomiuri Giants – the 'Manchester United' of Japanese baseball – play in it. The two league champions play off in the best-of-five Japan Series.

Football

Japan has joined the rest of the world in soccer mania. The J. League was formed in 1993 and now comprises two divisions, imaginatively called J. League 1 (18 clubs) and J. League 2 (15 clubs). Below the J. League, the Japan Football Association operates the even more imaginatively named Japan Football League (18 clubs), which is made up of amateur, semi-professional and university clubs. Any J. League or Japan Football Association team may enter the annual Emperor's Cup, a knock-out competition inaugurated in 1921.

The best-supported team in Japan is Urawa Red Diamonds, which is based in Saitama. Its average gate of 46,000 being the highest in Asia. The Diamonds were runners-up in J. League 1 in 2004, 2005 and 2007, but have won it only once, in 2006. They also won the Emperor's Cup that year (and in 2005) and the Asian Champions League in 2007, when they came third in the FIFA Club World Cup. Other strong teams are the Kashima Antlers (five-times league winners), Júbilo Iwata and Yokohama F. Marinos (both three-times winners), Tokyo Verdy (twice) and Gamba Osaka (once).

Japanese football fans have adopted some of the customs of European fans, borrowing their songs and developing their own variations on them, but fortunately not their indulgence in hooliganism.

Golf

With over 2,400 18-hole golf courses, Japan is a golfer's paradise – or, at least, a rich golfer's paradise. In the years before the Asian economic crash, golf became a sport for the dealmakers of the corporate world. The price of club memberships rose astronomically as they became yet another commodity to be traded for profit. In 1993, annual membership of the Koganei Country Club cost over ¥350mn (US$3.5mn), and several other clubs weren't a lot cheaper. When the bubble burst, fees collapsed, many golf clubs went out of business and the number of golfers declined.

Recent years have seen a gradual recovery in player numbers, especially as baby boomers retire and more women are becoming interested in the sport, and membership fees are more reasonable, although still beyond the reach of the vast majority of Japanese: the average membership fee at the 650 clubs in the Tokyo region is just under ¥2mn (US$20,000) and the Koganei Country Club now charges a 'mere' ¥60mn (US$600,000).

Many clubs have been forced to abandon their members-only policy and will allow visitors to play a round on weekdays – if they can afford to fork out almost ¥1,000 (US$10) per hole!

> **Japan's most exclusive golf club, the Koganei Country Club, is one of several that still bar women from membership.**

If you don't have the time or money to play a real round of golf, you can get a feel for the game at one of the country's many driving ranges – easily recognised by the vast areas of green netting strung up around them, often four or five storeys high.

The Japanese at Play

Winter Sports

Given Japan's plentiful snow and mountains, it's no surprise that skiing and snowboarding are high on the list of 'things to do' in winter. Among its 600-plus ski stations are some world class resorts, including two that have hosted the Winter Olympics (Sapporo in 1972 and Nagano in 1998). All-day lift passes typically cost between ¥3,500 and 5,000 (US$35-50).

Japan has a strong line-up of female figure skaters, who compete with the best in the world. To many Japanese, who take pride in their winter sports, their generally poor performance at the 2006 Winter Olympics was redeemed only by Shizuka Arakawa's gold medal.

Other Sports

- **Basketball, Ice hockey & Volleyball** – Japan has professional or semi-professional leagues in all three sports and matches are occasionally televised.

- **Judo** – Japan takes great pride in having developed this international sport, a pride which must be upheld by success in Olympics and World Championships.

- **Martial arts** – Another iconic Japanese activity, which in the last few years has taken to TV in the form of professional mixed-discipline tournaments called 'K1' and 'Pride'. These also attract sell-out stadium audiences.

- **Motorsports** – It isn't surprising that Japan, a world leader in automotive manufacturing, has a lively bike and car racing scene. Perhaps the most famous circuit is Suzuka, where the Japanese Formula 1 Grand Prix has traditionally been held, although this event moved to Fuji Speedway (Oyama) in 2007.

- **Rugby** – Japan has more rugby players than almost any other country in the world due to its popularity at high school level. The semi-professional Top League consists of 14 teams, sponsored by large Japanese companies such as Sanyo, Toshiba and Toyota. Many star players from major rugby-playing countries play in these teams, and the Japanese national team has many players 'imported' from other countries.

- **Table-tennis** – The popularity of this sport has been maintained by public interest in its 'cute' female prodigy, Ai Fukuhara.

- **Tennis** – Japan is much stronger on the world stage in women's tennis than men's, although Kimiko Date, who 'retired' in 1996, was their last top-ten player and her recent return

The Japanese at Play

to competition is unlikely to alter that record. It's a popular game nevertheless, with both artificial and real grass courts throughout Japan.

Sporting Events

The following annual sporting events are the most important in the Japanese calendar:

Baseball – High School Baseball Tournament, Koshien Stadium, Kobe (August) and the Japan Series Final, played in the league champions' stadiums (October)

Formula 1 motor racing – Japan Grand Prix, Oyama (May)

Grand Prix motorcycling – Grand Prix of Japan, Motegi, (early September)

Golf – Japan Open Golf Championship, Fukuoka (mid-October)

Running – Hakane Ekiden, Hakone to Tokyo (January)

Sumo – bi-monthly basho (see above), Tokyo (January, May & September), Osaka (March), Nagoya (July) and Fukuoka (November)

Tennis – AIG Japan Open Tennis Championships, Tokyo (early October)

Hunting & Fishing

Although hunting isn't a popular sport, there are those who go out into Japan's plentiful forests to shoot boar and deer. Fishing is a popular pastime among older Japanese males, even if it involves catching minuscule fish in Tokyo's public parks.

Gun-owners must apply for a licence and are subject to regular psychological evaluations.

Onsen

There are over 27,500 officially recorded hot springs (*onsen*) in Japan, of which almost 19,000 are in use as 'spas' (5,000 naturally occurring and 14,000 pumped from sources under the ground). Only 91 of these have been designated by the Ministry of the Environment as 'Hot Spring Health Resorts', which means that their waters are considered to have healing properties. This is of little significance, however, to most Japanese, who firmly believe in the benefits of immersion in *onsen* waters – whether or not granted official recognition – and will travel hundreds of kilometres to visit their preferred *onsen*.

Onsen facilities vary greatly, some being extensive resorts with a range of pools, others boasting little more than a rustic hut for changing in. Typically, an *onsen* belongs to a *ryokan*, a traditional Japanese inn, and the 'package' includes food and overnight accommodation as well as immersion in the soothing water. Every year the Japanese spend a total

Onsen bath

of some 140mn nights at *onsen* and millions more visit them on day trips.

Onsen aren't to be confused with Japanese public baths, or *sento*, which make no claim to use geo-thermally heated water.

> 'What could be more sublime than sitting in a mountain hot tub at night, sipping *sake* and conversing with your close ones while gazing at the stars through snow-clad branches?'
>
> Robert Neff, *Japan's Hidden Hot Springs*

Like most Japanese customs, a visit to an *onsen* involves certain rituals and taboos, including the following:

- **Nudity** – Most *onsen* are segregated by sex and bathers are naked, although family-style *onsen* and mixed *onsen* can also be found.

- **Tattoos** – Many *onsen* ban tattoos because of their association with *yakuza* (the Japanese mafia), although smaller establishments are less likely to be fussy.

- **Towels** – In large establishments towels are included, but in smaller ones you should bring two towels: a large one for drying yourself and a smaller one for taking into the baths (see below).

- **Washing** – You must wash your body (and rinse all the soap off) before entering the water. Some country *onsen* lack washing facilities, in which case there will be a small bucket full of water to slosh over yourself before getting in.

- **Bathing** – Although you're usually naked when bathing, you should cover your private parts with your towel while walking around, but beware of letting it come into contact with the *onsen* water; when you take your dip, roll it up and place it on your head. Covering up isn't so necessary in female-only *onsen*. It's considered bad form to 'swim' in an *onsen* – find a spot and stay put. Some *onsen* allow you to adjust the temperature of the water using hot and cold water taps, although you should ask the other bathers before doing so.

THE ARTS

The fine arts are highly valued in Japan, where you'll often see painters in groups or by themselves in public parks, and where exhibitions of Western art – especially those of famous artists – are extremely well attended. Traditional Japanese styles include *shodo* (calligraphy) and *sumi-e* (traditional scenes painted in charcoal ink). Japanese watercolour and silk scroll painting are also world-famous.

The traditional domestic arts of the tea ceremony and flower arranging are also highly prized, and both are taught in junior and senior high schools throughout Japan.

Western classical music, jazz concerts, ballet, theatre and traditional dance performances are popular in the main cities.

Booking

Though tickets for almost everything are expensive, events are often sold out. To be sure of getting a seat it's therefore wise to book, although this usually requires a reasonable grasp of Japanese. Tickets can be obtained in advance in the following ways:

- **ATMs:** Many convenience stores have an electronic ticketing machine at which almost anything can be booked. Unfortunately the instructions are entirely in Japanese.

- **Discount ticket stands:** These are found at major railway stations and sell left-over and returned tickets. These may be cheaper than face value or, if only a few remain, more expensive.

- **Online:** The best site for booking events is ⌨ http://t.pia.jp, the website of the Japanese magazine *Pia* (in Japanese only).

- **Telephone:** For smaller events it may be possible to book by phone and pay for your ticket when you collect it.

Cinema

The golden age of Japanese cinema is long past, and what remains is a somewhat shallow film industry. Although a few high-quality Japanese films occasionally win awards at international film festivals, they aren't generally well known in Japan, where Western blockbusters dominate. Fortunately for foreigners, these are usually shown with Japanese subtitles rather than in dubbed versions. In larger cities it's possible to see foreign 'independent' films, but be prepared for a long wait before they reach Japan. Even Hollywood movies can take up to a year to appear in Japanese cinemas.

> With tickets for regular sessions costing around ¥1,800 (US$18), seeing a film is expensive, but there are ways to cut the cost. On the first of every month all seats are ¥1,000 (US$10), and many cinemas have a 'ladies' night', usually on Wednesday, when women receive a discount. (Unfortunately, there isn't a corresponding 'gentlemen's night'!) Also, there are ticket booths near major rail stations that sell tickets for certain films for ¥1,200-1,300 (US$12-13).

Popcorn and drinks are commonly sold in Japanese cinemas, and drinks include beer and, in some modern cinemas, wine and champagne. Some

The Japanese at Play

other peculiarities of Japanese cinema-going are listed below:

- **Air-conditioning** – In summer, cinemas can be like fridges, therefore it's advisable to take a sweater or jacket.

- **Food** – You can usually take food into a cinema, but not always, so it's best to check. When you leave, you should do as the Japanese do and take your litter with you.

- **Location** – many of Japan's cinemas are on the upper storeys of skyscrapers.

- **Disabled access** – Wheelchair access and seating areas for the disabled are rare in Japanese cinemas.

- **Times** – First sessions are at around 11am, the last showing at around 7pm, to allow cinema-goers to catch the last train home. It's considered impolite to arrive late for a show and, although you'll usually be allowed in, you'll be unpopular if you push past people's legs to get to your seat.

- **Noise** – Japanese audiences are quiet and respectful. Scarcely a whisper will detract from your viewing pleasure, and many Japanese stay right to the last roll of the credits.

Theatre & Opera

A variety of theatrical entertainment is on offer in Japan, including the following.

Bunraku

Although *Bunraku* has come to mean any kind of puppet theatre in Japan, it originally referred to a particular troupe in Osaka. The puppets are generally between two and four feet tall and each is controlled by two or three puppeteers who stand on stage dressed in black. The themes of *Bunraku* include stories from Japanese folklore and dramatisations of historical events, but most common are tales that involve lovers' suicides.

Kabuki

Kabuki is a highly stylised form of classical Japanese dance-drama. Kabuki theatre is known for the stylisation of its drama and costumes, the elaborate (white) make-up worn by some of its performers and the strangulated vocal delivery.

> In 1629 women were banned from performing *Kabuki* because some had become involved in prostitution. As a result, boys took on the female roles – in more ways than one. Twenty-three years later, they too were therefore banned, leaving men as the only performers legally allowed to continue the *Kabuki* tradition.

Noh

A form of masked musical theatre that developed in the 14th century, *Noh* has changed little since that time and is distinguished by slow, stylised movements accompanied by the sound of traditional stringed instruments. Performances are often given at outdoor theatres.

Takarazuka Revue

A less traditional but no less unique theatrical institution in Japan is the Takarazuka Revue, a group that stages large-scale, glitzy, Broadway-style musicals in which all the roles are played by women. The Revue was founded in 1913 by the president of a railway company who wanted to increase passenger numbers on the Takarazuka line, in Hyogo prefecture. It remains popular to this day among Japanese women, who make up the vast majority of the audience.

As well as classic musicals such as *Guys and Dolls* and *The Sound of Music*, the Takarazuka Revue has performed adaptations of films and even operas, such as *Gone with the Wind* and *Aida*. All productions are in Japanese.

Western Productions

Translated Western plays and musicals are often performed in the major cities. These range from Shakespearean tragedies (Tokyo even has its own replica of the Globe theatre) to *Cats* and *Mamma Mia*.

As a major stop on the international tour, Tokyo also gets its share of touring productions in the original language. At the other end of the scale are the Tokyo International Players (www.tokyoplayers.org), who have been putting on plays in English since 1896.

Museums & Art Galleries

Japanese art galleries are well funded and have excellent permanent and short-term exhibitions. Museums of science, technology and other topics are also common. Even small towns usually have several museums, dedicated to local history or industry. Some of the smaller museums are among the strangest in the world, being devoted to such subjects as parasites, buttons, laundry and baseballs. Japan also has some impressive open-air museums, displaying historic buildings from various regions and periods.

The following general information applies to most Japanese museums and galleries:

- **Opening hours:** These are fairly consistent throughout Japan: museums and galleries open at 9.30-10am, close at 5pm and are nearly always closed on Mondays, with the exception of public holidays. Last access is usually 30 minutes before closing time and visitors are asked to leave 10 or 15 minutes before the museum closes. Late evening opening is rare.

- **Entrance fees:** Most museums charge between ¥500 and 1,600 (US$5-16), with discounts for students and seniors.

- **Security:** Typically, security is lacking in comparison with measures common in the West. There are usually lockers or a cloakroom in the foyer where you can leave bags and other items. There are usually umbrella racks outside.

- **Disabled access:** Most major museums have disabled access, although you must sometimes ask to use a lift or stair lift.

- **Shops & restaurants:** All museums and galleries have a shop where you can buy merchandise relating to the displays, and most also have a restaurant.

- **Noise & crowds:** Japanese museum visitors are generally quiet. However, museums can be very busy – the best times to visit are soon after opening time and on weekdays.

> In Tokyo you can buy a 'Grutt Pass' for ¥2,000 (US$20), which allows entry to most of the city's museums, aquariums and parks for a two-month period.

Beach, Okinawa

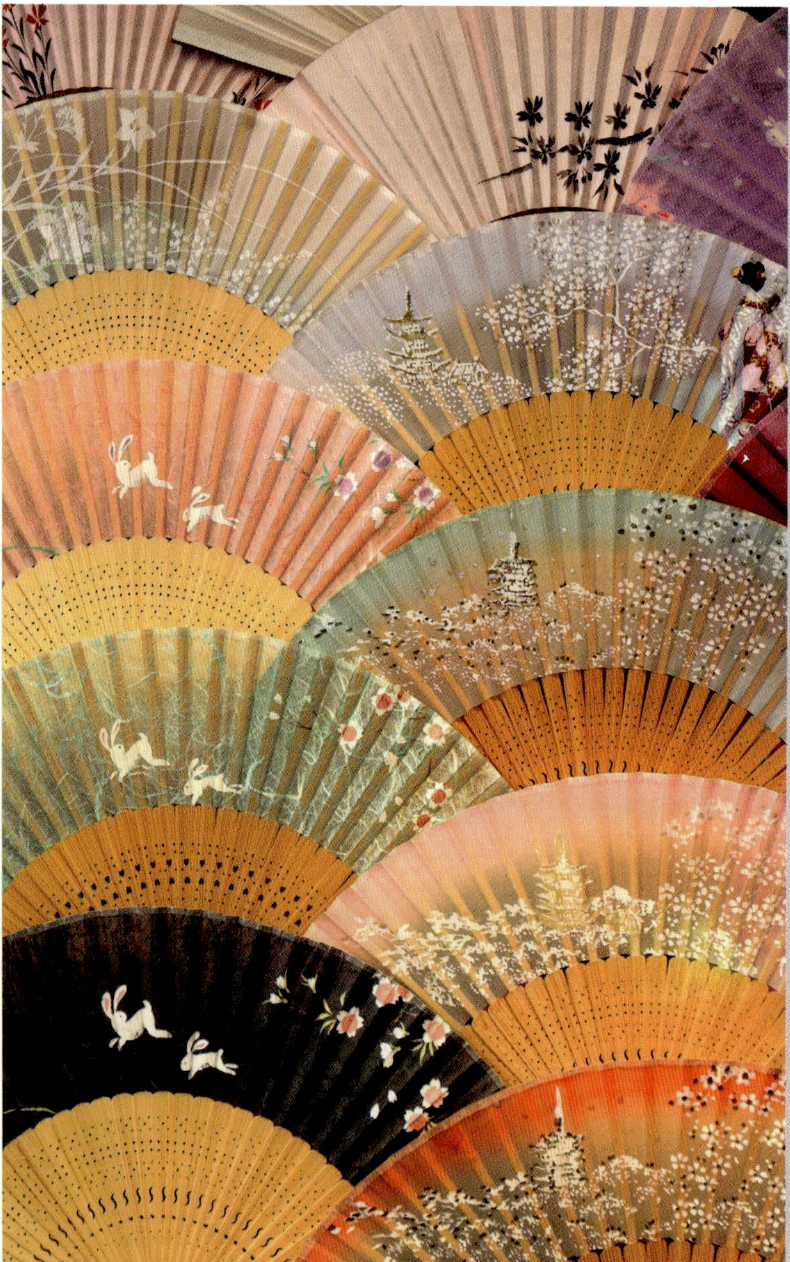

9.
RETAIL THERAPY

Shopping in Japan is a fascinating experience, especially if you have plenty of money to spend. However, even if you don't, you can have a great time just browsing and inspecting all the weird and wonderful offerings that make Japan such a shoppers' delight. Shopping is regarded as a recreation in Japan, where the major stores are open seven days a week; from sophisticated sprawling malls to chic and trendy departmental stores, exclusive boutiques to vast markets, Japan has something for everyone.

> You need to add the 5 per cent consumption tax to the price tag in Japan.

Japan is a shopper's paradise, offering everything from high-tech gadgetry and electronics (a techie's Aladdin's cave) to traditional arts and crafts. Popular buys include cameras, watches, CD players, hi-fi equipment, silk goods, lacquer ware, Japanese dolls, and woodblock prints. Not only are products high quality and beautifully crafted, whether clothes, accessories, homewares, electronic goods or handicrafts, customers are treated as Gods in Japan – greeted royally, never harried or hurried and bowed out of shops with infinite courtesy.

However, whether you're buying or just browsing, you'll need to know about Japanese shopping 'etiquette', which is discussed in this chapter.

CUSTOMER SERVICE

Japanese companies pride themselves on their customer service. They will do their utmost to help and if they cannot they will apologise as if they're personally to blame for the company's failure. For example, if you ask for a product that a shop doesn't stock, you'll be given profuse – and sincere – apologies. However, staff are less likely to show initiative by suggesting where you may be able to find it. If you ask for something to be delivered locally, it will invariably be delivered on the day and at the time specified.

Most shops gift-wrap items free of charge. While in some cases this involves merely popping the item into a 'gift bag' and closing it with a tie, in many cases great care is taken and the process is a joy to watch. Gift wrapping is an art in Japan, where your purchases are beautifully wrapped in layers of protective hand-made paper and finally luxury paper displaying the store's name (which is totally acceptable, particularly if it's a prestigious store), tied with special cords (*mizuhiki*) made of rolled paper or ribbon, and finally put in a 'made-to-measure' bag. The paper and cord colour will depend on the occasion and even the wrapping technique may vary depending on the purpose of a gift.

> In Japanese shops, it's usual to be greeted by a chorus of *irasshaimase* (welcome), whether shouted with cheery gusto or spoken with decorum. It isn't necessary to answer this greeting verbally – eye contact and a nod are sufficient.

OPENING HOURS

Major stores in Japan are usually open from 10 or 11am (usually on the dot) until 7 or 8pm every day, including Saturdays and Sundays. Some are closed one day a week (often Wednesdays), but most open seven days a week and also on public holidays other than *Obon* and New Year. Some large shops even remain open during these holidays. However, many smaller specialty shops are closed on weekends, national holidays and over traditional Japanese holiday periods.

QUEUING

In Japan people queue in an orderly, patient manner, whatever they're waiting for. There may be a single queue (line) for several counters or one for each; look to see which system is being used before joining a queue. The Japanese tend to be robotic about waiting, often queuing where everybody else is, leaving some lines miraculously clear for those quick to spot the opportunity.

In banks and post offices there's usually a ticket machine that issues a queue number. Be careful not to miss your turn, as it's bad manners to 'push in' after your number has been displayed (there may be a chime each time the display changes).

SALES & DISCOUNTS

Bartering is virtually unknown in Japan – even where it's widely believed that you can ask for (and get) a discount, as in the electronic selling district in Akihabara, Tokyo. There are, however, sales (*baagen seiru*, which is a corruption of 'bargain sale'). The biggest sales are held during the New Year holiday, starting on or after 1st January, when goods may be sold at up to 50 per cent discount. The other major sale time is mid-summer, around the *Obon* holiday.

Some sales run for just a few days, others for a week or more. A common feature of these is the 'sale bag' (*fukubukuro*), containing an assortment of surplus goods at a considerable discount. The catch is that you usually don't know what's in the bag! There are also 'pop-up' promo stores that appear in designated spaces in some of the larger stores, where a clothes, shoes, kitchen, homewares or gift supplier will set up shop for a week or two, and then disappear to be replaced by another supplier.

> Japan has a strong cash culture and it's common to see people carrying large amounts of cash (thanks to the low crime rate). It's only recently that credit cards have become more popular and foreigners may still encounter difficulties using foreign credit cards.

Duty- & Tax-free Shopping

Duty-free shopping is only available in Japan's international airports, but tax-free shopping is possible in urban centres at authorised tax-free stores. In these stores, purchases of over ¥10,000 (US$100) on selected items are exempt from Japan's 5 per cent consumption tax, but it's worth comparing prices at discount stores and bargain markets before buying.

Bear in mind that many electrical and electronic products sold in Japan are designed solely for the domestic market, therefore you need to confirm the voltage and system requirements for your home country. You may also wish to check that an expensive item, such as a camera or computer, has an international warranty.

TYPES OF SHOP

In the countryside, where people tend to own cars, large shopping centres have put local shops out of business, leaving town centres dead. The cities still have vibrant shopping areas, mainly near the railway stations, and it's here that you'll find the most interesting selection of shops. Typical Japanese shops include the following:

- *Hyaku en*: ¥100 shops where almost everything costs just ¥100 (see below).

- *Konbini*: convenience store (see below).

- *Kudamono-ya*: fruit and vegetable shop. These often have lower prices and better quality produce than can be found in a supermarket.

- *Kusuriya*: pharmacy. These range from tiny establishments selling only medicines to emporiums stocking a range of toiletries and foodstuffs as well, sometimes cheaper than at supermarkets.

- *Tofu* **shop**: If you're lucky enough to live near a shop that makes its own tofu (assuming you like the stuff), you can try a different variety each day.

- **Japanese cake shop:** stocking a selection of *wagashi*, red-bean confections and green-tea flavoured *mochi*, the products vary with the season. Popular as presents.

¥100 Shop

As the name suggests, a ¥100 shop (*hyaku en*) is a store where almost everything costs ¥100 (US1$) – actually ¥105 when the consumption tax is added. ¥100 shops buy goods in huge volumes from China and further afield, where manufacturing and labour costs are low, thus allowing them to sell them at low prices and still make a profit. They stock a vast array of items, including stationery, household goods, clothes, leisure products, tools, gardenware, kitchenware, tableware and much more. They are a great place to 'furnish'; a new home as well buy cheap souvenirs – and many shops have recently begun selling fruit and vegetables at correspondingly low prices.

The ¥100 shops gained popularity during the recession in the '90s and have since gone from strength to strength and now rival convenience stores in numbers. Nowadays there are thousands of 100 Yen Shops across Japan, ranging in size from multi-storey 'department stores' to small corners in shopping malls. Market leader Daiso operates over 2,000 stores nationwide and pursues an aggressive expansion policy.

Convenience Stores

Japan has over 40,000 convenience stores (*konbini*), which are usually open 24 hours a day, seven days a week. There's strong competition between the major operators such as Seven Eleven, Lawson and Family Mart, which makes for keen prices and innovative products and services, and makes Japanese convenience stores truly convenient.

Convenience stores primarily sell food including a large range of meals, snacks and sweets, such as *onigiri* (rice balls), sandwiches, bread, chips, candy, *obento* (lunch boxes), instant *ramen*, microwave meals and hot foods such as fried chicken, *nikuman* and *oden*. Some cold foods, such as *onigiri*, can be heated up by the store staff. Stores also sell hot and cold beverages including soda, coffee, tea, water, sport drinks, juice, milk and vitamin drinks, and many also sell alcohol including beer, *happoshu*, *chuhai*, *nihonshu*, *shochu* and wine. Other goods available include body care products, cosmetics, batteries, CDs and tapes, umbrellas, newspapers, magazines and comics.

Convenience stores also offer a wide range of services, many of which can be accessed through automated multi-purpose terminals, such as ATMs, copier/fax machines, ticket reservations, digital camera prints, a bill payment service, postal services, and delivery and pick-up services (Takuhaibin). Instructions are only in Japanese, but staff will be happy to help you if they aren't busy.

> Gift giving became so great in the '80s that many gifts were unused and companies were established specifically to buy unopened gifts – at a fraction of their original cost!

VENDING MACHINES

Japan is famous for its vending machines (*jidoohanbaiki*), which sell everything under the sun – and then some! There are over 6mn vending machines in Japan – one for every 20 people – with sales of over ¥50bn (US$500mn) a year. With so many people on the run at all hours of the day and night, it's the best way to make sure that people can always find what they need – and caters to the bashful when buying 'intimate' items – and the machines always work!

Drinks (soft drinks, coffee, tea, and vitamin drinks), cigarette and snack machines are the most common, but you may also come machines selling beer, *sake*, videos, condoms, instant *ramen*, fried food, eggs, pornography, Ipods, hot food, live lobsters, sex toys, batteries, CDs, disposable cameras, fortunes (*omikuji*), chewing gum, ice cream, milk, newspapers, pornographic magazines, paperbacks, *manga* comics, rice, tampons, travel insurance, toilet paper, umbrellas, flowers, clothing, chocolate and rhinoceros beetles (*kabuto-mushi*) – to name but a few items!

While the machines all take coins, most also accept common notes (some even accept ¥10,000 banknotes) and give change. And if you do need change, there's a machine for that also. Cell phones can also be used to pay for items bought from vending machines.

In 2008, a smart card (called *Taspo*) was implemented in the majority of tobacco vending machines across the country to restrict sales of cigarettes from them. From such machines, cigarette purchases may only be made by those in possession of a smart card, which is issued to adults (which in the case of Japan, is 20 years of age). The card is read by a sensor after payment has been made.

Used Panties

You can buy almost anything from vending machines in Japan but the most famous product, used panties, is no longer available. The machines, catering to the schoolgirl obsession (*bura-sera*) of many Japanese men, first appeared in 1993. The soiled underwear, also available in specialist *bura-sera* shops, is often accompanied by a photograph of the panties' former owner – like a seal of authentication. The machines were met with public outcry, but there was no direct statute banning the trade. However, some traders were (creatively) charged under the Antique Dealers Law, requiring dealers in second-hand goods to obtain permission from the local authority, and the panties disappeared from the streets overnight.

MARKETS

Street markets aren't common in Japan, but you may see occasional advertisements on community notice boards and in the classified sections of publications such as *Metropolis* for 'free markets'. These aren't markets where all the goods are free, but are in fact flea markets (*nomi-no-ichi*), which, due to the difficulty the Japanese have pronouncing the letter 'L', is often 'translated' into *romaji* as 'free market'.

Flea markets are common in Japan, where they are usually held in the grounds of temples and shrines and at parks, parking lots and in department stores. They open from early morning to later afternoon and feature a wide range of goods, from antiques (usually poor quality) to inexpensive crafts. Typical wares include used clothes, accessories, toys, shoes, books, potteries, pictures and much more. You may also be able to find souvenirs at reasonable prices.

Among the largest and most famous flea markets are Togo-no-Mori Nomi-no-ichi at Togo Shrine in Tokyo on the first Sunday of the month, just a few minutes walk from JR Harajuku station; Kitano Tenman-gu Tenjin-san at Kitano Tenman-gu Shrine in Kyoto (30 minutes by bus from JR Kyoto station) on the 25th of the month; and Kyoto To-ji Temple Koubou-ichi at Toji Temple in Kyoto (five minutes walk from Kintetsu To-ji station) on the 21st of the month.

Many large flea markets are organised by associations such as the Japan Garage Sale Association (☏ 06-6362-6322), the Japan Flea Market Association (☏ 06-6531-8417), the Tokyo Recycle Campaign Citizen's Association (☏ 03-3384-6666) and the Recycle Campaign Citizens' Association (☏ 03-3226-6800). Most markets are held irregularly, so be sure to check the schedule before you go, and bear in mind that they may be cancelled during wet weather.

Fujitsu, Mitsukoshi and Shiseido have teamed up to bring a virtual, real-time makeover machine to Japanese department stores, in order to give women a chance to test out a smorgasbord of shades on their virtual face before buying.

DEPARTMENT STORES

Japan has a wealth of department stores (*hyakkaten* or *depāto*), of which the most famous chains include Daimaru, Hankyu, Isetan, Mitsukoshi, Seibu, Sogo and Takashimaya. Japan's department stores were once symbols of modernity. The first 'Western-style' department store in Japan was Mitsukoshi, founded in 1904, which has its root as a *kimono* store called Echigoya dating from 1673. Its flagship store (Nihombashi, Tokyo) was the first building in Japan to have central heating and escalators, and one of the first large shops in the country to allow customers to wear shoes indoors. Seibu in Ikebukero (Tokyo) is one of the largest department stores in the world, while Matsuzakaya (Ginza, Tokyo) is a sprawling store occupying a ten-storey building and one of the oldest and most elite stores in the city.

The major *depātos* are very classy stores and sell all the leading international fashion names in spacious 'in house' stores (stores in stores) and offer a wide range of goods and services such as foreign exchange, travel reservations, and ticket sales for local concerts and other events. In addition to the usual departments, they offer a range of traditional Japanese products, including *kimonos*, *mingei* (local crafts including kites and folk toys), *Kyoto* silks, fans, screens and dolls; religious articles such as Shinto and Buddhist artifacts; paper lanterns, pottery and lacquerware. The basement is usually an international food hall, with a bread shop, café and fast-food outlets, while upper floors usually have a restaurant and café. They also have children's playgrounds, so that parents can get on with the business of spending money.

Japanese department stores are bastions of cultural conservatism and gift certificates for prestigious department stores are frequently given as formal presents in Japan. However, since the '80s, they have faced fierce competition from supermarkets and convenience stores. Many stores are seen as outdated and customers are deserting them in favour of speciality clothing stores and malls. A combination of increasing competition, high prices, falling sales, low productivity and high operating costs, almost certainly mean that the days of the *hyakkaten* are numbered – at least in their current form.

SUPERMARKETS

Modern Japanese supermarkets are organised in much the same way as their Western counterparts. They offer all kinds of goods such as fresh fruit and vegetables, fresh seafood, meat and tofu; pickled, dried and canned food; bread, dairy products, snacks and ready-to-eat meals; alcoholic and non-alcoholic beverages; and household articles.

Their products are usually beautifully presented and of excellent quality, although price can be high. The sizes of packaged goods and portions are usually smaller than comparable products sold abroad (e.g. in Europe and North America), although prices may be higher, particularly for non-standard Japanese fare. However, traditional Japanese foodstuffs can be relatively inexpensive.

Supermarkets are few and far between in central Tokyo and other city centres, although most department stores have excellent food halls, usually located in the basement.

> While the yen's recent strength against the dollar has been a cause for anxiety among Japan's exporters, some supermarkets have turned the situation to their advantage. For example, Aeon, Japan's largest retailer, has been holding 'strong yen sales' with markdowns on imported wines, meat and fish.[a]

Shopping in Supermarkets

When shopping in a Japanese supermarket, note the following practices:

- You can enter by either the exit or the entry doors. Strict anti-shoplifting measures such as are common in Western countries aren't found in Japan, although you'll see the odd security guard wandering around (perhaps paying closer attention to foreigners than to locals).

- Westerners will be surprised at the comically small supermarket trolleys used in Japan. Japanese households tend to shop daily, buying small amounts to ensure that they always eat fresh produce. Besides which, fridges in Japanese homes are small and separate freezers are virtually unheard of, making regular shopping trips a necessity.

- Trolleys are designed to accommodate baskets – usually one at the top and one at the bottom – and you should put all your purchases in these rather than in the trolley itself. At the checkout you place the basket(s) on the counter, where the cashier takes the goods out, runs them by the barcode reader and puts them in another basket. When you pay, you'll be given a number of plastic bags and should take the basket(s) of goods to a 'packing' area by the exit, where you put your purchases into the bags.

If you don't want a plastic bag, you should say to the cashier *sono mama* (literally 'in the original state').

FOOD

Fish

Japan is famous worldwide for its fish, particularly sushi and sashimi (see **Icons – Food & Drink** in Chapter 2), and Japanese supermarkets pride themselves on having a well stocked fish section, where a wide variety of fresh and sometimes live fish are on display.

In Tokyo, a visit to Tsukiji Market is a fascinating experience, where merchants from across the city arrive long before dawn to select the best seafood of the day – you need to arrive before 5am to witness the unloading and selling. If it swims or crawls in the sea, it's likely that you'll find it at the Tsukiji Market, which also sells a wide variety of produce.

Eating whale meat is a thorn in Japan's relationship with the rest of the world, although the annual catch is limited to 1,000 whales for 'scientific research'. There is, however, political pressure to keep it on the menu, as whale meat is an integral part of many festivals and traditions.

Fruit & Vegetables

High quality fruit and vegetables are also available, although items grown locally can cost more than produce imported from China and even the US. Vegetables commonly found in the West are widely available, though they may look quite different. Japanese radishes (*daikon*), for example, can be two feet long, while aubergines (eggplants) tend to be small; mandarin oranges are often green and you'll even see square watermelons (*shikaku suika*) grown in glass boxes – although at ¥10,000 (US$100) each they're a luxury few can afford. The variety of mushrooms may astonish you – and not a 'button' mushroom in sight.

Small fruit and vegetables are sold by the kilo, while larger items, such as cauliflower and broccoli, by the piece. They're weighed at the checkout.

Meat

Japan is a land of small, hygienic packages, and nowhere is this more evident than when it comes to buying meat. It's unusual for a supermarket to have a butcher's counter; meat is almost always pre-packed. It may be difficult to

Metric/Imperial Conversion

Weight

Imperial	Metric	Metric	Imperial
1 UK pint	0.57 litre	1 litre	1.75 UK pints
1 US pint	0.47 litre	1 litre	2.13 US pints
1 UK gallon	4.54 litre	1 litre	0.22 UK gallon
1 US gallon	3.78 litres	1 litre	0.26 US gallon

Capacity

Imperial	Metric	Metric	Imperial
1 UK pint	0.57 litre	1 litre	1.75 UK pints
1 US pint	0.47 litre	1 litre	2.13 US pints
1 UK gallon	4.54 litres	1 litre	0.22 UK gallon
1 US gallon	3.78 litres	1 litre	0.26 US gallon

Note: An American 'cup' = around 250ml or 0.25 litre.

find cuts of meat that you're familiar with, but you can be sure that it will be cleanly cut with the most appetising side up.

The cheapest meat is chicken, which is sold whole, in halves or in pieces: breast (with or without the skin) and leg (with bones). There's a huge difference between Japanese and imported meat, both in quality and price. Japanese meat (e.g. including the famous Kobe or Hyogo and Wagyu beef) is marbled with fat, whereas that imported from the US and Australia is leaner (and cheaper). American pork is commonly available, as are various kinds of ham, sausage and bacon. The Japanese also eat raw horse meat (*basashi*), although its consumption is in decline.

It's advisable to avoid meat imported from China and Chinese-made frozen or processed food, which nowadays make up a large proportion of Japan's food merchandise. Not only is it often of inferior quality, but there are numerous health scares associated with Chinese foods and their safety and quality standards don't match up to those in Japan and many other countries. Better to buy imported meat from Australia, New Zealand and the US, if you cannot afford Japanese meat.

Milk & Dairy Products

Surprisingly for an Asian country, Japan has a well-developed dairy industry. This is because Hokkaido, the northernmost of Japan's islands, is too cold to grow rice, so agriculture is largely given over to dairy production. Most milk (*miruku*) is 'full cream', although low-fat milk is available (and cheaper). Due to the local method of homogenising, milk may taste slightly different from what you're used to. Fresh cream isn't widely available and is expensive.

When it comes to cheese, the most common varieties are grated and cream cheese, although Japan produces an excellent 'camembert', which is cheaper than the French brands found in almost every supermarket. Cheddar is expensive, sold in small (100-200g) packs and rarely available in supermarkets; it's possible to have it home delivered in 1kg packs at any time by Costco's online store in Japan (🖥 www.theflyingpig.com), which works out cheaper even allowing for the delivery charge. For other imported cheeses, you must go to a specialist cheese shop (in an main city) – and be prepared to pay a premium.

Be sure to learn the *kanji* (ミルク) for milk so that you don't accidentally buy 'reconstituted milk', made by adding water (and calcium and other minerals) to milk powder.

Organic Food

A small but growing proportion of Japanese consumers are aware of organic food, but it isn't as widely available as in most Western countries. The largest supermarkets have an organic section and you can find free-range eggs and chicken in most supermarkets, although of course such products are more expensive than their non-organic equivalents.

Foreign Foods

Some foreign foods are widely available, and Japanese versions of them have become part of the Japanese diet. In fact, the most popular dish in Japan is 'curry rice', a lightly spiced brown gravy with the odd bit of meat served with rice and eaten with a spoon, while pizzas, pasta and 'Italian' sauces can be found in almost any supermarket – there's even a Japanese brand of tinned 'Bolognese' sauce. For more authentic home comforts, there's usually an expensive foreign food store in the major city centres, and the food halls in the basements of department stores have a high proportion of imported foods – along with every type of Japanese food imaginable.

> The widest choice of (and often the cheapest) foreign foods, and other goods, are to be found in the few Costco (www.costco.co.jp/eng) and Carrefour branches scattered around Japan.

ALCOHOL

Beer, Wine & Whisky

The Japanese make some excellent beers (*bīru*) – the best is produced by small breweries, although even their major brewers are now making good 'special' beers. There are a surprisingly large number of breweries in Japan as the Japanese seem to be developing a taste for 'boutique' beers. Unfortunately major supermarkets stock only the major brands (Asahi, Kirin, Sapporo and Yebisu), which means that connoisseurs must go to the area where the specialist beers are made.

Japan has a small wine industry (mostly red), but its quality is generally low. However, imported wine is popular and a wide range is available in convenience stores, supermarkets and liquor stores at reasonable prices (although expensive compared with Europe and the US). Japan is the largest export market for '*Beaujolais nouveau*', nearly a quarter of all production being shipped there. (Desperate?) French wine-growers even created a rosé *primeur* specifically for the Japanese market, which was reportedly popular among women.

Japan also makes good whisky, the best of which some say can hold its own with Scotland's finest (but don't try telling a Scot!).

Nihonshu & Shochu

Known in the West as *sake* (which in Japanese means simply 'alcohol'), *nihonshu* is produced by over 1,500 companies, so there are enough brands to keep you 'tasting' for several years. *Shochu*, a spirit made from sweet potato, wheat or rice, has in recent years overtaken *nihonshu* as the second most popular alcoholic drink after beer. (See also **Icons – Food & Drink** in **Chapter 2**.)

CLOTHES

Shibuya (Tokyo) is a major shopping area and a must see for anyone interested in Japanese fashion; not only are there many trendy fashion stores but you'll also see many young Japanese people wearing the latest (and often simply outrageous) fashion in the streets. Another popular Tokyo shopping street is Takeshita-dori (Opposite Harajuku Station), which represents the cutting edge of fashion where you'll see the latest in Japanese street fashion in the wealth of boutiques.

Shibuya 109 Building (Ichimarukyū) shopping centre is packed with fashionable stores is popular among young people, especially teens, and famous as the origin of the *kogal* subculture. *Kogals* are known for wearing platform boots, miniskirts, copious amounts of makeup, hair colouring (usually blonde), artificial suntans and designer accessories. *Kogals* aren't to be confused with the *Ganguro* subculture, although they're similar. *Ganguro* is an alternative fashion trend of blonde or orange hair and tanned skin among young Japanese women, which peaked in popularity around the year 2000 but remains evident today. Another fashion trend among Japanese girls is *Yamanba* or *Manba* – the term comes from mythology and refers to a mountain-ogress – which is an extreme form of *Ganguro* fashion. Starting with the bleach-white hair and heavy tan of the *Ganguro* girl, the *Yamanba* adds white lipstick and eye makeup and sometimes blue contacts. The result is a caricature of a blond Caucasian woman.

Gothic Lolita is a fashion style popular among Japanese youth. Usually worn by girls, the image is that of a Victorian doll, with pale skin, neat hair, knee or mid-thigh Victorian dresses, pinafores, bloomers, stockings and shoes or boots. Sub-styles include elegant gothic Lolita or EGL (with a monochromatic palette), classical or country gothic Lolita (pastels), elegant gothic aristocrat (EGA) and industrial gothic Lolita (including PVC, leather, zippers, chains and other Punk fashion elements.)

Among the many unusual Japanese fashions are loose socks (*rūzu sokkusu*), which are popular among Japanese school girls, and the *tabi* sock that splits the big toe from the rest of the toes, thus allowing the wearer to also wear *zori* (tatami sandals with a separation between the big toe and other toes). The *yukata* is a type of clothing worn by the Japanese, especially women, at firework festivals and other summer events. It's a kind of casual *kimono*, also commonly worn after the bath at Japanese-style hotels (the word literally means bath robe or bath clothing). A *yukata* is a cooling garment to wear, consisting of one large piece of cloth with two wide sleeves and an *obi* (belt) to keep it from falling open. A special type of sandal (*geta*) with a single strap is traditionally worn with the *yukata*.

The majority of clothes sold in Japan are made in China, and although their quality is generally high, there may not be the range of styles and colours you're used to seeing. Prices may also be higher than you might expect. High-end shoppers are well served, however, as all the major fashion houses are represented in the up-market retailing districts of major cities, where prices are even higher than in Paris or Milan.

Sizes

It can be difficult for Westerners to find clothes that fit in Japan, as (not surprisingly) most clothes are made to fit the Japanese body shape, which is generally slimmer and shorter in the leg. The range of sizes available is limited, the tall and the large being poorly catered for, although in the major cities there are shops specialising in clothing for people of 'above-average' stature.

Although the sizing system used in Japan may seem familiar, e.g. S, M, L and XL, a Japanese M is roughly equivalent to an S in Western countries, an L is more like an M, and an XL equates to an L. Men's trousers are graded by waist size (in centimetres), but again Westerners may find they have to move up a size as their usual size is likely to be tight on the buttocks and thighs and short in the leg.

Conversion charts for men's and women's clothing sizes can be found on www.onlineconversion.com/clothing_mens.htm and www.usatourist.com/english/tips/Womens-Sizes.html respectively.

Japan's most famous designer, Issey Miyake, makes exclusive one-size shirts that stretch to fit the wearer. Shirts are factory-packaged in transparent plastic tubes and purchased from a transparent machine.

Clothes Size Comparisons

Women's Clothes

Continental	34	36	38	40	42	44	46	48	50	52
UK		8	10	12	14	16	18	20	22	24	26
US		6	8	10	12	14	16	18	20	22	24
Japan		9	11	13	15	17	19	21	23	-	-

Men's Shirts

Continental	36	37	38	39	41	42	43	44
UK/US	14	14	15	15	16	17	17	18
Japan	87	91	97	102	107	112	117	122

Retail Therapy

Shoe Size Comparisons (Men's & Women's)
European	35	36	37	37	38	39	40	41	42	42	43	44	45
British	2	3	3	4	4	5	6	7	7	8	9	9	10
US		4	5	5	6	6	7	8	9	9	10	10	11	11
Japan (cm)	21.5	22.5	22.5	23	23	24	24.5	25.5	25.5	26.5	27.5	27.5	28.5

Shoes

A good range of shoes is available in Japan, with many imports from Italy and other European countries. Some quality shoes are made in Japan, cheaper footwear not surprisingly coming from China. Shoe sizes in Japan are in centimetres, which is a convenient system once you get used to it, although if your foot is over 28cm (11in) long, you may have to buy your shoes abroad!

A traditional Japanese form of footwear not often seen nowadays, are *Zori*, which are sandals made from rice straw or lacquered wood worn with a *kimono* on formal occasions.

Children's Clothes

A good range of children's clothing is available at prices that range from reasonable to ridiculous, but styles tend to be 'cute' rather than practical. Japanese garments such as *jimbe* (loose pyjamas), *kimono* and *yukata* (a cotton *kimono*) are all available in children's sizes.

Alterations

If you buy clothes for work in a department store, any necessary alterations will usually be done by the shop. For all other alterations, you must ask at a dry cleaner's (which are widespread) or try to find a tailor.

BOOKS, NEWSPAPERS & MAGAZINES

English-language books (and books in other foreign languages) are expensive in Japan, therefore you would be wise to stock up before arriving. However, there are special departments in for English-language books in some shops of the Maruzen chain (e.g. in central Tokyo and Kyoto), the Kinokuniya chain of bookshops (e.g. Shinjuku and Subuya areas of Tokyo and Umeda railway station in Osaka), the Jena bookshop in the Tokyo Ginza area, the Byblos bookshop in Tokyo's Takada-no-Baba area, and the Avanti bookshop near Kyoto station. Book First (Bunkamura-dori) is one of Tokyo's largest bookstores and carries a good range of foreign language magazines, as does Tower Records (Shibuya). You can also buy English-language books via the internet from booksellers such as Amazon (💻 www.amazon.com) – often cheaper even after paying the postage.

Japan has a many English-language newspapers, including *The Japan Times* (💻 www.japantimes.ja), the *Mainichi Daily News* (💻 http://mdn.mainichi.jp), the *Daily Yomiuri* (💻 www.yomiuri.co.jp/dy) and the *Asahi Evening News* (💻 www.asahi.com/English). (See also the list in **Appendix B**.) International newspapers and magazines are available from hotel kiosks and major bookshops. International newspapers such as the English weekly *Daily Express*, *Daily Telegraph* and *Guardian* are a good way to keep up with British and foreign news. You can also read most newspapers via the internet – see 💻 www.onlinenewspapers.com. When you buy a book in Japan, you'll often be asked if you want to have it covered in paper. This is because it's thought that you may want to keep the title of the book private when reading it in public.

COLLECTABLES

As may be expected of the land of the geek and the cult of cuteness, Japan is a Mecca for certain kinds of collector. Shops devoted to collectables of one kind or another are easy to find. Most common are those selling cartoon figures – from lasciviously proportioned, moon-eyed *anime* characters to threatening robots and spacecraft.

Japanese antiques are very collectible, although prices are high and you may find better pickings abroad, e.g. in the UK or US.

MAIL-ORDER SHOPPING

There's a huge mail-order market in Japan, including companies that cater specifically to the expatriate community.

Internet

Internet shopping in Japan is big business, the leading online retailer being Rakuten (💻 www.rakuten.co.jp – in Japanese only) – whose founder, Hiroshi Mikitani, is one of the world's richest men. Other Japanese mail-order companies include Cecile (💻 www.cecile.co.jp) and Dinos (💻 www.dinos.co.jp). You can, of course, order products from abroad, but import charges can significantly increase the cost; as well as The Flying Pig (see **Food & Drink** above), the Foreign Buyers' Club (💻 www.fbcusa.com) has a Japanese base (in Kobe) and can deliver quickly and cheaply.

Online auctions are also popular, the largest in Japan (in English) being Yahoo! Japan Auctions (💻 www.rtecec.com).

Catalogues

Catalogue buying has a long tradition in Japan, where almost anything can be bought from a catalogue. Most catalogue companies have websites as well as printed catalogues, but both tend to be only in Japanese (apart from the pictures). One of the largest is Nissen (💻 www.nissen.jp), which sells everything from clothes to furniture. There are even 'mail order shops' where you can consult a variety of catalogues and place your order.

Home Deliveries

Most major shops make home deliveries, especially if you're buying large items such as furniture or kitchen appliances. Delivery may be free and will almost always be on the day and time specified.

RETURNING GOODS

Given their almost obsessive customer focus, Japanese shops are usually happy to replace defective or damaged goods without question, even if they've been damaged by the customer. Provided, you still have the receipt with the shop's stamp (*inkan*) on it and the item is within its warranty period (usually between six months and a year), you should receive satisfaction, although you should always remain calm and it helps to take along a Japanese-speaker if you don't know the relevant vocabulary. Items are not always easy to return to shops, even with a receipt, and you may have to argue your case when you consider service is unsatisfactory (for example, dry-cleaning).

Refunds

Refunds are rarely made, and a damaged or defective item will generally be replaced with an identical or similar product. Goods bought from door-to-door salesmen, telemarketers or on 'special offer' normally offer a cooling-off period, during which you can cancel your order for any reason and receive a full refund. This period varies between 8 and 20 days, depending on the type of transaction.

Complaints

The National Consumer Affairs Centre of Japan provides information relating to retailing and deals with complaints through its Local Consumer Centres, listed on its website (💻 www.kokusen.go.jp/map/index.html – in Japanese only).

Retail Therapy 183

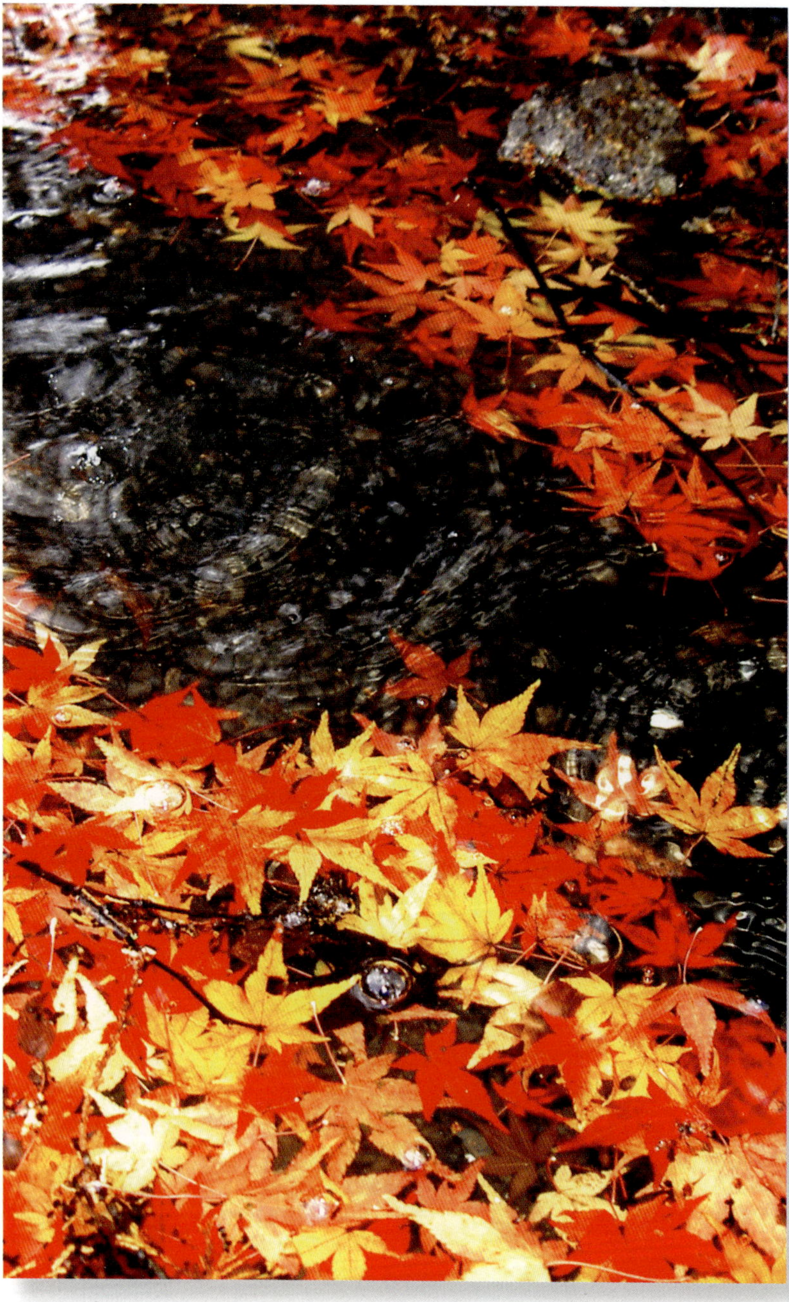

10.
ODDS & ENDS

A country's culture is influenced by various factors and reflected in myriad ways. Among the principal influences are its geography, climate and religion, which are considered here along with miscellaneous cultural manifestations, including crime, the national flag and anthem, government and international relations, pets, tipping and toilets.

> Spring and autumn in Japan are like a reward for suffering through the other two seasons, and the Japanese treat them as such, celebrating them in poetry and song.

CLIMATE

Most of Japan has four clearly defined seasons: a hot and humid summer, a freezing winter, and a comfortable spring and autumn (see below). The severity of winter depends on the latitude and the coastal orientation. In the far north, Hokkaido has sub-arctic weather patterns that give it snow for three months of the year. Similarly the coast of Honshu, which faces the East Sea, gets heavy snow brought in by freezing winds from Siberia. These winds drop all their moisture over the Japanese Alps, leaving the Pacific Ocean coasts clear but chilly. Far to the south, Okinawa has a sub-tropical climate, which gives it a mild winter (the average temperature rarely dips below 15°C) and a hot summer, cooled only by the ocean breeze.

The most comfortable summers in Japan are undoubtedly in Hokkaido, where the daytime temperature is typically in the mid- to low 20s. Most of the rest of Japan has average temperatures in the mid- to high 20s, but it's the humidity that makes the summers uncomfortable, especially in the major cities, where humidity averages over 70 per cent from June to September and days of 90 per cent humidity aren't uncommon.

With a population of 35mn crammed into an area of 13,500km^2 (5,200mi^2), the Tokyo-Yokohama urban area is the greatest concentration of people on the planet. One result of this excessive aggregation is the 'heat island' phenomenon. A combination of internal combustion engines, breeze-blocking skyscrapers and heat-trapping concrete has driven up Tokyo's average temperature by three degrees in the last century (compared with less than one degree for the world as a whole).

There are now over 35 days with temperatures over 35°C a year, in contrast to only 14 in 1975. To combat this, Tokyo regulations stipulate that new buildings must devote a percentage of roof-top space to greenery, schools in the Tokyo area must replace their clay or concrete playgrounds with grass, and 'cooler' types of asphalt are being developed. Only time will tell whether these measures help beat the heat.

The Gentle Seasons

Spring and autumn are like a reward for suffering through the other two seasons, and the Japanese treat them as such, celebrating them in poetry and song. Spring brings the famously ephemeral cherry blossom – and hordes of Japanese to admire them. *Hanami* (flower-watching) parties – for company employees and groups of friends – are commonly held under the cherry trees in parks and on river banks, where they're planted en masse. Autumn too is ablaze with colour. The welcome return of cooler weather brings a range of hues to the trees, from the fierce red of the maples to highlighter-yellow of the ginkgo trees – as well as legions of admiring Japanese. Temples, shrines and national parks famous for their autumnal colours become particularly crowded.

Sake nakuta
Nan no onore ga
Sakura kana

**Without flowing wine
What good to me are lovely
Cherry trees in bloom?**

anonymous 17th-century haiku

The Rainy Season

Strangely, the Japanese rarely mention that their country has a fifth 'season': the rainy season. This lasts around six weeks, starting in June, when prevailing weather patterns park a long band of cloud over the whole of Japan except Hokkaido, usually resulting in continual downpours. The amount of rain that falls varies from year to year; occasionally the front is blown offshore and the 'season' passes almost unnoticed, but it's usually very wet.

Typhoons

An average of 27 typhoons are spawned each year between August and October in the Northwest Pacific Ocean, of which three can be expected to make landfall in Japan. These bring heavy rains that cause flooding and landslips, and winds strong enough to shut down railways and cause cities to grind to a halt. In recent years the number and strength of typhoons have been increasing. The most expensive year so far for typhoon damage was 2004, when ten typhoons hit Japan, three of which ranked among the five most powerful ever recorded. In total they were responsible for 214 deaths and damage valued at over ¥700bn (US$7bn).

The (relatively) good news is that typhoons are predictable – up to a point. News broadcasts will warn of an approaching typhoon, showing its likely path and strength (in terms of wind speeds), so you have time to take avoiding action.

CRIME

Japan is internationally renowned for its low crime rate. This doesn't mean that crime is non-existent, but people in general are honest. It isn't unusual, for example, for a dropped wallet to be returned intact to its owner. On the other hand, certain crimes are common, e.g. bicycle theft, and for women there's the constant threat of wandering hands on crowded trains. However, it's safe for women as well as men to walk at night almost anywhere in Japan.

Organised Crime

The mafia isn't confined to Italy and the US, but is also thriving in Japan. Japan's organised crime groups (*Yakuza* or *Gokudō*) control hostess bars and gambling establishments, drug and gun smuggling, and run various extortion rackets – from forcing local shops to pay for 'protection' (from themselves of course) to blackmailing major companies by threatening to embarrass them at their AGMs.

Originating in the 16th century, the *Yakuza* became powerful after the Second World War, when Japan's central government was weak. They're notorious for their intricate tattoos, many members being covered from neck to ankles.

There are an estimated 110,000 *Yakuza* members in Japan, organised into some 2,500 'families'. By way of comparison, in the US, where the population is over twice as high as Japan's, there are 'only' 20,000 organised criminals. The *Yakuza* have a firm alliance with right-wing nationalists and various individuals with political and financial power, and their influence extends to other Asian countries as well as the US.

FLAG & ANTHEM

Anthem

The words of Japan's anthem (see box), *Kimi ga yo* – the 'Reign of the Emperor' – are taken from a tenth-century poem that was set to music in 1880 by Hiromori Hayashi. Although it has been used as a national anthem since its first performance in the same year, it wasn't legally recognised until 1999. The anthem is controversial, because it became associated with Japanese militarism during the Pacific War, an association that is remembered by many today, on both the left and the right of the political spectrum.

The controversy came to a head when, in October 2003, the Tokyo Board of Education decreed that the national anthem (and flag) should feature in school assemblies. Teachers who refused to comply because of its association with Japan's imperial past were threatened with pay cuts and 're-education' classes, and the case went to court. In 2006 the Tokyo District Court found in favour of the 401 teachers who had challenged the government, ruling that the Board of Education had violated the constitutional guarantee of 'freedom of thought and conscience'.

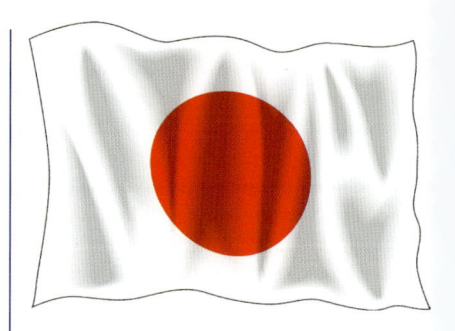

In 1868 it was chosen as the civil ensign for Japanese ships and became the de facto national flag of Japan, although (surprisingly) it wasn't until 1999 that it was officially acknowledged by a parliamentary bill.

GEOGRAPHY

Japan's location in the world is captured by its name, *Nihon* (or *Nippon*), which means literally 'sun's origin'. Japan stands off the eastern edge of the Asian continent, and seen from there the dawn does indeed break behind its four main islands, making it the 'Land of the Rising Sun'. The word 'Japan' comes from the Chinese pronunciation of *Nippon*, 'jih pun', by which the land became known to Portuguese sailors, who were the first Europeans to develop trading links with the Far East, in the 16th century.

Japan is a larger country than many think. The 3,000 islands within its territory give it a greater land area than Germany's and a coastline of 29,751km (18,594mi), the sixth-longest of any country in the world. These islands stretch some 2,500km (1,560mi) from Okinawa,

---

Japanese National Anthem – *Kimi ga yo*

Romaji	English
Kimi ga yo wa,	May the Emperor's reign,
Chiyo ni,	continue for a thousand,
Hachiyo ni;	eight thousand generations;
Sazare-ishi no,	until the pebbles,
Iwao to Nari-te,	grow into boulders,
Koke no musu made.	lush with moss

Flag

The Japanese flag (*hinamaru*) consists of a red disc, representing the rising sun, on a white background. Its earliest recorded use is in the 12th century, when it was used by various warlords.

over 1,500km south-west of Tokyo, to the northernmost tip of Hokkaido island, 950km from the capital. The four main islands of Hokkaido, Honshu, Kyushu and Shikoku are dominated by mountains that sweep down their spine, forming the Japanese Alps. Over 73 per cent of Japan is mountainous, restricting the space available for habitation, agriculture and industry. Restrictive housing regulations and a disinclination to build on sloping land, aggravate the notorious clutter of its cities.

The shortage of habitable land has meant that for many years the Japanese have been reclaiming land from the sea. In Tokyo Bay alone, 249km^2 (97mi^2) of land has been created over the four centuries of the capital's existence, and four Japanese airports are built entirely on artificial islands. With many other multi-million dollar projects involving the creation of land where once there was sea, Japan is one of the most heavily modified countries in the world.

Away from the heavily populated coastal areas, however, Japan has extensive stretches of wilderness. The Japanese Alps are covered in forests of beech, cedar and pine, making Japan the most heavily wooded of the developed countries. Its numerous rivers are short and wide and over the millennia have carried sediment from the mountains to form the flatlands where the majority of the 128mn population live. Japan's countryside is therefore an unusually peaceful place to be.

Administratively, Japan is divided into 47 areas. Three of these are metropolitan or urban areas – Tokyo, Kyoto and Osaka – and the remaining 44 are prefectures, or *ken*. The prefectures on the main island, Honshu, are grouped into regions. The northern prefectures are in the Tōhoku region; the Kanto region covers the area around the two largest cities in Japan, Tokyo and Yokohama; Chubu straddles the middle of the island, including some of Japan's most mountainous terrain in addition to the industrial city port of Nagoya, the country's fourth-largest city, and Hiroshima, rebuilt after its destruction at the end of the Pacific War to become the tenth-most-populous city in Japan; finally the Kansai region contains the ancient seats of power, Kyoto and Nara, along with the third-largest city, Osaka, and the important port of Kobe. Historically, this region has been the main political and economical rival to Kanto, but due to Tokyo's predominance often yields to it, much to the chagrin of its inhabitants.

The various regions have distinct dialects and customs, which developed over centuries of isolation from each other. It's only in recent decades that the depopulation of rural areas and improved communications have started to break down their differences.

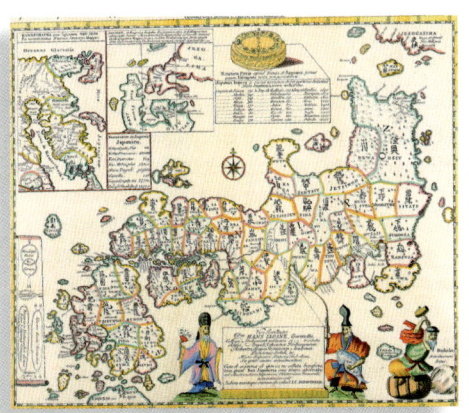

Earthquakes

Perhaps the most widely known 'geographical' feature of Japan is its propensity for earthquakes. No fewer than five tectonic plates meet within the country's borders, and three of them intersect in the Tokyo area, making it the most at-risk city in the world. Throughout its history, Tokyo has been levelled by a major earthquake approximately every 70 years; the last, in 1923, caused nearly 150,000 deaths. Geologists give Tokyo a 90 per cent chance of suffering another Big One within the next 50 years.

Earthquakes occur regularly not only in Tokyo but throughout Japan. The largest in recent years was in 2003. It measured 8 on the Richter scale but caused little damage because it struck a remote northern area. The last earthquake to cause substantial damage and loss of life was in 2004. It measured 6 on the Richter scale and hit Niigata on the east coast, causing 39 deaths and derailing a bullet train, putting the line out of action for almost two months.

How often you're likely to feel the earth move depends on where you are in Japan. In Tokyo it's possible to go several months without noticing one, or there may be several minor tremors in a week. In other places you may sense nothing for years, but this doesn't mean there's no risk. Kobe was widely regarded as a 'quiet' zone in seismic terms until the Great Hanshin Earthquake of January 1995 destroyed large parts of it, killing 5,100 people. Nowhere in Japan is safe from a serious quake.

Natural Disasters

Since 1605 there have been at least 20 natural disasters in Japan (earthquakes, tsunami, typhoons, famines and fires) in which the death toll has numbered in the thousands. Among these were eight catastrophes in which between 20,000 and 150,000 people lost their lives.

Volcanoes

As if the threat of earthquakes weren't enough, Japan is home to 10 per cent of the world's active volcanoes – 108 to be precise – though the term 'active' includes all volcanoes that have erupted in the last 10,000 years and only 30 of Japan's volcanoes are monitored. Those near inhabited areas include Miyake Island (which last erupted in 2000, causing 4,000 people to be evacuated) and Unzen (whose 1991 eruption killed 43 people). Japan's tallest (3,776m/12,460ft) and most famous mountain, Mount Fuji, which is a mere 100km (60mi) from Tokyo, last erupted a mere 300 years ago. The earthquakes that preceded the 1707 eruption unleashed tsunamis that killed 30,000 people, and over the 16 days the eruption lasted it spewed out 700mn cubic metres of magma, damning rivers and laying waste to the surrounding land for 100 years. Although Fuji has been quiet since then, it occasionally makes worrying rumbles. In 2000, monitoring stations logged almost 200 low-level tremors over a few months – one of the signs of an imminent eruption. There was a collective sigh of relief when the tremors died down, but they prompted furious bureaucratic action to develop contingency plans.

If there's an upside to the precarious geographical position occupied by Japan, it's in the vast number of hot springs (*onsen*) that can be found throughout the archipelago (see **Chapter 8**).

GOVERNMENT

Japan has a constitutional monarchy with a parliamentary government. The emperor is the symbol of the state and the representative of the people. The pillars of government are as follows.

The Constitution

Japan's constitution is a legacy of the American occupation, which lasted from 1945 to 1952. As well as setting out the rights of the people and the structure of the government and ensuring the independence of the judiciary, the constitution retained the emperor – which undoubtedly helped it to be accepted. Although the constitution renounced war as an expedient, a 1954 law enabled the Japanese to develop 'self-defence forces', in which members of the armed services are officially civil servants and defence spending is limited to 1 per cent of GNP. This created a tension between the existence of armed forces and the pacifist constitution, which most recently surfaced in relation to Japan's role as a supporter of America's military intervention in Iraq. Japanese politicians have periodically vowed to amend the constitution to allow the military to exist but this invariably causes opposition from neighbouring countries, the Japanese public and opposition parties. Prime Minister Abe has most recently declared this intention, and as a first step upgraded the Japanese Defence Agency to a full ministry within the government cabinet in January 2007.

The Diet

The Japanese parliament, known as the Diet, comprises an upper House of Councillors and a lower House of Representatives. The latter has 480 seats, of which 300 are single-seat constituencies that are elected on a 'first past the post' system and the remainder are derived from eleven electoral blocks, selected by proportional representation. Members of the lower house serve four-year terms, unless the Prime Minister dissolves parliament before this period has elapsed. The Prime Minister is elected by the majority party or coalition in the House of Representatives.

The House of Councillors has 242 members, 144 of whom are elected from the 47 prefectures by a single, non-transferable vote and the remainder from a single national party list. Upper house members serve six-year terms, which cannot be reduced by the Prime Minister. However, the House of Councillors has less power than the House of Representatives, whose decision on important matters is final.

The role of the emperor is purely ceremonial. He opens and closes parliament and makes a speech that outlines the governing party's programme for the session. He must promulgate all laws passed by the Diet and has no right of veto.

Political Parties

Dissatisfaction with corrupt political practices and the slowness of economic reform resulted in changes to the electoral system in 1993. The previous system had encouraged a situation in which one party dominated and the opposition was fractured. The new system was supposed to encourage a system in which two parties vie for power, but it has been only partially successful to date.

The principal Japanese political parties are:

- **Liberal Democratic Party** (LDP) – This has been the dominant political force since its formation in 1955. It's a right-wing party, traditionally drawing its support from rural areas. Dissatisfaction with its allegedly corrupt practices led to a brief spell out of power in 1993-4, but since then it has been the major partner in the ruling coalition.

- **Democratic Party of Japan** (DPJ) – Formed in 1998, this is the second-largest party and the main opposition to the LDP. It tends towards social-liberalism and opposes the LDP on such issues as sending troops to Iraq.

- **New Komeito** – a right-wing party supported principally by a Buddhist sect (the Sokka Gakkai). It has the third-largest representation in parliament and is a member of the current ruling coalition.

- **Japanese Communist Party** (JCP) – Having formed in 1922, this is the oldest party and Japan's fourth largest.

- **Social Democratic Party** (SDP) – a moderate social-democratic party and a partner in the ruling coalition.

The Judiciary & the Law

There are five levels of court, the highest being the Supreme Court, comprising a 'Grand Bench' of 15 judges selected by the cabinet. The Grand Bench is divided into three 'Petty Benches' of five judges, which consider whether cases should be brought before the Grand Bench. At all other levels of the Japanese court system, cases are currently decided by a panel of three judges, but this will change in 2009, when a jury system will be introduced for serious crimes such as murder, arson and hit-and-run incidents.

INTERNATIONAL RELATIONS

Considering the importance of its economy to the world, Japan has been curiously absent from international politics until recently. Japan's enforced alliance with the US after World War II meant that she followed their lead in international matters. As recently as 1991, Japan provided US$13bn to support the US's action in the First Gulf War. The following year, a bill was passed that allowed Japanese Self Defences to participate in United Nations peacekeeping operations. In accordance with this statute, Japan sent troops abroad for the first time since the end of the Pacific War – to Cambodia in 1992-3 to supervise elections – and since then has participated in other UN missions in Asia and Africa. More controversially, Japan sent 1,000 troops to Iraq in 2003, a move that many saw as illegal since it wasn't a UN-led mission.

At the same time as taking on a role more commensurate with her economic power, Japan has been among the nations aiming to reform the UN, the first step being to earn a permanent seat on the UN Security Council. This is a controversial move for many Japanese, who don't think the country is ready for such a role, despite being the second largest financial contributor to the UN.

Neighbour Relations

Japan has also been taking a more active role in its own regional affairs. In the Asian financial crisis of 1997, Japan paid heavily to shore up Thailand's finances. At that time Japan proposed the creation of an Asian Monetary Fund to counter future crises, and despite opposition from the US persisted in negotiations with other Asian countries to establish it. After the devastating tsunami of December 2005, Japan worked closely with UN agencies to set up a tsunami alert system to cover the Pacific Ocean.

One of the biggest 'local' issues which Japan has had to deal with is the withdrawal of North Korea from the Nuclear Non-Proliferation Treaty in 2003, and it has contributed to the diplomatic effort to reduce tension along with the United States, China, South Korea and Russia. Japan's involvement has been complicated, however, by the admission of Kim Jong-il (Chairman of North Korea's National Defence Commission) in 2002 that it abducted 13 Japanese citizens to act as language teachers in North Korea. Not surprisingly this disclosure outraged the Japanese, and efforts are ongoing to discover what happened to these 'teachers', and to others who are suspected of being kidnapped.

Japan's relations with her South East Asian neighbours are fraught with tension due to lingering resentment of her aggression from the 1890s to 1945. Reminders of a brutal past surface regularly, particularly in the Koreas and China. The Koreans, for example, are still seeking compensation for women who were forced to work in brothels for the Imperial Army (so-called 'comfort women') during Japan's colonisation, and Japanese government-approved text books which brush over such inhumanities continue to rankle. As recently as 2003, Japan paid US$2.5mn in compensation to 43 Chinese villagers who were poisoned by mustard gas left by the Imperial Japanese Army in north-eastern China decades earlier.

Territorial Disputes

Japan has several unresolved disputes with its neighbours over territory, including the following:

- **Dokdo/Takashima Islands:** Both Japan and Korea have historical ties to these islands. Korea erected a lighthouse in 1953, and there are conflicts over rights to the rich fishing in the area.

- **Kuril Islands:** Russia moved into these islands north of Hokkaido, claimed by Japan (which refers to them as the Northern Territories), at the end of the Second World War and its continued occupation of them is the main reason a peace treaty between the two countries has not been signed since the end of the Pacific War.

- **Okinotori:** China refuses to recognise this group of rocks as an island as Japan does – and therefore disputes the latter's 200km exclusion zone around them.

- **Senkaku/Diaoyu Islands:** Another dispute between Japan and China over ownership of these islands is heightened by the large reserves of oil and natural gas in the area.

PETS

The Japanese love their pets and often treat them as a member of the family. The most popular pets are small pedigree dogs (the Japanese place little value on 'mongrels'), which can sell for exorbitant prices, but cats (e.g. Japanese bobtail) are also popular. For children, especially small boys, large insects are popular pets, and there are plenty of Japanese of all ages who hold a fascination for 'exotic' animals, such as snakes, turtles and large spiders.

> As in other countries, pet ownership in Japan is subject to fads. Often a cute example of a particular animal in a popular TV advert or programme will cause demand to soar, no matter how poorly suited it is to the life of a pet. Often these unfortunate creatures are then abandoned in parks or quiet places.

RELIGION

The Japanese aren't particularly religious people, but religious institutions and beliefs play a role in the major events in their lives. Unlike most Westerners, the Japanese tend to 'adopt' a religion to suit the occasion. For example, they usually hold birth ceremonies at Shinto shrines and funerals at Buddhist temples. In December, parents give their children 'Christmas' presents and at New Year most go to either a Shinto shrine or a Buddhist temple to pray for good fortune for the new year. Marriages have traditionally been sanctified by Shinto priests, but these days Christian-style weddings predominate, two-thirds of marriages in Tokyo being celebrated in this way.

Temples or shrines are also visited at times of need or sorrow. Certain Shinto shrines supposedly bring luck to those taking examinations, for example, or foster fertility, while in Buddhist temples you may find small statues that represent the departed souls of aborted foetuses. In many villages, towns or suburbs, traditional festivals, or *matsuri*, are conducted by Shinto priests (see **Chapter 8**), and many households and businesses have a small Shinto or Buddhist altar; some have both.

As you will have been gathered, the two main religions in Japan are Shinto and Buddhism, the former being the country's 'native' religion, while the latter was introduced from Korea in the 6th century. There are also around 2mn Christians (less than 2 per cent of the population). Although not strictly a religion but a moral system, Confucianism has shaped the character of the Japanese no less than any religion and is also included below.

Shinto

Shinto holds sacred many Gods, which are inherent in natural phenomena such as Mount Fuji, an ancient tree or a prominent rock (see box). It doesn't have a set of prayers or dogma but consists of a series of practices that are supposed to help humans relate to the Gods. Shinto was made the state religion during the Meiji revolution of 1868, when it was used to deify the emperor and unite the country behind him. The 1952 constitution expressly removed this association, making Japan the secular state that it is today.

By some counts there are over 800,000 Shinto Gods. The primary deity is Amaterasu, the Sun Goddess, who's considered the divine ancestor of the emperor. She sent her grandson to rule Japan with gifts of a sword, a mirror and a jewel, which became the three sacred treasures of Shinto. It's thought that the mirror now resides in the Grand Shrines of Ise, in Mie-ken, the sword in Atsuta Shrine near Nagoya and the jewel in the Imperial Palace in Tokyo. Nobody knows for sure because only the emperor and certain priests are allowed to view these items and they aren't letting on.

Buddhism

While Shinto was always the religion of the people,

Buddhism was first taken up by the ruling and military classes and spread from above. Between the 6th and 17th centuries different varieties of Buddhism were introduced into Japan, each enjoying varying levels of acceptance among the ruling elite of the time. In contemporary Japan there are many Buddhist sects, ranging from those with just a handful of members to the Soka Gakai, whose affiliated political party (called the 'New Komeito') has become the third-largest in Japan (see **Politics** above).

Although there were some early conflicts with Shinto, it didn't take long for Buddhism to be accommodated with the native religion. In fact, they became entwined to such an extent that it took a decree to separate Buddhist temples and Shinto shrines after the Meiji Restoration.

Christianity

Christianity was brought to Japan by missionaries in the mid-16th century. Francis Xavier established the first church in 1549 in Kagoshima, Kyushu. After the conversion of local warlords, Christianity was seen as a threat by the *Shōguns* and the first edict banning Christianity was passed in 1587. On the suppression of a revolt by Christian warlords in Shimabara in 1637, Christians were forced underground. The restoration of the emperor in 1868 brought freedom of religion, and Christians who had been secretly practising Christian rites for two and a half centuries could once more practise in public.

Confucianism

Like Buddhism, Confucianism was introduced to Japan in the sixth century, probably via Korea, but it was the Neo-Confucianism adopted as the state ideology by the Tokugawa *Shōguns* in the early 17th century that has had a lasting impact on Japanese society. Neo-Confucianism defined a hierarchical class structure and the relationships between ruler and ruled, parents and offspring, men and women, and so on. It emphasised the importance of satisfaction with one's station in life and ritualised actions.

During the long period of peace during the Tokugawa regime (1603-1867), concepts such as *bushido* (way of the warrior), *sado* (way of making tea) and *shodo* (way of writing) became entrenched. In present day Japan such aspects as respect for authority, student behaviour in the education system, family relationships and the relatively low status of women can be traced back to Japan's Confucian heritage.

Aum Shinrikyo

On 20th March 1995 Japan woke to the shocking news that a nerve gas attack on its subway had killed 11 and injured hundreds more. There was further disbelief when it was revealed that the crime had been was perpetrated not by some international terrorist organisation, but by a 'religious' group among whose members were some of Japan's brightest university graduates. Nor was it the first time Aum Shinrikyo had resorted to extreme acts; its members had already murdered several people who tried to leave or prosecute the cult. Aum Shinrikyo still exists under the name 'Aleph' and was recently reported to have some 2,000 members.

TIME DIFFERENCE					
MADRID	**LONDON**	**JO'BURG**	**SYDNEY**	**AUCKLAND**	**NEW YORK**
04.00	03.00	05.00	14.00	16.00	22.00

TIME DIFFERENCE

Japan is nine hours ahead of GMT and doesn't adjust its time in summer. The time in winter (October to March) in a selection of foreign cities when it's noon in Tokyo is shown in the table above.

Arabic numerals are usually used for times, and timetables commonly use the 24-hour clock, with a colon separating the hours from minutes.

TIPPING

Tipping isn't expected in Japan (Americans please note!). If you were to leave some money on a restaurant table, for example, it's likely you'll find a waiter rushing after you to return it. In some high-class *ryokan* (traditional inns) it's acceptable to put some money in an envelope for the person who tidies your room or provides room service, but even here it isn't usual.

TOILETS

Although public toilets (*toire*) aren't plentiful in Japan, they can be found quite easily if you know where to look. The first place to check is the local convenience store, which often has toilets (though it's less likely in city centres). The small public parks that dot urban areas also have basic facilities and toilets are to be found in most department stores and railway stations. You don't usually need to pay in a public toilet, but there may be only cold water for hand washing and nothing to dry your hands on. Somewhat paradoxically, the word for toilet in Japanese is *tearai* (literally 'hands wash'), but *toire*, the *katakana* pronunciation of 'toilet', is used just as often and if you say 'toilet' in English, your will be understood.

There are two kinds of toilets commonly found in Japan: the oldest type is a simple squat toilet, which is still common in public conveniences. However, after WWII modern Western-style flush toilets and urinals became common. The current state of the art for Western-style toilets is the bidet toilet or washlet (*woshuretto*), which are installed in most Japanese households. Washlets commonly have heated seats (great in winter), and wash and dry your private parts after you have done your business. Other features may include automatic flushing and lid closing after use, massage options, water jet adjustments, automatic lid opening, wireless control panels, and heating and air conditioning for the room. These features are accessed by a control panel that is either attached to one side of the seat or on a wall nearby, often transmitting commands wirelessly to the toilet seat.

Toilet Signs

Signs are sometimes written in *romaji*, as follows:

Romaji	English
Tearai or Toire	Toilet
Resutoroumu	Restroom
Suisenshiki	Flush toilet
Joseiyou	Ladies
Danseiyou	Gentlemen

Washi paper doll

Odds & Ends

Kinkakuji temple, Kyoto

Koi carp

APPENDICES

APPENDIX A: EMBASSIES & CONSUALTES

In Japan

Listed below are the contact details for the embassies of the main English-speaking countries in Tokyo. A full list of embassies and consulates in Japan is available from the website of the Ministry of Foreign Affairs of Japan (🖥 www.mofa.go.jp/about/emb_cons/protocol/index.html).

Australia: 2-1-14, Mita, Minato-ku, Tokyo 108-8361 (☏ 813 5232 4111, 🖥 www.australia.or.jp/english/index.html). Consulates are located in Fukuoka, Nagoya, Osaka and Sapporo.

Canada: 7-3-38, Akasaka, Minato-ku, Tokyo 107-8503 (☏ 813 5412 6200, 🖥 www.canadanet.or.jp/english.shtml). Consulates are located in Hiroshima, Nagoya and Sapporo.

Ireland: Ireland House, 2-10-7, Kojimachi, Chiyoda-ku, Tokyo 102-0083 (☏ 813 3263 0695, 🖥 www.irishembassy.jp). A consulate is located in Osaka.

New Zealand: 20-40, Kamiyama-cho, Shibuya-ku, Tokyo 150-0047 (☏ 813 3467 2271, 🖥 www.nzembassy.com/japan). Consulates are located in Fukuoka, Nagoya, Osaka, Sapporo and Sendai.

South Africa: Oriken Hirakawa-cho Building, 3-4F., 2-1-1, Hirakawa-cho, Chiyoda-ku, Tokyo 102-0093 (☏ 813 3265 3379, 🖥 www.rsatk.com). Consulates are located in Nagoya and Sapporo.

United Kingdom: 1, Ichiban-cho, Chiyoda-ku, Tokyo 102-8381 (☏ 813 5211 1100, 🖥 http://ukinjapan.fco.gov.uk/en). Consulates are located in Nagoya and Osaka.

United States of America: 1-10-5, Akasaka, Minato-ku, Tokyo 107-8420 (☏ 813 3224 5000, 🖥 http://usembassy.gov). Consulates are located in Fukuoka, Nagoya, Naha, Osaka-Kobe and Sapporo.

Abroad

Listed below are the contact details for Japanese embassies in the main English-speaking countries. A full list is available at 🖳 www.mofa.go.jp/about/emb_cons/over/index.html.

Australia: 112 Empire Circuit, Yarralumla, Canberra ACT 2600 (☏ 02-6273 3244, 🖳 www.au.emb-japan.go.jp).

Canada: 255 Sussex Drive, Ottawa, Ontario K1N 9E6 (☏ 03-241 8541, 🖳 www.ca.emb-japan.go.jp).

Ireland: Nutley Building, Merrion Centre, Nutley Lane, Dublin 4 (☏ 01-202 8300, 🖳 www.ie.emb-japan.go.jp)

New Zealand: Level 18, Majestic Centre, 100 Willis Street, Wellington 1 (☏ 04-473 1540, 🖳 www.nz.emb-japan.go.jp).

South Africa: 259 Baines Street, corner Frans Oerder Street, Groenkloof, Pretoria 0181 (☏ 12-452 1500, 🖳 www.za.emb-japan.go.jp).

United Kingdom: 101-104 Piccadilly, London, W1J 7JT (☏ 020-7465 6500, 🖳 www.uk.emb-japan.go.jp).

United States of America: 2520 Massachusetts Avenue NW, Washington DC, 20008-2869 (☏ 202-238 6700, 🖳 www.us.emb-japan.go.jp).

> The business hours of embassies vary and they close on their own country's national holidays as well as on Japanese public holidays. Always telephone to confirm opening hours before visiting.

APPENDIX B: FURTHER READING

English-language Newspapers & Magazines

Asahi Shimbun & International Herald Tribune (☎ 0120 330 843, 🖳 www.asahi.com/english) Daily newspaper and weekly magazine.

The Daily Yomiuri (☎ 0120 431 159, 🖳 www.yomiuri.co.jp/dy). Daily Newspaper.

J@pan Inc (☎ 03 3499 2099, 🖳 www.japaninc.com). Bimonthly business and technology magazine.

The Japan Times (☎ 03 3453 5312, 🖳 www.japantimes.co.jp). Daily newspaper.

Japan Update (☎ 098 921 2052, 🖳 www.japanupdate.com). Weekly newspaper published in Okinawa.

Japanzine (☎ 052 788 2123, 🖳 www.seekjapan.jp). Free monthly magazine, published in Nagoya.

Kansai Time Out (☎ 078 393 7044, 🖳 www.japanfile.com). Monthly publication focussing on the Kansai region.

Kyoto Journal (☎ 075-761-1433, 🖳 www.kyotojournal.org). Magazine published in Kyoto, three issues a year.

Kyodo News (☎ 03 6252 8306, 🖳 http//home.kyodo.co.jp). News agency.

Mainichi Daily News (☎ 03 3212 0321, 🖳 http://mdn.mainichi.jp). Weekly newspaper.

Metropolis (☎ 03 4550 2929, 🖳 www.metropolis.co.jp). Free weekly magazine.

The Nikkei Weekly (☎ 03 5255 2312, 🖳 www.nni.nikkei.co.jp). Weekly business magazine.

Outdoor Japan (☎ 03 3481 6139, 🖳 www.outdoorjapan.com). Free bimonthly magazine.

Tokyo Journal (☎ 03 3876 3574, 🖳 www.tokyo.to). Quarterly magazine, published in Tokyo.

Tokyo Weekender (☎ 03 5549 2038, 🖳 www.weekender.co.jp). Weekly magazine, published in Tokyo.

Books

The books listed below are just a selection of the hundreds written about Japan and the Japanese. The publication title is followed by the author's name and the publisher's name (in brackets).

Culture

Dave Barry Does Japan, Dave Barry (Random House)

Different Games Different Rules, Haru Yamada (Oxford)

Dogs and Demons, Alex Kerr (Hill and Wang)

Geisha, Gangster, Neighbor, Nun: Scenes from Japanese Lives, Donald Richie (Kodansha)

The Japanese Mind, Roger J. Davies & Osamu Ikeno (Tuttle)

Lost Japan, Alex Kerr (Lonely Planet)

Out, Natsuo Kirino (Kodansha)

Runaway Horses, Yukio Mishima (Vintage)

Silent Cry, Kenzaburo Oe (Kodansha)

Speed Tribes, Karl Taro Greenfield (Harper Perennial)

Tabloid Tokyo, Mark Schreiber (Kodansha)

The Wind-Up Bird Chronicle, Haruki Murakami (Vintage)

History

Geisha: The Secret History of a Vanishing World, Lesley Downer (Headline)

Hidden Horrors, Yuki Tanaka (Westview)

A History of Japan, Conrad Totman (Wiley-Blackwell)

Japan Before Perry, Conrad Totman (University of California Press)

Japan at War: An Oral History, Haruko Taya Cook and Theodore F. Cook (New Press)

The Making of Modern Japan, M.B. Jansen (Harvard)

A Modern History of Japan: From Tokugawa Times to the Present, Andrew Gordon (Oxford)

Multicultural Japan – Paleolithic to Postmodern, Mark Donaldson et al (Cambridge University Press)

Pink Samurai, Nicholas Bornoff (Trafalgar Square)

The Wages of Guilt, Ian Buruma (Phoenix)

Yoshimasa and the Silver Pavilion: The Creation of the Soul of Japan, Donald Keene (Columbia)

Appendices

Language

2001 Japanese and English Idioms, Nobuo Akiyama & Carol Akayama (Barron's)

A Dictionary of Basic Japanese Grammar, Seiichi Makino & Michio Tsutsui (The Japan Times)

Dirty Japanese: Everyday Slang from "What's Up?" to "F*ck Off!", Matt Fargo (Ulysses)

Essential Kanji: 2,000 Basic Japanese Characters Systematically Arranged For Learning And Reference, P. G. O'Neill (Weatherhill)

A Guide to Learning Hiragana and Katakana, Kenneth G. Henshall & Tetsuo Takagaki (Tuttle)

Guide to Writing Kanji & Kana Book 1, Wolfgang Hadamitzky & Mark Spahn (Tuttle)

Japanese for Busy People 1, Association For Japanese-Language Teaching (Kodansha)

Japanese The Manga Way: An Illustrated Guide To Grammar And Structure, Wayne P. Lammers (Stone Bridge)

Living and Working in Japan

Being a Broad in Japan: Everything a Western woman needs to survive and thrive, Caroline Pover (Alexandra Press)

Business Guide to Japan: A Quick Guide to Opening Doors and Closing Deals, Boye De Mente (Tuttle)

Ganbatte Means Go for It! Or. . . how to Become an English Teacher in Japan, Celeste Heiter (Global Directions Inc)

In the Know in Japan: The Indispensable Guide to Working and Living in Japan, Jennifer Phillips (Living Language)

Japan: A Working Holiday Guide, Louise Southerden (Roundhouse)

Living Abroad in Japan, Ruth Kanagy (Avalon Travel Publishing)

A Practical Guide to Living in Japan: Everything You Need to Know to Successfully Settle In, Jarrell D. Sieff (Stone Bridge Press)

Shopping Guide to Japan, Boye De Mente (Tuttle)

Tourist Guides

Getting Wet: Adventures in the Japanese Bath, Eric Talmadge (Kodansha)

A Guide to the Gardens of Kyoto, Marc Treib & Ron Herman (Kodansha)

Hiking in Japan, Mason Florence et al (Lonely Planet)

Japan: Eyewitness Travel Guides (Dorling Kindersley)

Japan's Hidden Hot Springs, Robert Neff (Tuttle)

Lonely Planet Japan, Chris Rowthorn et al (Lonely Planet)

Mishima's Sword: Travels in Search of a Samurai Legend, Christopher Ross (Da Capo Press)

The Rough Guide to Japan, Jan Dodd et al (Rough Guides)

Ryokan: Japan's Finest Spas and Inns, Akihiko Seki & Elizabeth Heilman Brooke (Tuttle)

Time Out Guide to Tokyo (Time Out)

cherry blossom

APPENDIX C: USEFUL WEBSITES

This appendix contains information about some of the most popular websites dedicated to Japan and the Japanese people.

Business

Japan Inc (🖥 www.japaninc.com). Japanese business, technology and people.

Japanese Business Federation (🖥 www.keidanren.or.jp).

JETRO (🖥 www.jetro.go.jp). The Japan External Trade Organization (JETRO) is the Japanese government's organization for helping foreigners do business in Japan.

Nikkei Net Interactive (🖥 www.nni.nikkei.co.jp). Business news from Japan's stock market.

Venture Japan (🖥 www.venturejapan.com/index.htm). Contains useful information about doing business and how to succeed in the Japanese market.

Web Japan (🖥 http://web-japan.org). Provides a wealth of interesting information about Japanese products and current trends.

Culture

The Black Moon (🖥 http://theblackmoon.com). Art, anime and Japanese culture.

Japan for the Uninvited (🖥 www.japanfortheuninvited.com). Japanese culture from a bemused foreign perspective.

The Japan Faq (🖥 www.thejapanfaq.com/FAQ-Primer.html). Japanese culture: A primer for foreigners.

Japan Foundation (🖥 www.jpf.go.jp/e). Specialises in international cultural exchange in Japan.

Japan Information & Culture Centre (🖥 www.us.emb-japan.go.jp/jicc/index.htm). Embassy of Japan, Washington DC.

Japanese Lifestyle (🖥 www.japaneselifestyle.com.au/culture/culture.html). An in-depth look at Japanese culture from this excellent Australian website.

Nihingo (🖥 www.nihongo.org/English). The people, culture, art and language of Japan.

What Japan Thinks (🖥 http://whatjapanthinks.com). Information and statistics about Japanese life.

Government

Cabinet Office (🖥 www.cao.go.jp/index-e.html). Japanese cabinet office.

Diet (🖥 www.shugiin.go.jp/index.nsf/html/index_e.htm). Website of the Japanese House of Representatives.

Ministry of Foreign Affairs (🖥 www.mofa.go.jp).

Prime Minister (🖥 www.kantei.go.jp/foreign/index-e.html). Website of the Japanese Prime Minister and his cabinet.

Public Relations Office (🖥 www.gov-online.go.jp/eng). Government of Japan.

Language

Engrish (🖥 www.engrish.com). Humour site dedicated to the strange English found in China and Japan.

Japanese Language (🖥 www.japanese-language.org). The most comprehensive Japanese language website.

Japanese-Language Education Overseas (🖥 www.jpf.go.jp/e/japanese/index.htm). From the Japan Foundation.

Japanese Links (🖥 www.japaneselinks.net). Learning resources for students of Japanese.

Japanese-Online (🖥 www.japanese-online.com). Free online Japanese study site.

LanguageSchool.net (🖥 http://learnjapanese.elanguageschool.net). Learn Japanese online.

My Japanese Translator (🖥 www.myjapanesetranslator.co.uk/japan.html). Guide to learning Japanese and much more.

Living & Working

Dai Job (🖥 www.daijob.com/en). Job website for bilinguals.

Education in Japan (🖥 www.education-in-japan.info). All about education in Japan.

Gaijin Pot (🖥 www.gaijinpot.com). This site is best for those looking for jobs and places to live in Japan. Includes forums where you can discuss Japanese issues.

Japan English Teacher (🖥 www.japanenglishteacher.com). Site specialising in English teaching jobs.

Japan Meteorological Society (🖥 www.jma.go.jp/jma/indexe.html). Weather, earthquakes, volcanoes, etc.

Japan Survival (🖥 www.japan.survival-links.com). Has a comprehensive list of links to websites for expats daily living needs.

Jobfinder (🖥 http://jobs.japantimes.jp). Job and career information from the *Japanese Times*.

Ohayo Sensei (🖥 www.ohayosensei.com). Has the best listing of English teaching and English related jobs in Japan.

Jobs in Japan (🖥 www.jobsinjapan.com). One of the best Japanese job websites.

Study in Japan (🖥 www.studyjapan.go.jp/en). Comprehensive guide to education in Japan.

Tokyo Apartments (🖥 www.tokyo-apartments.info). Apartments to rent in Tokyo.

Media

The Black Ship (🖥 http://theblackship.com/news). Japanese news, forum, views and features.

Hiragana Times (🖥 www.hiraganatimes.com). Japanese lifestyle magazine that 'introduces the real Japan to the world'.

Japan Centre (🖥 www.japancentre.com). Buy Japanese magazines online.

Japan Economy News (🖥 www.japaneconomynews.com). News and blog from Ken Worsley, a long-time resident of Tokyo.

Japan Today (🖥 www.japantoday.com). Japan news and discussion.

World Newspapers (🖥 www.world-newspapers.com/japan.html). Links to all Japanese English-language newspapers.

Miscellaneous

Japan 101 (🖥 www.japan-101.com). Excellent information resource for everything Japanese.

Japan Information Network (🖥 http://jin.jcic.or.jp). 'The portal to the world of Japan since 1985.'

Japan Reference (🖥 www.jref.com). Contains a wealth of information about Japan. Has a useful Japan Directory feature with links to thousands of websites.

Japan Stores (🖥 www.jp-stores.com/en). Shopping website.

Japanese Streets (🖥 www.japanesestreets.com). Online magazine about Japanese street culture and street fashion).

Japan Today (🖥 www.japantoday.com). A news site which specialises in Japanese news and allows readers to comment on the stories. Also includes forums where you can ask questions and discuss Japanese issues.

Japan Zone (🖥 www.japan-zone.com). Japanese culture, information and travel guide.

Kid Web Japan (🖳 http://web-japan.org/kidsweb). Japan for kids.

Tokyo Bazaar (🖳 www.tokyo-bazaar.com). Guide to Tokyo shopping.

Wikipedia (🖳 http://en.wikipedia.org/wiki/Japan). Wikipedia pages for Japan.

Tokyo Cube (🖳 www.tokyocube.com). Japanese lifestyle and shopping directory.

Web Japan (🖳 http://web-japan.org). One of Japan's most popular information sites.

Travel & Tourism

Asian Rooms (🖳 www.asiarooms.com/travel-guide/japan/index.html). Japanese travel and information.

Bento (🖳 www.bento.com/tokyofood.html). A complete guide to Japanese cuisine and eating in Japan, plus recipes, tours of Japanese markets, and tips on the best places to eat in Kobe, Kyoto, Osaka, Tokyo and Yokohama

Hyperdia (🖳 http://grace.hyperdia.com/cgi-english/hyperWeb.cgi). A timetable website for rail services in Japan.

Japan Airlines (🖳 www.jal.com/en). Japan's national carrier.

Japan Guide (🖳 www.japan-guide.com). A travelling and living guide for Japan, including a forum where you can ask questions.

Japan Hotels (🖳 www.japanhotel.net). One of Japan's most comprehensive hotel sites.

Japan I Can (🖳 www.japanican.com). Popular hotel and tours' website.

Japan National Tourist Association (🖳 www.jnto.go.jp/eng). The official Japanese tourism website providing a wealth of information, including upcoming events, accommodation and travel deals.

Japan Railways Group (🖳 www.japanrail.com). Book your rail tickets online.

Japan Roads (🖳 www.japanroads.com/index.htm). 'Getting you out of the bus and into the culture.'

Japan Travel (🖳 www.japantravel.co.uk). Website of the Japan Travel Centre in London.

Japan Visitor Blog (🖳 http://japanvisitor.blogspot.com). Blog for Kyoto, Nagoya, Osaka and Tokyo.

Japanese Lifestyle (🖳 www.japaneselifestyle.com.au). Japanese travel from an Australian perspective.

Tokyo Essentials (🖳 www.tokyoessentials.com). Tokyo travellers and tourist guide.

Appendices 211

APPENDIX D: PROVINCES & REGIONS

Japan is divided into nine regions (Chūbu, Chūgoku, Hokkaidō, Kansai, Kantō, Kyūshū, Okinawa, Shikoku and Tōhoku) and 47 prefectures (*ken*) which are listed below and shown on the map opposite.

Regions & Prefectures

Hokkaidō

1. Hokkaidō

Tōhoku

2. Aomori
3. Iwate
4. Miyagi
5. Akita
6. Yamagata
7. Fukushima

Kantō

8. Ibaraki
9. Tochigi
10. Gunma
11. Saitama
12. Chiba
13. Tokyo
14. Kanagawa

Chūbu

15. Niigata
16. Toyama
17. Ishikawa
18. Fukui
19. Yamanashi
20. Nagano
21. Gifu
22. Shizuoka
23. Aichi

Kansai

24. Mie
25. Shiga
26. Kyoto
26. Kyoto
27. Osaka
28. Hyōgo
29. Nara
30. Wakayama

Chūgoku

31. Tottori
32. Shimane
33. Okayama
34. Hiroshima
35. Yamaguchi

Shikoku

36. Tokushima
37. Kagawa
38. Ehime
39. Kōchi

Kyūshū & Okinawa

40. Fukuoka
41. Saga
42. Nagasaki
43. Kumamoto
44. Ōita
45. Miyazaki
46. Kagoshima

Okinawa

47. Okinawa

Appendices 213

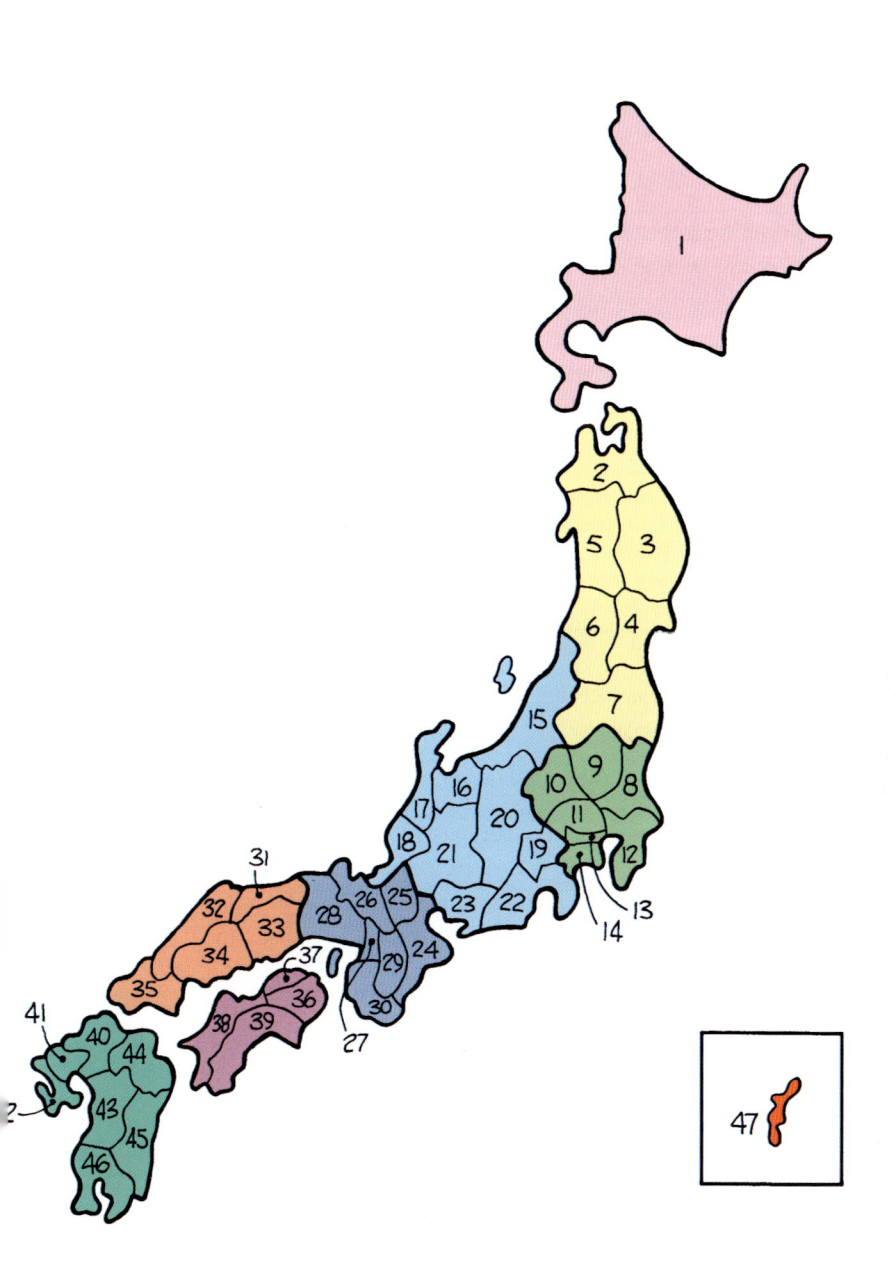

APPENDIX E: USEFUL WORDS & PHRASES

Asking for Help

Do you speak English? (Eigo wo hanashimasuka?)
I don't speak Japanese (Watashi-wa nihongo-wo hanashimasen)
Please speak slowly (Yukkuri hanashite-kudasai)
I don't understand (Wakarimasen)
I need ... (Watashi-wa ...ga irimasu)
I want ... (Watashi-wa....ga hoshii-desu)

Communications

Telephone & Internet

landline (kotei denwa)
mobile phone (keitai denwa)
no answer (rusu)
engaged/busy (hanashichyuu)
internet (intahnetto)
email (iimeiru)
broadband connection (burohdobando setsuzoku)
internet café/wi-fi spot (intahnetto kafe/waiyaresu supotto)

Post

post office (yuubinkyoku)
postcard/letter/parcel (hagaki/tegami/kozutsumi /stamps (kitte)
How much does it cost to send a letter to Europe/North America/Australia? (Yohroppa / amerika / ohsutoraria made-wa ikura-desuka?)

Media

newspaper/magazine (shinbun/zasshi)
Do you sell English-language media? (Eigo-no shinbun/zasshi/hon-wa arimasuka?)

Courtesy

yes (hai)
no (iie)
excuse me (sumimasen)
sorry (gomen-nasai)
I don't understand (Wakarimasen)
I don't mind (Daijobu-desu)
please (onegai-shimasu)
thank you (arigato)
you're welcome (doitashimashite)

Days & Months

Monday (getsuyobi)
Tuesday (kayobi)
Wednesday (suiyoubi)
Thursday (mokuyoubi)

Friday (kinyoubi)
Saturday (doyoubi)
Sunday (nichyoubi)

January (ichigatsu)
February (nigatsu)
March (sangatsu)
April (shigatsu)
May (gogatsu)
June (rokugatsu)

July (shichigatsu)
August (hachigatsu)
September (kugatsu)
October (juugatsu)
November (juuichigatsu)
December (juunigatsu)

Driving

car insurance (jidohsha hoken)
driving licence (unten menkyo)
hire/rental car (haiyah-wo yobu/kuruma-wo rentaru-suru)
How far is it to ...? (...made dorekurai-desuka?)

Can I park here? (Koko-ni chyusha shitemo iidesuka?)
unleaded petrol (gas)/diesel (gasorin)/(diizeru)
Fill the tank up please (Mantan onegaishimasu)
air/water/oil (ea/mizu/oiru)
car wash (sensha jou/jyo)
My car has broken down (Kuruma-ga koshou-shimashita)
I've run out of petrol (gas) (Gasuketsu-desu)
The tyre is flat (Panku-desu)
I need a tow truck (Kenin-sha-ga irimasu)

Emergency

Emergency! (Kinnkyu-desu!)
Fire! (Kaji-desu!)
Help! (Tasukete!)
Police! (Omawari-san!)
Stop! (Yamero!)
Stop thief! (Dorobo!)
Watch out! (Abunai!)

Health & Medical Emergencies

I feel ill/dizzy (guai-ga waruidesu/memai-ga shimasu)
I need a doctor/ambulance (oisha-san-ga hitsuyou-desu/kyukyusha-ga hitsuyoudesu)
doctor/nurse/dentist (isha/kangofu/haisha)
surgeon/specialist (gekai/senmonka)
hospital/healthcentre/A&E (byoin/iryosho)
kinkyuchiryoshitsu

Finding your Way

Where is ...? (...wa doko-desuka?)
Where is the nearest ...? (Chikaku-no ...wa doko-desuka?)
How do I get to ...? (...e-wa dou ikimasuka?)
Can I walk there? (Sokomade arukemasuka?)
How far is ...? (...wa dorekurai touidesuka?)
A map please (Chizu-wo onegai-shimasu)

I'm lost (Mayoi-mashita)

left/right/straight ahead (hidari/migi/massugu/opposite/next to/near (hantai/tonari/chikaku)

airport (kuukou)

bus/plane/taxi/train (basu/takushii/densha)

bus stop (basutei)

taxi rank (takushii noriba)

train/bus station (eki/basutei)

When does the ... arrive/leave? (...wa itsu tsukimasuka?/...wa itsu demasuka?)

one-way/return ticket (katamichi/kaeri-no kippu)

bank/embassy/consulate (ginko/taishikan/ryoujikan)

Greetings

Hello (konnichiwa)

Goodbye (sayonara)

Good morning (ohayo-gozaimasu)

Good afternoon (konnichiwa)

Good night (oyasumi-nasai)

In a Bar or Restaurant

Waiter! (sumimasen)

menu (menyu)

bill (kaikei)

vegetarian (bejitarian)

meat/fish (niku/sakana)

Numbers

one (ichi)

two (ni)

three (san)

four (yon)

five (go)

six (roku)

seven (nana)

eight (hachi)

nine (kyu)

ten (jyu)

Shinkyo (Sacred Bridge), Nikko

INDEX

A

Accommodation 53
   Buying a home 57
   Rented property 54
Alcohol 177
   Beer, wine &
   whisky 177
   Nihonshu & shochu 177
Alien registration card 52
Anthem 187
Appendices 201
A: Embassies &
consulates 201
B: Further reading 203
C: Useful websites 207
D: Map of provinces &
regions 212
E: Useful words &
phrases 214
Arts 160
   Booking 161
   Cinema 161
   Museums & art
   galleries 163
   Theatre & opera 162

B

Banking 70
Bars 144
Beer, wine & whisky 177
Birthdays 148
Body & sign language 98
   Bowing 98
   Gestures 98
   Personal space 99
Books, newspapers &
magazines 180
   About Japan 203
Bowing 98
Bread 142
Breaking the ice 75
Community life 75
Confrontation 87
Dealing with officials 88
Expatriate
community 86
Invitations 81
Meeting people 79
Respecting privacy 83
Sexual attitudes 77
Taboos 84
Buddhism 195
Bureaucracy 52
   Alien registration
   card 52
   Inkan or hanko 52
Buses 131
Buying
   a Car 58
   a Home 57

C

Cafes 143
Car insurance 63
Catalogues 181
Change of culture 13
   Culture shock 14
   Families in Japan 20
   Japan is different 13
   New life 21
Children 36
   Clothes 180
Christianity 196
Christmas & new year 149
Cinema 161
Civil servants 89
Classical period 24
Class system 36
Climate 185
   Gentle seasons 186
   Rainy season 186
   Typhoons 186
Clothes 177
Alterations 180
Children's 180
Shoes 180
Sizes 179
Clubs 153
Collectables 181
Community life 75
   Regulations 76
Confrontation 87
Confucianism 196
Constitution 191
Convenience stores 170
Conversation 84, 142
Council services 66
   Refuse/garbage
   collection 66
Crime 187
   Organised 187
Cult of cuteness 30
Culture shock 14
   Stages 15
Customer service 167
Cutlery 140

D

Dealing with officials 88
   Civil servants 89
   Police 89
   Teachers 89
Department stores 172
Determination &
endurance 33
Dialects & accents 97
Diet (government) 191
Doctors 61
Dress 86
Dress code 137
   At home 137
   Places of worship 138
Drinking 142
Driving 123
   Finding your way 126

Index

Japanese drivers 123
Japanese roads 124
Licences 125
Motorcyclists &
cyclists 128
Parking 127
Petrol 127
Road rules 124
Duty- & tax-free
shopping 169

E

Early modern period 25
Earthquakes 190
Eating 138
   Bread 142
   Conversation 142
   Cutlery 140
   Formal dining 139
   Grace 140
   Informal dining 140
   Meals 138
   Noises 141
   Seating 140
   Table manners 141
   Toasts 141
   When to start 141
Education 63
   Japanese education
   system 64
   Japanese or international
   school? 63
   University 65
Electricity 67
Embassies & consulates 201
Emergency services 58
Engagement parties 149
Expatriate community 86
   Advantages 87
   Disadvantages 87

F

Families in Japan 20
Family celebrations 148
   Birthdays 148
   Christmas & new
   year 149
   Engagement parties 149
   Weddings 150
Festivals & fairs 154
Finding your way 126
Fish 174
Flag & anthem 187
Food 174
   Fish 174
   Foreign 177
   Fruit & vegetables 175
   Meat 175
   Milk & dairy
   products 176
   Organic 176
Formal dining 139
Forms of address 99
   Children 100
   Names & titles 100
Fruit & vegetables 175
Funerals 152
   Dress 153
Further reading 203

G

Gambling 155
Gas 68
Gentle seasons 186
Geography 188
   Earthquakes 190
   Volcanoes 190
Gestures 98
Getting started 51
   Accommodation 53
   Banking 70
   Bureaucracy 52
   Buying or hiring a car 57
   Council services 66
   Education 63
   Emergency services 58
   Health service 59
   Immigration 51
   Insurance 62
   Staying informed 69
   Taxes 72
   Utilities 67

Government 191
   Constitution 191
   Diet 191
   Political parties 192
Grace 140
Greetings 101
Groupthink 31

H

Health insurance 62
Health service 59
   Doctors 61
   Hospitals 59
   Medicines 62
Home deliveries 182
Homosexuals &
transsexuals 79
Hospitals 59
Household insurance 63
Humour 35
Hunting & fishing 159

I

Icons 39
   Flora & fauna 44
   Food & drink 46
   People 39
   Places & structures 43
   Symbols 41
Immigration 51
Indirectness 32
Informal dining 140
Inkan or hanko 52
Inscrutability 34
Insurance 62
   Car 63
   Health 62
   Household 63
International relations 192
   with Neighbours 193
Internet 181
Invitations 81
   Making 83
   Receiving 81

J

Japanese
    Drivers 123
    Education system 64
    People 28
    at Play 137
    Roads 124
    at Work 105
Japanese at play 137
    Arts 160
    Cafes, bars & restaurants 143
    Clubs 153
    Dress code 137
    Drinking 142
    Eating 138
    Family celebrations 148
    Funerals 152
    Nightlife 147
    Popular culture 153

L

Language barrier 91
    Body & sign language 98
    Dialects & accents 97
    Forms of address 99
    Greetings 101
    Learning Japanese 91
    Other languages 96
    Slang & swearing 97
    Telephone, email & letters 102
Learning Japanese 91
    Children 96
    Know before you go 94
    Loanwords 93
    Once in Japan 94
    Spoken Japanese 93
    Tips for learning Japanese 95
    Why Japanese is essential 94
    Writing systems 92
    Yes or no? 92
Licences 125
Loanwords 93

M

Mail-order shopping 181
    Catalogues 181
    Home deliveries 182
    Internet 181
Making invitations 83
Maps 6, 212
Markets 171
Meals 138
Meat 175
Medicines 62
Medieval period 24
Meeting people 79
    Paying 81
    Where & when to meet 81
Men 77
Milk & dairy products 176
Modern
    Japan 27
    Period 26
Modesty 32
Motorcyclists & cyclists 128
Museums & art galleries 163

N

Names & titles 100
National icons 39
Neighbourly relations 193
Newspapers 70
Nightlife 147
Nihonshu & shochu 177

O

Odds & ends 185
    Climate 185
    Crime 187
    Flag & anthem 187
    Geography 188
    Government 191
    International relations 192
    Pets 194
    Religion 194
    Time difference 197
    Tipping 197
    Toilets 197
Onsen 159
On the move 123
    Cycling 128
    Driving 123
    Motorcycling 128
    Public transport 129
    Walking 133
Opening hours 168
Organic food 176
Organised crime 187

P

Parking 127
Paying 81
People 28
    Attention to detail 34
    Cult of cuteness 30
    Determination & endurance 33
    Groupthink 31
    Importance of spring 29
    Indirectness 32
    Inscrutability 34
    Modesty 32
    Politeness & rudeness 33
    Seniority rules 31
    Shyness 31
    Social obligation 32
    Worship of the new 29
Personal space 99
Petrol 127
Pets 194
Places of worship 138
Police 89
Politeness & rudeness 33
Political parties 192
Popular culture 153
    Festivals & fairs 154
    Gambling 155
    Hunting & fishing 159
    Music 155
    Onsen 159
    Spectator sports 156
Prehistoric period 24
Public transport 129

Index

Air 133
Buses 131
General
 information 129
Taxis 133
Trains 129
Trams 133
Underground
 (subway) 132

Q/R

Queuing 168
Radio 69
Rainy season 186
Receiving invitations 81
Refunds 182
Refuse/garbage collection 66
Religion 194
 Buddhism 195
 Christianity 196
 Confucianism 196
 Shinto 195
Rented property 54
Respecting privacy 83
Restaurants 146
Retail therapy 167
 Alcohol 177
 Books, newspapers &
  magazines 180
 Clothes 177
 Collectables 181
 Customer service 167
 Department stores 172
 Food 174
 Mail-order
  shopping 181
 Markets 171
 Opening hours 168
 Queuing 168
 Returning goods 182
 Sales & discounts 168
 Supermarkets 173
 Types of shop 169
 Vending machines 171
Road rules 124

S

Sales & discounts 168
 Duty- & tax-free shopping
  169
Seating 140
Seniority rules 31
Sexual attitudes 77
 Homosexuals &
  transsexuals 79
 Men 77
 Women 78
Shinto 195
Shoes 180
Shyness 31
Slang & swearing 97
Social obligation 32
Spectator sports 156
Spring, importance 29
Staying informed 69
 Internet 181
 Newspapers 70
 Radio 69
 Television 69
Supermarkets 173
 Shopping in 174

T

Table manners 141
Taboos 84
 Conversation 84
 Dress 86
Taxes 72
 avoidance 72
Taxis 133
Teachers 89
Telephone, email &
 letters 68, 102
Television 69
Theatre & opera 162
Time difference 197
Timeline 23
 Classical period 24
 Early modern period 25
 Medieval period 24
 Modern Japan 27
 Modern period 26
 Prehistoric period 24
Tipping 197
Toasts 141
Toilets 197
Trains 129
Trams 133
Types of shop 169
 ¥100 Shop 170
 Convenience stores 170
Typhoons 186

U

Underground (subway) 132
University 65
Useful
 Websites 207
 Words & phrases 214
Utilities 67
 Electricity 67
 Gas 68
 Telephone 68
 Water 67

V

Vending machines 171
 Used panties 171
Volcanoes 190

W

Walking 133
Water 67
Weddings 150
Who are the Japanese? 23
 Attitudes to
  foreigners 37
 Children 36
 Class system 36
 Humour 35
 Icons 39
 People 28
 Timeline 23
Women 78
Worship of the new 29
Writing systems 92

Survival Books

Essential reading for anyone planning to live, work, retire or buy a home abroad

Survival Books was established in 1987 and by the mid-'90s was the leading publisher of books for people planning to live, work, buy property or retire abroad.

From the outset, our philosophy has been to provide the most comprehensive and up-to-date information available. Our titles routinely contain up to twice as much information as other books and are updated frequently. All our books contain colour photographs and some are printed in two colours or full colour throughout. They also contain original cartoons, illustrations and maps.

Survival Books are written by people with first-hand experience of the countries and the people they describe, and therefore provide invaluable insights that cannot be obtained from official publications or websites, and information that is more reliable and objective than that provided by the majority of unofficial sites.

Survival Books are designed to be easy – and interesting – to read. They contain a comprehensive list of contents and index and extensive appendices, including useful addresses, further reading, useful websites and glossaries to help you obtain additional information as well as metric conversion tables and other useful reference material.

Our primary goal is to provide you with the essential information necessary for a trouble-free life or property purchase and to save you time, trouble and money.

We believe our books are the best – they are certainly the best-selling. But don't take our word for it – read what reviewers and readers have said about Survival Books at the front of this book.

**Order your copies today by phone, fax, post or email from:
Survival Books, PO Box 3780, Yeovil, BA21 5WX, United Kingdom.
Tel: +44 (0)1935-700060, email: sales@survivalbooks.net,
Website: www.survivalbooks.net**

Buying a Home Series

Buying a home abroad is not only a major financial transaction but also a potentially life-changing experience; it's therefore essential to get it right. Our Buying a Home guides are required reading for anyone planning to purchase property abroad and are packed with vital information to guide you through the property jungle and help you avoid disasters that can turn a dream home into a nightmare.

The purpose of our Buying a Home guides is to enable you to choose the most favourable location and the most appropriate property for your requirements, and to reduce your risk of making an expensive mistake by making informed decisions and calculated judgements rather than uneducated and hopeful guesses. Most importantly, they will help you save money and will repay your investment many times over.

Buying a Home guides are the most comprehensive and up-to-date source of information available about buying property abroad – whether you're seeking a detached house or an apartment, a holiday or a permanent home (or an investment property), these books will prove invaluable.

For a full list of our current titles, visit our website at www.survivalbooks.net

Living and Working Series

Our Living and Working guides are essential reading for anyone planning to spend a period abroad – whether it's an extended holiday or permanent migration – and are packed with priceless information designed to help you avoid costly mistakes and save both time and money.

Living and Working guides are the most comprehensive and up-to-date source of practical information available about everyday life abroad. They aren't, however, simply a catalogue of dry facts and figures, but are written in a highly readable style – entertaining, practical and occasionally humorous.

Our aim is to provide you with the comprehensive practical information necessary for a trouble-free life. You may have visited a country as a tourist, but living and working there is a different matter altogether; adjusting to a new environment and culture and making a home in any foreign country can be a traumatic and stressful experience. You need to adapt to new customs and traditions, discover the local way of doing things (such as finding a home, paying bills and obtaining insurance) and learn all over again how to overcome the everyday obstacles of life.

All these subjects and many, many more are covered in depth in our Living and Working guides – don't leave home without them.

The Expats' Best Friend!

Culture Wise Series

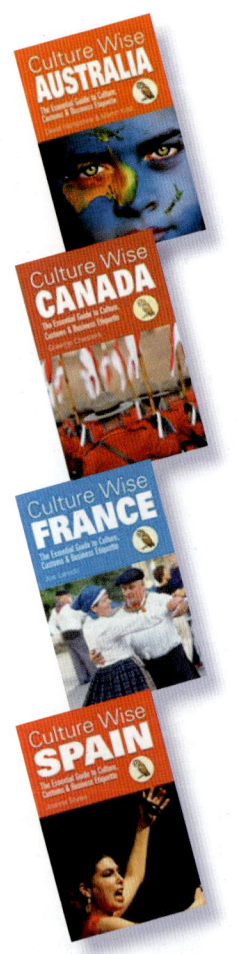

Our **Culture Wise** series of guides is essential reading for anyone who wants to understand how a country really 'works'. Whether you're planning to stay for a few days or a lifetime, these guides will help you quickly find your feet and settle into your new surroundings.
Culture Wise guides:

- Reduce the anxiety factor in adapting to a foreign culture
- Explain how to behave in everyday situations in order to avoid cultural and social gaffes
- Help you get along with your neighbours
- Make friends and establish lasting business relationships
- Enhance your understanding of a country and its people.

People often underestimate the extent of cultural isolation they can face abroad, particularly in a country with a different language. At first glance, many countries seem an 'easy' option, often with millions of visitors from all corners of the globe and well-established expatriate communities. But, sooner or later, newcomers find that most countries are indeed 'foreign' and many come unstuck as a result.
Culture Wise guides will enable you to quickly adapt to the local way of life and feel at home, and – just as importantly – avoid the worst effects of culture shock.

Culture Wise – The Wise Way to Travel

The essential guides to Culture, Customs & Business Etiquette

Other Survival Books

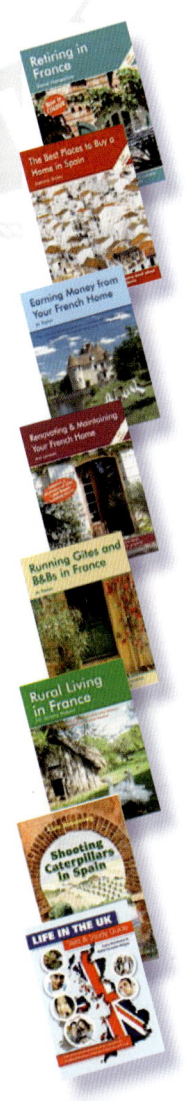

The Best Places to Buy a Home in France/Spain: Unique guides to where to buy property in Spain and France, containing detailed regional profiles and market reports.

Buying, Selling and Letting Property: The best source of information about buying, selling and letting property in the UK.

Earning Money From Your French Home: Income from property in France, including short- and long-term letting.

Investing in Property Abroad: Everything you need to know and more about buying property abroad for investment and pleasure.

Life in the UK - Test & Study Guide: essential reading for anyone planning to take the 'Life in the UK' test in order to become a permanent resident (settled) in the UK.

Making a Living: Comprehensive guides to self-employment and starting a business in France and Spain.

Renovating & Maintaining Your French Home: The ultimate guide to renovating and maintaining your dream home in France.

Retiring in France/Spain: Everything a prospective retiree needs to know about the two most popular international retirement destinations.

Running Gîtes and B&Bs in France: An essential book for anyone planning to invest in a gîte or bed & breakfast business.

Rural Living in France: An invaluable book for anyone seeking the 'good life', containing a wealth of practical information about all aspects of French country life.

Shooting Caterpillars in Spain: The hilarious and compelling story of two innocents abroad in the depths of Andalusia in the late '80s.

For a full list of our current titles, visit our website at
www.survivalbooks.net

CULTURE WISE INDIA

The Essential Guide to Culture, Customs & Business Etiquette

- vital reading for visitors who want to understand how India really works
- helps newcomers quickly find their feet and settle in smoothly
- reduces the anxiety factor in adapting to Indian culture
- explains how to behave in everyday situations in order to avoid cultural and social gaffes
- helps you make friends and establish lasting business contacts
- enhances your understanding of India and its people

Culture Wise India will help you adapt to the Indian way of life and enable you to quickly feel at home.

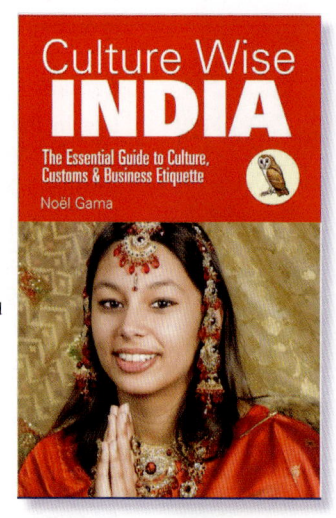

Survival Books - The Expats Best Friend

CULTURE WISE AUSTRALIA

The Essential Guide to Culture, Customs & Business Etiquette

- vital reading for visitors who want to understand how Australia really works
- helps newcomers quickly find their feet and settle in smoothly
- reduces the anxiety factor in adapting to Australian culture
- explains how to behave in everyday situations in order to avoid cultural and social gaffes
- helps you make friends and establish lasting business contacts
- enhances your understanding of Australia and its people

Culture Wise Australia will help you adapt to the Australian way of life and enable you to quickly feel at home.

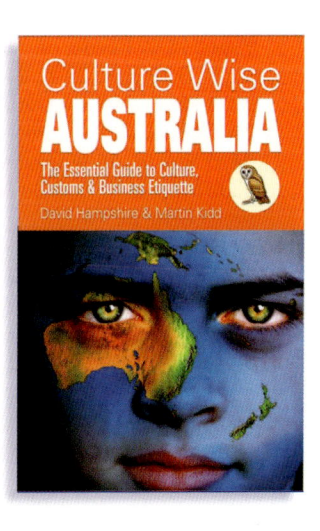

Survival Books - The Expats Best Friend

PHOTO

www.dreamstime.com

Pages 15 © Exvise, 16 © Razvanjp, 18 © Mosich, 25 © Jsanchez_bcn, 27 © Grosremy, 28 © Briancweed, 30 © Daniel_m, 33 © Beckyabell, 37 © Beckyabell, 39 © Maxfx, 40 © Fabinus08, 42 © Briancweed, 43 © Photoclicks, 48 © Wellmony, 49 © Flashon, 50 © Razvanjp, 53 © Elenaray, 55 © Nruboc, 56 © Mmette, 58 © Bright, 70 © Jojojojo, 72 © Cookelma, 73 © Mocker, 77 © Phildate, 90 © Ellebell, 95 © Wildcat123, 97 © Tadija, 98 © Geotrac, 101 © Lightpainter, 103 © Ozawa, 104 © Mmette, 108 © DnDavis, 110 © Graytown, 111 © Nruboc, 112 © Svanhorn4245, 113 © Razvanjp, 115 © Itinerantlens, 116 © Zhudifeng, 117 © Devonyu, 119 © Pemotret, 122 © Sersei, 127 © Mccarthystudio, 130 © Yujiro, 133 © Razvanjp, 134 © Kroppix, 140 © Radist, 143 © Tiberius, 144 © Rockpig, 146 © Hemul, 148 © Dubassy, 149 © Zts, 151 © Apollofoto, 153 © Sorinus, 154 © Tinoni, 156 © Joeygil, 159 © Smack, 160 © Pdtnc, 163 © Chaser, 164 © Og_vision, 165 © Ippeito, 172 © Smack, 173 © Spanishalex, 174 © mypokcik, 176 © Xylke, 180 © Smack, 181 © Photol, 183 © Razvanjp, 186 © Barsik, 187 © Neon1974, 188 © Suljo, 190 © Yujiro, 191 © Puentes, 193 © Razvanjp, 195 © Lightpainter, 197 © Jojojojo, 198 © Razvanjp, 199 © Swtbeb4lyfe43, 206 © Ikeda, 211 © Tashfoto, 230 © Awcnz62, 230 © Pxlar8, 230 © Erickn, 231 © Nsilcock, 231 © Elkeflorida, 232 © Yujiro

CREDITS

www.shutterstock.com

Pages 10 © Hiroshi Ichikawa, 12 © mypokcik, 20 © Kirk Peart PI, 22 © Jorgen, 26 © Richard Sergeant, 31 © Holger Mette, 35 © Scott Milless, 41 © Elnur, 44 © Craig Hanson, 45 © Frances A. Miller, 46 © Nataliya Peregudova, 47 © Images Hunter, 60 © Tom Grill, 62 © Iofoto, 63 © WizData,inc, 64 © Thomas M. Perkins, 67 © mypokcik, 68 © Dash, 74 © Ilya D. Gridnev, 78 © Patricia Malina, 80 © Szefei, 82 © Radu Razvan, 85 © mypokcik, 87 © Phil Date, 88 © Just ASC, 92 © Mario Babu, 96 © Thomas M. Perkins, 106 © Iofoto, 121 © Ilya D. Gridnev, 125 © James B. Adson, 129 © Alexey Averiyanov, 135 © Mike Liu, 136 © Mikhail Pozhenko, 158 © Anna Jurkovska, 166 © Can Balcioglu, 168 © Ronen, 169 © Jose Gil, 170 © Igor Sivolob, 178 © Craig Hanson, 182 © mypokcik, 200 © Irina Fukuoka, 218 © mypokcik, 230 © Dmitry Pichugin, 231 © Yury Zaporozhchenko

Culture Wise Series

Current Titles:

America
Australia
Canada
England
France
Germany
India
Japan
New Zealand
Spain
Turkey

Coming soon:

Cyprus
Dubai
Greece
Holland
Hong Kong
Ireland
Italy
Switzerland

Culture Wise - The Wisest Way to Travel